"In these remarkable seminars Jean-Max Gaudill
ters with madness – in the clinical setting, in liter
of scientists, philosophers, social scientists, psycho.
a way of following the 'erased traces' of the storie
official history. Moving among literary narrative
globe, conceptual thought, personal biographies, ...u ms own clinical experiences, Dr. Gaudillière teaches us to recognize in madness a 'research tool' into
catastrophic pasts, a *showing*, in personal lives, of what has been muted and
remains unspeakable within a larger History. At the heart of this stunning book
is the exchange by which the 'mad' and the listener (in clinical settings, rituals,
literature, and conceptual writing) can together participate in the inscription of
these collective traumas. What is ultimately at stake in this utterly innovative
work – in Dr. Gaudillière's profound and moving listening, reading and telling –
is the possibility of making the frozen time of lost histories move again, and
fighting the perversion by which history is lost. In a time in which we face the
renewed threat of totalitarian violence, the lessons of madness that emerge from
this book point not only to crucial personal, but also political truths."

Cathy Caruth, Frank H. T. Rhodes Professor of Humane
Letters at Cornell University

"In the first of two volumes, seven years of seminars taught by Jean-Max
Gaudillière demonstrate the links between psychosis, literature, language,
history, and the psychoanalyst's courage and persistence in understanding
madness in the clinical encounter. Moving between fiction, clinical stories,
and theory from a wide range of authors, Gaudillière brings the force of
both death and life into the psychoanalytic field of understanding trauma
and madness. Françoise Davoine has organized and transcribed the seminars in a masterful way, allowing the reader to enter the profound depth of
Gaudillière's thinking about the erasure of history and the production of
madness. Clinicians who work with patients who are delusional, traumat-
ized, or psychotic will find the book opens a space for new and fresh thinking about the meaning of madness. Full of humanity, wisdom, and
creativity, *Madness and the Social Link* teaches clinicians to listen simultaneously to what is said and what cannot be said because of the rupture of
the social link. This is a critically important book."

Jane G. Tillman, PhD, Evelyn Stefansson
Nef Director of the Erikson Institute

"This lively and erudite double volume on psychosis showcases the work of
a master teacher and clinician who was already a post-Lacanian psychoanalyst in Paris while Lacan was still alive. Psychosis is the patient's investiga-
tive tool, shared in the transference with the analyst, for naming the
traumatic catastrophe that has stopped time and destroyed all social links.
The author shows this process of inscription through many generous clinical
examples and by extensive examples from literature, political texts, social

thought, and other psychoanalysts. This rich work provides a much-needed thoughtful perspective for those who work with patients."

John Muller, Senior Erikson Scholar, Austen Riggs Center

"Françoise Davoine's transcriptions of the seminars she conducted with Jean-Max Gaudillière for thirty years in Paris brilliantly illuminate the psychic territory where the cataclysms of history intersect with personal story in trauma, breakdown, and psychosis. Here, the texts of Cervantes, Sterne, Strindberg, Pirandello, Charlotte Beradt, Kenzaburō Ōe, Toni Morrison, and others, along with the words and gestures of particular patients, reveal the individual link to collective horror, horror that cannot be assimilated or thought but is nevertheless embodied and enacted. It seems to me that in this moment of global political nightmares, the lessons to be learned from reading *Madness and the Social Link* are urgently needed."

Siri Hustvedt, American novelist

Madness and the Social Link

This book provides a psychoanalytic reading of works of literature, enhancing the illuminating effect of both fields.

The first of two volumes, *Madness and the Social Link: The Jean-Max Gaudillière Seminars 1985–2000* contains seven of the "Madness and the Social Link" seminars given by psychoanalyst Jean-Max Gaudillière at the École des hautes études en sciences sociales (EHESS) in Paris between 1985 and 2000, transcribed by Françoise Davoine from her notes. Each year, the seminar was dedicated to an author who explored madness in his depiction of the catastrophes of history. Surprising the reader at every turn, the seminars speak of the close intertwining of personal lives and catastrophic historical events, and of the possibility of repairing injury to the psyche, the mind, and the body in their wake.

These volumes expose the usefulness of literature as a tool for healing, for all those working in therapeutic fields, and will allow lovers of literature to discover a way of reading that gives access to more subtle perspectives and unsuspected interrelations.

Jean-Max Gaudillière studied classical literature at the École normale supérieure (ENS) in Paris before becoming a psychoanalyst. He was a professor at the École des hautes études en sciences sociales (EHESS) and was a member of the Center for the Study of Social Movements (CSSM), founded by Alain Touraine, research director at the EHESS.

In the weekly seminar called "Madness and the Social Link," held for forty years at the EHESS, Gaudillière combined his clinical work with the exploration of literary works dealing with the madness of war. The focus of his clinical work was the impact of historical catastrophes on personal lives.

He is the co-author of two books written with Françoise Davoine: *History Beyond Trauma* (2004) and *A Word to the Wise* (2018, Routledge).

Madness and the Social Link
The Jean-Max Gaudillière Seminars
1985–2000

Jean-Max Gaudillière

Transcribed by Françoise Davoine
Translated by Agnès Jacob

Routledge
Taylor & Francis Group

LONDON AND NEW YORK

First published in English 2021
by Routledge
2 Park Square, Milton Park, Abingdon, Oxon OX14 4RN

and by Routledge
52 Vanderbilt Avenue, New York, NY 10017

Routledge is an imprint of the Taylor & Francis Group, an informa business

Published in French by Hermann 2020

British Library Cataloguing-in-Publication Data
A catalogue record for this book is available from the British Library

Library of Congress Cataloging-in-Publication Data
Names: Gaudillière, Jean-Max, author. | Davoine, Françoise, transcriber. |
Jacob, Agnès, translator.
Title: Madness and the social link : the Jean-Max Gaudillière seminars
1985-2000 / Jean-Max Gaudillière ; transcribed by Françoise Davoine ;
translated by Agnès Jacob.
Other titles: Lectures. Selections. English
Description: London ; New York, NY : Routledge, 2021. | "Published in
French by Hermann 2020"–Title page. | Includes bibliographical
references and index.
Identifiers: LCCN 2020015256 (print) | LCCN 2020015257 (ebook) |
ISBN 9780367523282 (hardback) | ISBN 9780367523299 (paperback) |
ISBN 9781003057468 (ebook)
Subjects: LCSH: Psychoanalysis and literature. | Psychic trauma in literature. |
Literature and mental illness. | Literature and mental illness. | War and
literature.
Classification: LCC PN56.P92 G3813 2021 (print) | LCC PN56.P92 (ebook) |
DDC 809/.933561–dc23
LC record available at https://lccn.loc.gov/2020015256
LC ebook record available at https://lccn.loc.gov/2020015257

ISBN: 978-0-367-52328-2 (hbk)
ISBN: 978-0-367-52329-9 (pbk)
ISBN: 978-1-003-05746-8 (ebk)

Typeset in Times
by Swales & Willis, Exeter, Devon, UK

To Jeanne, Batiste, Emile, Kalea, his grandchildren

Contents

Prologue

This book contains seven of fourteen seminars given by Jean-Max Gaudil-lière at the École des hautes études en sciences sociales (EHESS) between 1985 and 2000, transcribed from my notes, since Jean-Max spoke without preparing a written text. The other seven seminars, given between 2001 and 2014, are published by Routledge in *The Birth of a Political Self* (2020). We held these weekly seminars alternately for nearly forty years, until his death in March 2015. The seminars were held under the auspices of the Center for the Study of Social Movements (CSSM), founded by Alain Touraine. Our research, conducted under the title *Madness and the Social Link*, was based on our experience as psychoanalysts in public psychiatric hospitals. Although we were neither psychologists nor psychiatrists – our background was in classical literature and sociology – we had joined Jacques Lacan's École freudienne and were welcomed by Edmond Sanquer, psychiatrist and psychoanalyst, to work in the departments he directed in three successive hospitals over thirty years.

The idea of transcribing my notes was born on the occasion of a memorial for Jean-Max organised in the fall of 2015 by our friends at the Austen Riggs Center, a clinic devoted to the psychoanalysis of psychoses, located in Stockbridge, Massachusetts. In 1979, we had been invited there to speak about Lacan, by John Muller, director of training, Jim Gorney, a psychoanalyst now practising in Knoxville, Tennessee, and philosopher William Richardson, then director of research, who were introducing Lacan's teachings. At Austen Riggs, we met psychoanalysts working with madness, from different orientations, particularly those of Harry Stack Sulli-van and Frieda Fromm-Reichmann, neither of whom we had heard of until then. Regular visits to the United States followed.

In July 2017, Jane Tillman, director of the Erikson Institute of Research at Austen Riggs, and Jerry Fromm, its first director, invited me to transcribe my notes of Jean-Max's seminars while in residence as an Erikson scholar. This book is the result of that work.

Each chapter of the book is a seminar focusing on an author who lets madness speak, at a time when the word "trauma" was not yet in fashion. In Erasmus' *The Praise of Folly*,[1] she starts by saying: "For who can set me out better than myself?" and ends her praise by asserting: "… if I shall seem to have spoken anything more boldly or impertinently than I ought, be pleased to consider that not only Folly but a woman said it."

Our seminars were not recorded. But recently, one of the participants gave me some photos he took, by chance, at the last seminar given by Jean-Max in February 2015. On a video recording, he can be seen speaking happily while I am busy trying to take notes as fast as I can, like in a Charlie Chaplin slapstick. Bursting out laughing, I remembered that laughter was part of our seminars, where we transmitted the lessons taught by madness on the catastrophes of history, on whatever scale.

Our national jester Raymond Devos claimed that laughter works on the edge of tears, when silenced stories are expressed; it also works through delusions, "at the crossroads of personal history and world History," as one of my patients said. Often these stories are related to the war, whose traces I bear myself since my early years in my native valley in the Alps. These traces resurface unexpectedly in my work as an analyst, resonating with something I am being shown, when there are no words to say it.

Madness teaches us that it emerges out of the destruction of otherness, and attests to truths without a witness in order to inscribe them in a narrative. The word "transference" illustrates the search for this "other" without whom no inscription is possible. For a long time, transference was thought impossible in psychosis, and therefore no psychoanalysis could take place. But in truth, it takes a different form, in which the place of the other has to be created from scratch.

Each one of our weekly seminars spoke through the voice of a writer acquainted with madness, whose voice resonated with our practice and allowed us to preserve confidentiality. We followed Freud's advice, recalling that he called writers our "valuable allies," for they know "a whole host of things between heaven and earth" of which our institutes have no idea.[2] Every other year, one of us chose a writer as a guide. For me, it was Don Quixote, Wittgenstein and the medieval theatre of fools; these became the subject of books that have been published. Now the time has come to prevent the lessons learned from the authors who guided Jean-Max from disappearing without a trace.

Their experience with madness intersects with that of the pioneers in the psychoanalysis of psychosis, around the time of World War I. The seminars provide a dialogue between writers and psychoanalysts, and are presented in chronological order.

The first one is based on the work of Japanese writer Kenzaburō Ōe, author of *Teach Us to Outgrow Our Madness*. He responds to this request by showing that his heroes outgrow madness through an enquiry into the upheavals in the history of Japan.

The second seminar focuses on psychoanalyst Gaetano Benedetti, who worked with schizophrenia in Basel. Being of Sicilian origin, he would often refer to Pirandello when we used to visit him in Basel at Carnival time. So, the third seminar is about the lessons of Pirandello, who drew inspiration for his short stories of madness from sundry news stories in the local papers. The stories were transformed into plays after 1915, constituting what he called his "theatre of war."

The fourth seminar is a dialogue between Toni Morrison's novel *Beloved* – on the complete destruction of the social link by slavery in the Southern United States – and the psychoanalyst of madness Frieda Fromm-Reichmann at Chestnut Lodge, near Washington where she had fled Nazism – an experience which resonated with her patients' traumatic life experiences.

The fifth seminar discusses the impressive testimony given by Swedish writer August Strindberg about his delusions in Paris, analysed day by day through his book *Inferno*, written in French, all the way to its resolution. For indeed, one can heal from madness when its tools are no longer needed, since it is possible for the truths it insists on revealing to circulate in an exchange again and, to use our leitmotif, find a way to be inscribed.

The sixth seminar examines *The Regeneration Trilogy* written by British author Pat Barker. The hero is the famous neurologist/anthropologist William Rivers. He becomes another pioneer of the psychoanalysis of psychosis and traumas – pursuing the same field of research – when he is drafted as a military doctor to work at the Craiglockhart Hospital in Scotland, a treatment centre for officers returning from the front. He reads Freud and modifies his technique, to find a way to reach suppressed zones in his patients. One of Rivers' disciples was John Rickman, Wilfred Bion's second analyst. Bion is the subject of the opening seminar in the second volume, *The Birth of a Political Self*, composed of seven other seminars given by Jean-Max Gaudillière at the EHESS.

These seminars have a common, insistent theme: the battle fought by madness against a ruthless agency that erases traces by stopping time. The authors quoted in this book show that it is possible to set time in motion again, in spite of desperate and pessimistic diagnoses. Interaction in the transference produces what Benedetti calls a "transitional subject," which we might also call a "political subject" since it emerges from resistance to totalitarian perversion. This is the main focus of the seventh seminar on the work of Hannah Arendt, which sets the stage for the second volume, entitled *The Birth of a Political Self*.

The text I submit to the reader is not an exact reproduction of my notes. As I transcribed them, I could not help pursuing my dialogue with Jean-Max by inserting references and ideas like in the good old days of our conversations. I also had to modify the oral exchanges with seminar participants, who year after year shared their experience with us. Unfortunately, I was unable to convey the atmosphere of freedom and gaiety that reigned during our gatherings.I remain grateful to the participants for their enthusiasm, which helped this book to take shape.

When I chose the title *Madness and the Social Link* for the first book of the seminars, I was thinking, of course, of Erasmus' *The Praise of Folly*. Now that they are about to become public, I invoke his and her protection, as well as that of Charlie Chaplin.

Françoise Davoine
August 20, 2019

Notes

1 Erasmus, D., *The Praise of Folly*, Aeterna Publishing, 2010.
2 Freud, S., *Delusions and Dreams in Jensen's Gradiva*, S.E. 9, Hogarth Press, 1907.

1 Seminar 1: 1985–1986 Kenzaburō Ōe (1935–)

Teach Us to Outgrow Our Madness

This seminar will examine two books: *Teach Us to Outgrow Our Madness* (1977)[1] and *The Silent Cry* (1967).[2]

The first title is that of a collection of short stories, which in the Japanese original also contains other texts. The English translation contains four short stories. The second one, "Prize Stock," earned Ōe, at the age of 23, the highest literary distinction in his country. The title of the third story is the one that was chosen for the book. The last story is called "Aghwee the Sky Monster," and the first "The Day He Himself Shall Wipe My Tears Away." In Japanese, the title of the second book is *Football in the First Year of Man'en*, the start of a new era (1860) just before Japan was opened to trade with foreign countries by Emperor Meiji, that is, a century before the time frame of the stories in the book. These facts were supplied by Akira Mizubayashi, who has had several books published in French translation by Gallimard, with the most recent being *Un amour de mille ans* (*A Thousand-Year Love*) in 2017.

I. *TEACH US OUTGROW OUR MADNESS*: AN ANALYSIS OF MADNESS AND TRAUMA

In "The Day He Himself Shall Wipe My Tears Away," the narrator distinguishes several periods in the years of extreme poverty of his childhood. The shortest period is the one in which he accepts his father's madness, calling it his "Happy Days," after the title of an American song. After a violent scene between his parents, his father – whom his mother would call "a certain party" from then on – closes himself up in a storehouse, where the child joins him.

The war has just ended; Japan is on the brink of collapse. The boy's father, who is obese and has bladder cancer, sprays the child with bloody urine. At the same time, the boy is made witness to his father's madness. To be saved, the emperor must be killed. A delusion takes shape; the child never stops searching for its inscription. At the age of 10, he witnesses his father's death, when the latter is killed by machine-gun fire on August 16, 1945, the only occasion on which he ventured out, with officers who had deserted, to bomb the imperial palace after the capitulation of Japan.

At the beginning of the story, the narrator thinks he will die of liver cancer at the age of 35. He dictates a "history of the age" to an "acting executor of the will," who, at the end of the story, is revealed to be his wife. The writer highlights the political dimension of the delusion present in the psychoanalysis of madness and trauma, a process in which the patient and the analyst are co-researchers, in a field of historical catastrophes whose inscription is the aim of the therapeutic process. The writer provides tools designed to encourage what British psychoanalyst Wilfred Bion, based on his experiences in World War I, called "psychotic transference," at work in madness and trauma.

This very particular transference brings into question the frame of reference of traditional psychoanalysis when benevolent neutrality is attacked by tempestuous outbursts. Recourse to family history is of no use since time has stopped in the zones of catastrophe; causality is irrelevant, since it needs the past for the cause and the future for the effect; the destruction of all otherness obliterates identity and leads to absolute loneliness. Unconscious processes such as repression are not expressed in words – signifiers in Lacan's terms – since speech is no longer trustworthy; they are expressed through sensory images that survived the catastrophe.

The madness of Ōe's characters is not an illness, but a strength which impels them to fight against the erasure of traces. This madness uses specific tools to explore the silent zones of catastrophe, at the crossroads of their subjective and *historical* origins, and to inscribe them by means of fictional creations. What is at stake here, the historical truth, is political in nature, as are the stakes in the psychoanalysis of psychoses and traumas. A catastrophe is a near-history, something which could have become History, but fell short. It could have been History. In January 1946, God came down from the sky. That day, the emperor spoke over the radio "in a mortal voice," declaring that "he was of human essence." The Japanese were devastated and cried as they listened to their radios. The emperor was no longer a god. History could instead have consisted of a bomb being dropped on the palace, and the catastrophe would have been averted. This is the father's delusion in "The Day He Himself Shall Wipe My Tears Away."

For the narrator, this near-history took shape at the moment when he became the puppet of this delusion in a space of arrested time he calls his "happy days." This song title also made its appearance in my work as an analyst at the psychiatric hospital where I used to go every Monday.

Happy days at the psychiatric hospital

I had been seeing this delusional patient for twenty years. In the beginning, for several months, he did nothing but swear at me, or he refused to speak to me. At that time, he was very friendly with the intern, but he distrusted me greatly.

Suddenly, he started to tell me about his delusion. I can reconstitute some elements of his account. His father was a film projectionist, and his mother a cinema usherette. He had seen a great number of movies, and I presume that the segments he described afterwards to compose delusional stories were taken from various films. He dresses as a woman to play the heroine, using make-up. He creates images that he puts inside the television. The television then speaks to him by showing him these images.

The content of the delusion concerns some members of his mother's family, who are Nazis. His uncle is Hitler or Mussolini. We can suppose this to be a metaphor, but it isn't any longer. His suffering is real. He was letting himself die of hunger in his bed when I was asked to help him. That same day, when we talked again, he was critical of his delusion: "Everything I said was a lie. My uncle is not Hitler, all of that doesn't exist, it was put in my head by someone else."

A thought comes into my head. He has placed the origin of his delusion in another person, another madman. How will I be able to become this other madman in my work with him, to be truly in touch with his madness? He describes the moment when he stops identifying his own mind as the source of his delusion, but places this source in someone else. He has lent a record to his uncle's family, when they came to visit him; it was a recording of the song "Happy Days." Well, one may well be used to such coincidences, but they are still startling. What can I do with this particular coincidence? I relate the story written by Ōe, whom I happen to be reading at the time.

We start to talk. The other one – the mad one, who may still be positioned in the television or the radio – usually displays intense psychic activity. Since I don't know what else to say, I ask myself out loud what I could be thinking of. He looks at me and says with great conviction: "Why, nothing at all, of course." We stop there. He stops having delusions.

The coincidence created a social link at the place of a ruthless agency from which his delusion was trying to escape.

Making use of coincidences

Coincidences are one of the tools of transference when we work with those who are attempting to inscribe a cutaway history. They come from who knows where, and pull at the analyst, grabbing him by some particularity that ties him to the zone of catastrophe: in this case, two words: "happy days."

In our youth, a stock phrase among psychoanalysts was: "It's not by chance that ..." Well, precisely, I see no determinism of any kind here, not even unconscious, unless I go mad myself. And I think that the old word "asylum," once used to designate psychiatric hospitals, was not so preposterous, since these coincidences must be housed somewhere. In other cultures, ritual spaces exist to provide a locus for them, for otherwise they would be unbearable.

When I am tired, after months of work, I notice that patients who do not know each other use the same word or the same image as a connecting element between their sessions with me, as if they pass each other the word unknowingly.

The British anthropologist William Rivers,[3] who worked as a psychoanalyst with officers returning from the trenches during World War I, said of this phenomenon that on such occasions, he functions like a "pipe." Similarly, I find myself in the game of "the exquisite corpse" – *"le jeu du cadaver exquis"* – in which a paper is passed around, where everyone writes a sentence and folds the page before handing it to the next person. But here, so to speak, I am the paper which holds the impression of a word or thing. In the absence of a narrative that patients are at a loss to produce, they use me as their tool, in their attempt to tell a story.

Coincidences punctuate the moments of what could be called a "degree zero" of the encounter with the analyst, from which psychoanalysis may proceed. Is this the "objective chance" surrealists talked about? Hanged if I know! All I know is that the word "surrealism" was invented by Apollinaire, the poet "with a starry head," wounded by a bullet in the trenches during World War I.

And so, when the patient and I – here, we could speak of Harry Sullivan's concept of *self*, designating the space of our interaction – were talking about what I could possibly have in my head, something happened all at once: the coincidence of the American song, which produced a sudden encounter and put an abrupt end to the delusion, something that leaves one speechless.

In Lacanian terms, we can say that coincidences are an approach to the Real, described as "that which never stops not being written," or the impossible-to-write. Lacan also says: "The Real is the impossible, it always returns to the same place."[4] Still, this impossible is not destiny.

Paradoxically, the absence of symbolic articulation leaves no void, but only a bottomless, compact pit filled with senseless productions, allowing no interplay. Coincidences create an unprecedented interval – uncanny, *Unheimlich* – which opens the possibility of an intermediary space, a time-space called *ma* or *aida* in Japanese, and a "potential space" in Winnicott's writing.[5] This time-space creates the possibility of otherness in the extreme solitude of madness, for which no Other answers – except a ruthless intruding agency.

In such a space, a chance encounter triggers an interference with a possible other. Our patients often ask us: "By what chance did I meet you?"

Conversion of a chance encounter with the witness of an unwitnessed event

"Aghwee the Sky Monster" recounts the fate of a poor student paid by a banker to accompany his delusional son on his walks. Designated by the initial "D," the madman is a musician-composer whose problem, similar to that of the author, is the birth of an abnormal baby with a large lump on his head. But unlike Ōe's baby, the composer's baby did not survive.

D speaks to this infant, who has become a huge baby he alone can see when it comes down from the sky. His father has named him Aghwee, simply because between his birth and his death, he only spoke once, to say "aghwee" (p. 241). D makes the student the terrifyingly generous offer of changing places, by confiding his secret.

Ōe introduces this transformation in two stages: that of the gradual unfolding of transference, first in the literal sense, as they continue to take their walks, and then by writing the story more than ten years later. These two stages are punctuated by two accidents. First, on the road while the two young men are walking, D is struck and killed by a truck as he crosses the street. Ten years later, the narrator is blinded in one eye by children who throw stones at him for no reason. This is a recurrent theme in Ōe's work, in which often the narrators write in this blind state, explicitly called at the end of the story "a gratuitous sacrifice" (p. 261).

As long as the student has two good eyes, imaginary stereoscopy can build fictions and resistances, as it does for each of us. The first is that of the diagnosis. "Depression? Schizophrenia?" the student asks himself, while listening to the objective description the banker gives him of his son's case. This initial fiction sets the medical framework in which the disturbances caused by the madman in public places can be given a socially acceptable name. This diagnosis, always differential, answers the question: "Is there or is there not psychosis?"

At first, the narrator complies: "I was to be a moral sentinel guarding the family against a second contamination by the poisons of scandal" (p. 227). The second resistance comes in the form of well-meaning neutrality. The student waits for the patient's nurse to tell him what to do. She advises him to "play dumb" and not "get involved" (p. 237). After this, the student keeps a sort of "clinical distance": "I discovered that I was loving my job. Not loving my employer or his phantom baby the size of a kangaroo. Simply loving my job" (p. 244).

This reassuring distance can last forever, like psychoanalyses where nothing happens, where the patient and the analyst grow old together: the analyst likes his job. The composer, however, doesn't want this distance to persist, although he shows great understanding regarding his companion's difficulties. But he finds the situation very tiring.

Transformations of a relationship always take place when all forms of resistance and understanding have been exhausted – through seminars, supervisions, or comparisons with the stories of other patients. The tough hide softens little by little, until the process comes to resemble a striptease at the end of which the analyst finds himself naked.

The day when all imaginable limits are reached is a strange day. I don't know if it's a "happy day," or a "day of anger," a *Dies Irae*, quite unpredictable. On that day, the analyst faces what Raymond Devos calls "the hard reality of fiction," since he is called upon to become "the witness of events without a witness," an expression coined by the analyst Dori

Laub, one of the creators of the Fortunoff Video Archive for Holocaust Testimonies at Yale University. At the end of Ōe's story, the student joins the composer in the sphere the latter inhabits "outside of time."

Entering an anti-time

"I am a coded man of the anti-past." These are the words with which I was greeted by the patient I mentioned, the first time I saw him in his hospital bed, where he seemed to be completely disoriented. I had introduced myself, telling him my name and saying that I was a psychoanalyst on the ward. The team had told me: "We don't understand what he says." This coding was not the result of some logical reasoning that could give him perspective on what was happening to him. It came to him directly from the sphere he inhabited, when he had to face me, as someone who was supposed to investigate his past. The problem was that past had not passed. So he was coded by this anti-past. This is how he identified himself. Recourse to anamnesis and family history was of no use. This is why, in our seminar and with our patients, we cannot do without literature, where this particular time-space unfolds.

In fact, Freud gave us this advice. At the start of his text *Delusion and Dream in Jensen's Gradiva*, in which the madness of the young hero awakens the phantom of a young girl who had been buried in the ashes of Pompeii, Freud wrote in 1907 that "creative writers are valuable allies and their evidence is to be prized highly, for they are apt to know a whole host of things between heaven and earth of which our philosophy has not yet let us dream."[6]

The gigantic baby in Ōe's short story moves between heaven and earth, to say the least. In this intermediary space, the analyst will not, as many believe, look for the cause of madness by sifting through endless memories, but will work on the erased traces on the anti-trace road.

D tells the student who accompanies him on his walks: "[...] since I'm not living in present time, I mustn't do anything here in this world that might remain or leave an imprint" (p. 239). The only question he must not be asked is the one pertaining to cause: "'But why have you stopped living in present time?' I asked, and my employer sealed himself up like a golf ball and ignored me."

The analyst must not ask why either, but rather: "What am I doing in this with you, presuming that there is something I can do?" As they continue their meanderings side by side, the student changes places and testifies, in his own name, to the need for D's vision, in order to "outgrow our madness." When, at the end of the story, he visits the dying composer, this shared vision is exposed for the first time in a final exchange: "Then my throat was clogged with tears and I was surprised to hear myself shouting, 'I was about to believe in Aghwee!' At that moment [...] I saw a smile appear on D's darkened, shriveled face" (p. 260).

Ten years later, after the loss of his eye, the student confirms the validity of his discovery, when the violence of their two stories intersected:

> When I was wounded by those children and sacrificed my sight in one eye, so clearly a gratuitous sacrifice, I had been endowed, if only an instant, with the power to perceive a creature that had descended from the heights of my sky.
>
> (p. 261)

The critical moments in an analysis of madness or trauma, the moments when something changes, occur when we survive the patient's madness, which is by then also ours, at the intersection of catastrophic zones, on both sides.

A new agency of alterity is created in those circumstances, not without difficulty, as Ōe illustrates in his first short story, "The Day He Himself Shall Wipe My Tears Away," which I mentioned earlier.

The psychoanalysis of madness: joint research

In this short story, the one who fills the function of the "other" also has impaired vision. His vision is permanently blurred because he never takes off the "underwater goggles with cellophane covering the lenses," which had belonged to his father. He "had originally prepared them to observe a solar eclipse in Manchuria" during the war (p. 64).

We might think that this is a metaphor for their common inability to see. But metaphors are not possible when "a certain party," as the mother calls him, has become a perfect stranger who greets his son's arrival in the storehouse "with an angry Shhh! as if he were shooing a chicken away." Metaphors can't function outside the symbolic foundations of exchange with a reliable other. The diving equipment covers the narrator's eyes to adjust his perception to the gaze of the alien, who cannot adjust to the catastrophe suffered by Japan, as he tries to write the "history of the age" (p. 8). The artefact of the goggles tends towards inscription of the catastrophe, but does not depict it.

To carry out his writing, twenty-five years later, the narrator needs someone to act as "executor of the will," and to take down everything he relates (p. 9). It is not easy to hold the place of "the other," and they fight constantly. "Must I put down even that kind of silliness?" she asks, infuriating him. He can't tolerate any questions from her, particularly those concerning the man who bears such a strange designation. "Why do you keep calling him *a certain party*? Can't I change to 'father'?" (p. 49). When she is fed up with his demands, and when "he" insists on keeping this violent designation – thereby excluding the name of the father – she says that this name makes him sound "like an imaginary figure in a myth or in history."

For once, the narrator agrees to the need for creating imaginary figures of myth and fiction when everything has collapsed. Out of the ruins of the couple his parents once were, the child remains, in the place of the absent message. And the child will never stop searching for the erased traces of the phantom that haunts him:

> When I left the valley once and for all and moved to a place where there were no traces of *a certain party*, I gradually began to wonder myself [...] if I hadn't created *a certain party* entirely in my imagination [...]. At times, I've thought to myself maybe I have been mad since I was three [...] and someday if I recover my sanity the phantom tormenting me I call *a certain party* will disappear. But I feel differently now; if I'm a madman, fine, I'm resolved to stay that way and continue sharing life with my favorite phantom, *a certain party*. Ha! Ha! Ha!
>
> (p. 50)

Madness never stays where it has been put by an institution or a diagnosis. The narrator's madness prompts him to consult official military documents, as well as unofficial, reactionary sources, in which he comes across "*a certain party's* name frequently in accounts of anti-Tojo operations." (Hideki Tojo was the general of the Imperial Japanese Army and Prime Minister during World War II.) Ōe does not stick to the foreclosure of the name of the father, exhibited by the no-name "a certain party." The same thing applies to analytic work with madness: the analyst may seize the initial moment when the signifier of the name of the father was pulled out of the symbolic chain, the moment when everything fell apart, creating a psychotic structure, according to Lacanian theory. In practice, structure is quickly reduced to an illness, as if one could have foreclosure in the same way one might have chronic whitlow on one's toe. But what of it?

Ōe goes beyond this stereotype, by uncovering the historical field where madness functions as a research tool. We have only to look at the landscape a patient shows us when he tries to lend us the glasses that will allow us to be his co-researchers. This is the start of a process in which the analyst's aptitude as a co-researcher is constantly tested, in which his attempts to imagine the unimaginable will pile up on the floor like a pool of tears, tears the principal investigator cannot shed. When all efforts prove useless, when the analyst loses all his qualities and asks himself why he does this work, this experience of worthlessness indicates that he has entered a sphere where time has stopped. I will give you another example.

A young man who was coming to see me could not locate himself in time, which had to be constructed in the sessions. He often changed his appearance. I estimated that he had twenty different faces, which he created with changes to his hair and beard. On some occasions I didn't notice it, and suddenly I would see the mask he had brought me.

One day, I saw a face he had never shown me before: he looked like a financier of the Second Empire – under Napoleon III in the second half of nineteenth century. Indeed, the bank sent him, at tax time, a portfolio of stocks, to lighten the assets owned by his father, who can thereby break the law, and then take the stocks back at the end of that fiscal period. Of course, the patient did not buy the stocks, for he had no money. By coincidence, he had just lost his credit card, and mine had just been stolen with my wallet. So I told him: "You put your card in my pocket, and that's where you lost it." He had given me something to lose so that we could both be losers in this business, instead of being associates in the stock market game neither of us understood.

Now we had constructed a place for an "other" who might lose, in a world governed by an all-powerful, lawless agency for whom the other does not exist. After this, he came out of his paralysis. Not only did he arrive on time for his sessions, but he wore several watches. He even started to think about becoming a father – but that's another story.

"My delusion emerges at the crossroads of my history and world history"

This statement was made by a delusional patient whose madness was elaborating its own theory. During periods of political upheaval, traitors and dropouts appear in family lines, as was the case for this patient, whose father's collaboration with the Nazis had been kept quiet. Ōe would no doubt agree, since he constantly portrays breaks in the social link.

On a world history scale, the grandfather of the boy who joined his father in the dark storehouse had been guilty of grand treason in 1912. He had been "involved in a plot which had been exposed" (pp. 42–43). In the next war, the boy's father plots with dissident officers to "defend the national polity" (p. 44). The foreclosure of this cut-out history resulted in its persistent repetition in the aftermath.

At the level of personal history, a telegram announces that the boy's half-brother has deserted. A violent quarrel breaks out between his father and his mother, the deserter's stepmother. Both parents send back telegrams, with opposite messages. Not understanding what is going on, the child becomes the recorder of the event, "as if he were tracking [the telegram delivery man] with a directional microphone" (p. 59).

The boy is then entrusted with the two cables in which his parents are "trying to help my deserter brother in their own way, by different routes" (p. 60). The father's aim is to have the deserter "shot quickly and treated as if he'd died in action so at least his ashes will come home to us." The mother tries to save him. She screams at her husband: "You're trying to have that child killed before he reaches the other side? You want your own child shot in the back?" (p. 61).

Instead of receiving reassurances, the child, who witnesses this breaking apart, enters a time "out of joint," the time which Hamlet entered after his father's ghost revealed his uncle's villainous betrayal. The child will have to fill the void that annihilates all symbolic points of reference: "An emptiness the volume of one obese adult had opened in this world" (p. 52). The child first tries to fill the void with food, which he keeps procuring and preparing for his father. Later, he tries to fill the void through his search for old documents, to fill the pages of his "history of an age," driven by a sense of urgency in the face of impending death. "Once [he] began searching for a meaning, [the emptiness] proved to be a vacuum powerful enough to pull in all of his thirty-five years of life that protruded from his *Happy Days*" (p. 52).

Forms on the edge of catastrophe

In his *catastrophe theory*, formulated in the wake of a depression suffered after being awarded the Fields Medal, mathematician René Thom described forms emerging on the edge of catastrophes. In Ōe's story, at the point of rupture of the symbolic chain, a form is transmitted in the family through calligraphy of haiku poetry: "There's never been anything special about my family, but we have produced a number of calligraphers" (p. 50).

A taste for the pleasure of language is passed down to the hero of the story: "For all I know, whatever rhetorical skill I may have even now originates in simple puns" (p. 55). When the tool with the name is broken, as Wittgenstein says, puns and doggerels attempt to convey that which is not finding inscription: "They say that certain manic-depressives are fascinated by puns and anagrams. You're suggesting I'm that type of madman, and that all my chatter until now has been nothing more than a madman's raving, that everything recorded here about my past is therefore untrue" (p. 55), the narrator says defiantly to the executor of the will.

A psychiatric diagnosis of psychosis, based on the use of neologisms, could be applied to linguist Ferdinand de Saussure (1857–1913) and his contemporary Jean-Pierre Brisset (1837–1919), both at times quasi-delusional. They were from opposite backgrounds: Saussure the son of an aristocratic family from Geneva, and Brisset a country boy who left school at the age of 12 to work on the family farm, and then fought in the Crimean War and the Franco-Prussian War. But they had one thing in common: their passion for wordplay and anagrams.

In 1878, Brisset published *The Logical Grammar*, based, he says, on the language of frogs; his works were discovered and enjoyed by the famous French novelist and playwright Jules Romains. Brisset was elected "Prince of Thinkers" in a rigged election set up by Romain's friends, and became the darling of the surrealists and of the college of pataphysics.

Saussure's *Course in General Linguistics*, published posthumously in 1916, is preceded by a text on *Anagrams*, which he thought to be the basis of Latin Saturnian verse. In 1971, Jean Starobinski recounted the circumstance of this delirious discovery: how the linguist found, out of millions of combinations, the foundation for the composition of these few lines, using wooden letter tiles. In 1909, he stashed this device away in a safe-deposit box in a Geneva bank. Stay put!

In Ōe's story, the child's mother tells him to shut his mouth. By shutting himself away with his father, he tries to regenerate the symbolic chain through a common sacrifice. But no one is there to validate the symbolic status of this sacrifice, "tied into the knot of world history" (p. 54).

The father first shut himself in the storehouse in January 1943, after Japan's defeat in the naval battles of Midway and Guadalcanal:

> Late in 1942, burdened with the hopes and expectations of [...] the invaders in Manchuria, [he] had boarded a special plane and secretly had returned to Japan as a member of an underground group determined [to meet] Prime Minister Tojo. [They were] secret police officers who had massacred proletarian activists at the time of the 1923 earthquake.

After the failure of this meeting with Tojo, *a certain party* had come back to the valley and "had confined himself in the storehouse" for the first time (p. 54).

When the son finds "various so-called secret military journals," he recognises his father's writing – very clear, in phonetic script in the style of a famous calligrapher. The reference to that year (1942) brings back vivid images of a time in the past that had existed for *a certain party* and for himself, which they had shared, when he had longed "to die a mutual death" (p. 51). These forms of words, letters and images that survive catastrophe have been called "surviving images, *Nachleben*" by art historian Aby Warburg, who went mad at the start of World War I, and did not recover until 1923, when he presented his *Lecture on Serpent Ritual* in Ludwig Binswanger's clinic in Switzerland, where he was a patient.[7] In his lecture, he answers the plea: "Teach us to outgrow our madness" by showing – through his description of the Snake Dance among the Hopis, whom he had visited at the end of the previous century – how "a real and substantial symbolism appropriates by actual gestures that symbolism which exists in thought alone."

The end of Ōe's story comes back to the question of "how to outgrow our madness" and to the theme of *The Silent Cry*, which we shall discuss later. In Aby Warburg's words:

> To render things palpable, a being saturated with demonic energy is needed, for a full understanding of mysterious events. What we have seen in this all too brief summary of the snake cult is intended to show the change from real and substantial symbolism which appropriates by actual gestures to that symbolism which exists in thought alone.

For Warburg, the *Lecture on Serpent Ritual* served as a personal ritual performed before the patients and staff of the clinic, allowing him to come out of his isolation and take up his research again. In 1921, in the grip of delusions that started during World War I, he was screaming that all Jews would be exterminated – that they were threatened by genocide like American Indians – after "the seismograph of his soul" had recorded, in his childhood, the rise of mass anti-Semitism in Germany, threatening his family of bankers in Hamburg in the years following the War of 1870.

Political stakes: what cannot be said can only be shown

The cover of a French edition of Jacques Lacan's seminar *Les écrits techniques de Freud* shows an elephant. This elephant that no one wants to see in the china shop of psychoanalytic discourse is History. Lacan's "Remarks on Psychic Causality," published in *Écrits* and delivered at the Bonneval Conference in September 1946 – one year after "the Emperor swiftly descended to earth to announce the surrender in the voice of a mortal man" (p. 98) – makes no mention of the war. Yet the aim of the psychoanalysis of madness and trauma is to detect the erasure of traces.

This is also the belief of the obese man at the crucial moment when he decides to be the eyes of "his chosen son." Just before dying in the suicide military mission of the officers – who drew him out of the storehouse to participate in the bombing of the imperial palace so that the emperor may be spared the humiliation of defeat – the father passes on this injunction to his son, who had been dragged along: "Have you seen what must be seen? For the next quarter-century that you will live remember always what you have seen. All has been accomplished, you have seen what must be seen. Survive and remember" (p. 101).

Like Don Quixote, the child wears "his *fake* helmet down over his ears and a rusty old broken bayonet tied at his side" (p. 89). In the prologue of the first book of *Don Quixote de la Mancha*, Cervantes calls his hero "my son," a "chosen son" charged with transmitting to the reader, in hallucinatory form, the author's successive visions of war and captivity, which were cut out once peace returned. These events, too often neglected by psychoanalysis, are recounted with precision by Ōe.

The executor of the will insists on specifying that it was on August 16 – "the day after the war ended," and not on August 15 – the day Japan surrendered – that the father was killed and the 10-year-old child "decided the responsibility was all his [for an] action that turned the country's history upside-down" (p. 103). This event was not the cause of his madness, but the start of a search for his co-researcher, the "acting executor of the will," who would be able to participate in his quest.

Of course, signifiers are missing from the account of what really took place, at the macro and the micro levels of history. But are they lost for everyone? Signifiers that have broken loose from the weave of history are referred to as "signifiers in the Real," and they cannot be brought back into the fold by the shepherd of the symbolic. They remain floating, sometimes for a very long time, trying to grab on to something – to lives, to bodies, to voices, to visions, to little things – until the day when a second catastrophe occurs, prompting the need to explore, in order to inscribe it, the original catastrophe that no one suspects. The son of the obese man searches for them in unofficial documents – because a signifier is something that floats and continues to live its life outside of the signifying chain. You'll probably ask: "Prove it then, show me a floating signifier." And I'll answer: "That would be too dangerous!" as we will see in Ōe's novel *The Silent Cry*.

Far from being rigidly embedded in the structure, madness is a means of investigation that finds, beyond the impossibility of inscription, a way to show that which cannot be said – for instance, phantoms coming through walls and mirrors, or from clouds, like Aghwee, the giant baby. But these forms have to be validated by another, who is guided by the "seismograph of his soul." Indeed, the "signifiers in the Real" are carrying violent affects with them, ever since they were pulled out of the symbolic chain. Paradoxically, these affects may not be felt, since the absence of the reflecting quality of mirrors eliminates the capacity to feel.

The philosopher Ludwig Wittgenstein can testify to this. After his return from the war and the suicide of his three older brothers, he spent ten years in Vienna in a post-traumatic state. Then he went back to Cambridge at the end of the 1920s and changed the last sentence of the *Tractatus Philosophicus*, written on the front lines, from "Whereof one cannot speak, thereof one should stay silent" to "... thereof one cannot help to show it." But shown to whom? The problem is to find an other who can grasp what he calls an "ostensive definition."

This relationship is depicted at the beginning of his *Lectures* on "Private Experience" and "Sense Data," written in 1934–1935. It begins with a meeting between the philosopher and somebody "who looks lost and speaks in a toneless voice," unable to "communicate his true sense of inferiority in any other way." The philosopher expresses his dismay: "There is something more about it, but you can't say it. It is this idea which plays hell with us." By sharing his impression, the philosopher is able to engage in dialogue with the person who has given up on the possibility of dialogue. He remarks that in these circumstances, the inside and the outside are not constituted. "Inside, outside!" the philosopher exclaims in exasperation.

As the *Lectures* continue, Wittgenstein describes the situation portrayed by Ōe, in which "we are tempted to say I have gone mad," when he develops the idea of placing glasses of different shapes on a child, naming a colour for each pair. For example, red for the round glasses, "in order for the child to see what the adult has never seen," like the son of the recluse father, and like the child Ludwig, whose family had repudiated its Jewish origins a century earlier. In these situations, Wittgenstein says, "the notion of an ego inhabiting a body must be abandoned." It is possible to feel someone else's pain; this is the origin of his famous phrase: "I don't choose the mouth which says I have toothache."

French child psychoanalyst Françoise Dolto (1908–1988) shared such an experience with Sioux medicine men we had invited to Paris. They had expressed the desire to come to Paris during one of our visits to the Rosebud Indian Reservation in South Dakota, where psychologist Jerry Mohatt, who spoke their language, Lakota, had invited us to his ranch for several summers. We had organised meetings at the École des hautes études en sciences sociales (EHESS) in Paris and at the Maison de la culture in Reims. One of them was held in our home, and we had invited Françoise Dolto, whom we did not know personally.

Medicine man Joe Eagle Elk described the ceremony he had performed at the request of doctors at a hospital in Nebraska for a Sioux child who was letting himself die, locked in a morbid state impossible to treat. The ceremony took place in his room, with several people from his tribe present, in accordance with the ritual we had attended on the reservation. First, the medicine man calls forth the spirits, his allies, and, speaking in old Lakota, he recounts the initial vision that set him on the path of becoming a medicine man. Then each of the people seated in a circle says what his own associations are, or skips his turn, saying only *"mitakuye oyasin"* ("all my relatives"), including kinship with animals, plants and rocks. On that occasion, Joe saw the child's body on the ceiling, alternately bathed in flashes of light and plunged into darkness. The spirits present were those of thunderstorms, called *heyoka*. After the ceremony, the child started to live again, to the surprise of the entire hospital staff.

What were Dolto's associations? To our surprise, she nodded and said simply:

> For me, it's exactly the same. When I'm faced with such a severe downturn, I feel in the place of the child and I describe the primary opposites of hot and cold, hard and soft, light and darkness, which he can't feel.

It was a joyful gathering, because laughter is part of the ceremonies. Gatherings are always held in the dark – a reminder that they were prohibited until recently. Laughter is heard when the lights come back on, while the person who requested the ceremony treats the participants to food such as boiled beef, fried bread and wild cherry jam. Jokes are shared to bring us back to earth. Likewise, ancient Greek drama included Aristophanes' comedies along with tragedies, and Kyōgen farces were part of Noh theatre in Japan, to allow spectators to come back to everyday life.

II. MADNESS AND TRAUMA IN *THE SILENT CRY*

This book is difficult to read, even in Japanese, as Akira Mizubayashi explained, suggesting that we give a brief summary of it. This difficulty was intentional on Ōe's part. When we met him at a conference he gave in Paris at the Japanese embassy, he insisted with great fervour on the influence of his teacher, Professor Kazuo Watanabe, a François Rabelais expert, and on his own strong will not to let his style go down, but "to raise it to a higher sense" – Rabelais' expression – to which we will return in Seminar 12. In the novel, he relates the confrontation between two brothers with unusual names, written in kanji characters. The first brother's name, Mitsusaburo, means "the secret," and the sign following the kanji indicates his position as third son, after two older siblings. Takashi means "falcon," and is the name of the fourth son. The brothers' names indicate opposite positions in the social link.

In the first chapter, "In the Wake of the Dead," Mitsu is sitting at the bottom of a pit in his yard, meditating on the suicide of a friend and on the birth of his own child, who has the same brain anomaly as Aghwee, and as Ōe's own son. His friend killed himself after returning from the US, where he met Mitsu's brother Takashi, who had gone to America as a member of a student theatre group. The members of the group had taken part in the political riots of 1960, aiming to stop the signing of the Japan–U.S. Security Treaty.

The second chapter, "Family Reunion," describes Takashi's return and his intention to take his brother and his brother's wife back to their native village, to the valley deep in the forest where, 100 years earlier, their great-grandfather's brother had led a peasant uprising and had disappeared mysteriously after it was suppressed. Takashi intends to sell the old family house, with its adjacent pavilion, and then lead a revolt similar to that of his ancestor. The confrontation between the two brothers reproduces the conflict between their great-grandfather and his younger brother.

Their arrival in their native village is the subject of the third chapter, "Mighty Forest." In the village, Takashi feels impelled to draw the young men of the valley out of their apathy by teaching them to play football, so that he can incite them to rebel. In the next chapter, "Dreams within Dreams," we learn that their older brother, killed when he returned from World War II, in which their father was declared missing, has not been given a funeral, and that their mother went mad and their sister killed herself.

The four chapters that follow recount the stages of a revolt against the director of a supermarket chain, including the plundering of the local store. While all this is going on, Mitsusaburo remains aloof, choosing to separate himself from these events and to reconstitute the historical truth of past events that his brother insists on enacting in the present. Takashi also insists on reviving a lost ritual, the dance for the invocation of "forest spirits," while Mitsusaburo isolates himself in the pavilion, leaving his wife alone with his brother.

Starting with the eighth chapter, "Truth Unspeakable," the chaos produced by the "communal madness" and the failure of the revolt drive Takashi to more and more violent acts, escalating, in the penultimate chapter, "A Way beyond Despair," to the point where he tells his brother the truth about their sister's suicide, before taking his own life. The book ends with the discovery of the cutaway truth about two successive rebellions, led in 1860 and 1871 by the brother of their great-grandfather, before and after the Meiji Restoration. These historical facts are discovered in documents stored in the village temple, as well as in an unknown cellar discovered when the pavilion was demolished. At the end of the novel, Mitsusaburo and his wife Natusko decide to leave the valley for good, and to raise the child they had placed in an institution.

The cutaway unconscious

Two opposite positions are involved: that of Takashi, who acts out like mad and revives a sacred dance in an attempt to perform gestures that could become symbolic in the realm of thought, and that of Mitsusaburo, who stands in the very precarious position of the other whom Takashi talks to in a psychotic transference, which against all odds sets time into motion again in the end.

Right at the start, the narrator, Mitsusaburo, who was blinded in one eye by a stone, crouches in a hole excavated in his yard. Though psychoanalysis associates blindness with the myth of Oedipus, let's not rush to invoke the famous complex: killing father, sleeping with mother – the hallmarks of neurosis and castration. Sophocles went far beyond that.

Two decades after *Oedipus Rex*, he wrote *Oedipus at Colonus*,[8] a play in which the blind Oedipus arrives with Antigone and Ismene in this Athenian suburb, where he will die. It is there that Sophocles (496–405 BC) was born and died. Legend has it that at the age of 90, when he was accused by his sons of losing his head, he read this play before the tribunal, which greeted it with acclamation and acquitted him. In 401 BC, his grandson had the play produced for the first time.

To reach the place where he intends to die, Oedipus crosses the "brass-footed threshold" and asks his daughters to go away: "Leave this place and do not think to look upon that which you must not, nor hear it" (v. 1640). He is left alone with Theseus, the king of Athens, described by the messenger with "his hand across his face uplifted, to withstand the sight of some dread vision which no eye of mortal might endure" (v. 1646). And he concludes: "For this tale if any deem me mad ... for such, I care not what they say" (v. 1665). The theme of the play is political since Colonus will be a source of prosperity for Athens. Oedipus tells Theseus:

> Keep the secret safe and when you come to the end of life, reveal it only to your closest heir, then let him teach his too, and so in perpetuity. Thus you will keep this town of Athens safe from Theban warriors.
>
> (v. 1530)

At the end of Sophocles' tragedy, like at the end of *The Silent Cry*, the social link is re-established. Fate, *atè*, – from the verb *aô*, to drive mad – encountered by both blind heroes, is thwarted through the cathartic ritual of ceremonial theatre.

The mind and the brain

The first chapter of *The Silent Cry*, "In the Wake of the Dead," starts with Mitsusaburo's meditation during the hours before daylight in a pit dug in his yard for a septic tank. Huddling at the bottom of the pit, he sees with his blinded eye that the suicide of his friend, who hung himself, is connected with the chance meeting his friend had with the narrator's brother Takashi, when they were both in the US. He also sees the accident that cost him his eye, and the expressionless gaze of his baby after the operation that removed the lump on his brain. At the conclusion of the novel, the narrator will take up this crouching posture again, at the end of the long way he has come. The first meditation is not introspection, but rather the observation of his own brain after the loss of his eye, which occurred in "a nasty, stupid incident, one morning [when] a group of […] hysterical school children flung a chunk of stone at [him]."

The blind eye has become a camera focused on his brain:

> I [assigned] a role to this eye: I saw it, its function lost, as being forever trained on the darkness within my skull, a darkness full of blood and somewhat above body heat. The eye was a lone sentry that I'd hired to keep watch on the forest of the night within me, and in doing so I'd forced myself to practice observing my own interior.
>
> (p. 2)

This observation is not unlike Freud's in *Project for a Scientific Psychology*, written in 1896 in pencil, on a train bringing him back to Vienna from Berlin, where he had visited his friend Wilhelm Fliess. Observing neuronal connections under a microscope, Freud describes a series of filters for the enormous quantity of energy coming from the outside, which he calls omega. The first filter of the primary process, called phi, is composed of "word and thing representations" that are eventually transformed by the secondary process into "representants of the representation" – called "signifiers" by Lacan.

Mitsusaburo's blinded eye analyses the primary filter, when he becomes aware that his "consciousness has caught something unexpected on its very outer edge" (p. 17). This unconscious on the edge of the conscious, at work in madness and trauma, is not the repressed unconscious, as Freud points out on several occasions – for instance, in *Gradiva*, a story of madness and trauma. It is constituted by "surviving images" that are not articulated through signifiers since the symbolic chain is broken. According to Ōe: "The factors that remain ill defined may sometimes lead a survivor to the very site of the disaster, but even then the only thing clear to anyone concerned is that he has been brought up against something incomprehensible" (p. 18).

For Ōe's hero, one of these factors is the red of the dogwood leaves, which remind him of the "picture of hell" his great-grandfather had commissioned (p. 70). He was to find the painting, at the end of the novel, in the temple of his native village, where it has been hanging ever since. Having survived the disaster relentlessly unfolding in the novel, the narrator understands this initial impression, and will be able to decipher its meaning during his second meditation:

> I'd seen the same flaming red on the backs of the dogwood leaves that day-break as I lurked in my pit in the garden. It had summoned up memories of the painting of hell back here in the hollow, and impressed me as a kind of signal. The meaning of that signal, uncertain then, was readily under-standable now. The "tender" red of the painting was essentially the color of self-consolation, the color of people who strove to go on quietly living their murkier, less stable, and vague every-day lives rather than face the threat of those terrifying souls who tackled their own hell head-on. Ultim-ately, I felt sure that great-grandfather had commissioned the hell picture for the repose of his own soul. And the only people who had drawn con-solation from it were those of his descendants who, like grandfather and myself, lived out their lives in vague apprehension, unwilling to allow the urgent inner demand for sudden, unscheduled leaps forward to grow to the point where action was necessary.
>
> (p. 271)

What has happened since? A story of madness at the crossroads of world history and the subjective history of the narrator.

The "sudden leap" referred to in Mitsusaburo's second meditation is the one his brother will take, impelled by something he doesn't understand. A leap over the catastrophes of History, which arrested time in the village for 100 years. Takashi explores this temporal discontinuity by identifying with an event, in a present that lasts a century, since the period before the opening of Japan by Emperor Meiji, which ended the country's isolation – *sakoku* – that had lasted since the seventeenth century.

On the level of personal history, a conflict between two brothers is repeated, four generations later, after the collapse in the war of all guarantees of the social link. Like in the psychoanalysis of psychosis and trauma, the Furies waiting in arrested time go wild without warning. The crisis falls on a fool because that's what folly is about, to show the unleashing of Furies. Still, there is nothing closer to madness than normalcy, said Harry Stack Sullivan. He was speaking from his experience as a psychoanalyst working with schizophrenics and from his personal experience as the grandson of Irish immigrants fleeing the Potato Famine on a boat. And he added: "Madmen are the subject of social sciences, at the breaking point of the elements holding society together."

Takashi appears to be a normal man. Nothing predisposes him to the tragedy that will befall him. But little by little, the reader becomes aware that, like in Greek tragedies, everything is timed with precision, like an "Infernal Machine," to quote the title of Jean Cocteau's play about Oedipus. Takashi is programmed to resolve the madness of the gaping hole left in the family history. He reveals the "code of this anti past" in a final confession to his brother, made in Chapter 11, "A Way beyond Despair": "Mitsu, I want to tell you the truth" (p. 234). Mitsusaburo chooses not to follow his brother on the path of self-sacrifice. Instead, to "outgrow madness," he resorts paradoxically to a beneficial loss of identity.

Identity loss

Everyone in the narrator's world has what it takes to go mad. His sister committed suicide. Takashi confesses: "Although she was half-witted, she was really a rather special kind of person" (pp. 235–236). She loved music and listened to every note, never forgetting a single one, and hearing even the intervals between the notes. She cried when she heard engine noises or vulgar songs (pp. 236–237). The narrator's wife is "a rather special kind of person" as well; she is drowning her sorrow in drink since the birth of the baby, and her husband does not try to stop her. In fact, thinking of his friend's suicide, he reflects: "I too have the seeds of that same, incurable madness" (p. 10). At the start of the novel, he is presented as he awakens:

> Whenever I awaken, I seek again that lost, fervid feeling of expectation [...]. Finally convinced that I'll not find it, I try to lure myself down the slope to second sleep: *sleep, sleep! – the world does not exist.* [...] *Sleep, sleep! – if you can't sleep then pretend you're asleep.* Fear threatens to engulf me.
>
> (p. 1)

This is the fear Winnicott described in his last article, "Fear of Breakdown": the fear of annihilation. This fear was experienced by Mitsusaburo as a child when he was struck in the eye:

> I lay where I fell on the sidewalk, unable to make out what had happened. [...] Even now, I've never felt I understood the true meaning of the incident. Moreover, I'm afraid of understanding. [...] I was already showing more and more clearly a quality of ugliness [...]. The lost eye emphasized the ugliness each day ...
>
> (p. 2)

Winnicott speaks of patients who fear a catastrophe when they wake up each morning. And he declares:

> [...] the breakdown [...] *has already been*. The unconscious here is not exactly the repressed unconscious of Freud's formulation [...], nor is it the unconscious of Jung. [...] In other words, the patient must go on looking for the past detail which is *not yet experienced*. [...] [But] if the patient is ready for some kind of acceptance of this queer kind of truth, that what is not yet experienced did nevertheless happen in the past, then the way is open for the agony to be experienced in the transference, in reaction to the analyst's failures and mistakes. [...] The patient needs to "remember" [the agony] but it is not possible to remember something that has not yet happened, and this thing of the past has not happened yet because the patient was not there for it to happen to. This past and future thing then becomes a matter of the here and now, and becomes experienced by the patient for the first time. [...] The experience of annihilation as a reaction to environmental factors could have caused a premature awareness awakened before birth because of a maternal panic.
>
> (p. 106)

The senseless incident that blinded Mitsusaburo in one eye did not happen "to him," because he was not there "for it." He had removed himself from his body in response to the incredible violence of the impact, which returns in the form of terrifying expectation. This past and future thing will become his experience for the first time if he can tie it in with the cutaway history of his family and of the valley. He will then abandon the role of passive victim, and become an active witness of the disaster, by deciding to survive.

His trajectory parallels that of the analyst who can't help making blunders when his ability to imagine is depleted. Aware of his uselessness and of the inadequacy of all his qualities, he acquires the status without status of the "true man of no rank," as defined by Zen master Lin Tsi, whose French translator Paul Demiéville compares him to Musil's *Man without Qualities*. In Chapter 2, "Family Reunion," when the narrator, his wife and a young couple are waiting for Takashi in a hotel room near the airport, the narrator is the only one who senses an impending catastrophe.

The red painting of hell, which until then had acted like a mirror thanks to its consoling tenderness, is no longer reflecting any image back to the narrator: "The present 'I' had lost all true identity. Nothing, either within me or without, offered any hope of recovery" (p. 58). The accusing voice of the young man beside him in the hotel room, a fervent admirer of his brother, blurts out: "You're just a *rat*."

Until then, the red colour in the painting had allowed him to keep the phantoms of history at bay. "When the tool with the name no longer exists," says Wittgenstein in section 41 of his *Philosophical Investigations*, "it is still possible to imagine a language-game," not necessarily verbal, "in the place of the name that has lost its meaning." In the language-game involving the painting commissioned by their great-grandfather, "in the place of the name of his brother which had lost all meaning," there are three possible roles to play: that allotted to Takashi, who will go mad and step through the frame to the other side; that of the great-grandfather and his great-grandson, who watch their brothers, seeing both their gentleness and their violence; and that of Mitsusaburo, who rejects this position and, at the limits of each attitude – between action and contemplation – decides, at the end of the novel: "I would live on [...], peering out timidly like a rat, with my single eye, at a dim and equivocal outer world ..." (p. 269).

His decision was already taking shape in an inaugural dream he had in the airport hotel while waiting for his brother. In the dream, he is watching a silent world filled with silent ghosts:

> Large numbers of people bumped into my [...] back incessantly [...]. All the people [...] were old. [...] I [was] struggling to remember something that troubled me. Then I realized that my friend who had hanged himself and the idiot baby consigned to an institution were both present among the old men who filled the street [...]. [They] were almost identical with the other old men [...]; all the old men who filled the street were in some way relevant to me. I tried to burst into their world, met some invisible resistance, and gave a cry of despair: "*I deserted you!*"
>
> (pp. 31–32)

For the first time, an "I" appears. It is the "I" that abandoned not only the ancestors and his son, but also his own self at the moment of extreme solitude of his accident, which was witnessed by no "other." At the end of the novel, he will decide not to abandon his son, or himself.

But first, when Takashi arrives, they all leave for the village in the forest, where ghosts will make their presence felt and bring to light the truth about the past, not only concerning their ancestors, but also concerning one of their older brothers and their sister who committed suicide.

Relinquishing causality

Noh theatre presents two characters, the *Waki*, a pilgrim who "at the crossroad of dreams" – as the little stage is called – witnesses the arrival of the *Shite*, with his white mask, coming through the bridge in between here and the beyond, to sing and dance untold stories of a remote past that has not passed. Takashi is the *Shite*, who embodies the phantom of their great-grandfather's brother. He enacts his uprising in the present under cover of training the youth to play football. Mitsusaburo is the *Waki*, who stands apart and sees, at the crossroad of dreams, the unfolding of cut-out truths.

Now, there is one question: "Why?" which must never be asked in a context of madness, but I can't help asking it: "Why are you doing this?" This question is repeated several times by Natusko, Mitsusaburo's wife, who will also come a long way as the story unfolds. Having become pregnant with Takashi's child while her husband shut himself away in the pavilion, she emerges from the abyss of alcoholism, after Takashi's suicide, decides to keep his baby, to leave the village with her husband, and to take back their son from his institution.

When the story begins, she follows her husband to the village knowing nothing about the family's tragedy. In addition to the mystery surrounding his great-grand-uncle, another enigma concerns his older brother, designated only by the initial "S." His story takes the reader back to World War II, in which S fought, was killed after his return to the village, and incinerated without any funeral rites.

The two brothers argue constantly about these things, as did their ancestors 100 years earlier. Takashi, the youngest, idealises their older brother, while Mitsusaburo, who was 10 at the end of the war, can testify to a cut-out truth: S took part in a raid on the Korean settlement where black market activities went on, and after a Korean man was killed, "he offered himself as a scapegoat to be lynched. [...] As a kid of ten, he says, I [wasn't] likely [to] have appreciated the inner motives for S's behaviour ..." (p. 76). Their mother, already quite crazy, refused to see her son's body and to give him a burial on the pretext that beforehand, he had tried to take her to a mental hospital.

Horrified by these stories, the narrator's wife is impelled to ask: "Why?" Takashi answers: "In my dreams, I've never had the slightest doubt why S had to play the role" (p. 77). Concerning this inevitable question, psychoanalyst Martin Cooperman, who worked with psychosis, used to say: "I never ask a patient why, for only God can answer that question. The only question possible is 'how?'" During the Pacific War, in which the father of the two brothers in the novel was killed, Cooperman was a young flight surgeon on the Wasp aircraft carrier shot down by the Japanese.

The question of how to deal with the death of S is answered the following summer by Mitsusaburo, who is 11 and performs a ritual ceremony. At that time, the nembutsu dance was performed every summer in honour of the "spirits." Takashi revives this obsolete custom in Chapter 7: "Every year during the Bon festival, they came," from the forest into the hollow, "in a single-file procession"; these figures:

> represented the malevolent "spirit" [...] of one of the village ancestors who had led a brutal life, or of some good man who had died an unhappy death [...] of men drafted from the valley who had been killed in battle [...] the "spirit" of a young man who had been working in a Hiroshima factory and was killed by the atomic bomb.

(pp. 124–125)

That summer, unbeknownst to his mother, Mitsusaburo had given the tatami-maker, who also made masks, his dead brother's winter uniform jacket. "The next day, the party that came down the gravel road from the forest included a 'spirit' wearing the jacket, dancing for all it was worth ..." (p. 125).

Lacan coins the phrase "a space between two deaths," to speak of this interval between biological death and a symbolic grave, in his seminar *The Ethics of Psychoanalysis*, in reference to Sophocles' Antigone, who enters her tomb alive. The ghost of the sister who killed herself haunts this space, in the last chapter called "Retrial," in which Takashi confesses the truth to his brother: "I'm going to tell you, Mitsu! [...] you may have dimly suspected there was something odd about her death" (pp. 234–235).

His confession comes after the failure of the revolt against the "emperor of the supermarkets." After the looting of the store, Takashi rapes and kills a young girl belonging to the group of young people he had led into revolt. It is then that he reveals to his brother that he had forced their sister into an incestuous relationship, to which she later participated willingly. She became pregnant and, after an abortion performed in the city, when she sought solace from him, he had slapped her. And she, who had never lied, told him: "It wasn't true what you said, Taka. It was wrong, even though we kept it secret." And the next morning she killed herself (p. 239).

His one-eyed brother had indeed seen "something odd," thanks to the loss of his identity. The visions produced by madness and trauma are not the kind that reflect themselves in mirrors. They can only be expressed when they have been caught in the net of an interference, which starts a narrative. As the story unfolds, Mitsusaburo, like all of Ōe's narrators, becomes an analyst and an "annalist," leading an inquiry on facts cut out from history. As Wilfred Bion says, after having recounted, when he was over 70, his war years in two autobiographical books, *The Long Week-End* and *All My Sins Remembered*, and in *A Memoir of the Future*, a book of fiction: "One is not born a psychoanalyst, but becomes one." One becomes a psychoanalyst by creating a new language-game that, for the first time, brings otherness into existence.

The different agencies of the other

What is a fiction as opposed to the thing, *das Ding*, which cannot be symbolised? Faced with the unnameable and unimaginable of historical discontinuity, the only possible approach is a work of fiction, telling stories. This is how myths are used in Greek tragedies, because it was forbidden to represent contemporary catastrophes on stage for fear that they may trigger traumatic revivals. Fools will tell you that they are creating fiction. When the fiction takes the shape of a delusion, they want you to answer the riddle: "Do you believe it or not?" This question resembles a *koan*, an aporia much appreciated in Zen practice, which poses a quandary in logical reasoning. If you answer "yes," you are thought crazy; if you answer "no," you are sent packing. In fact, the question is not about belief, but about trust: "Do you trust what I am showing you?"

Such a challenge was presented to us by Alain Touraine, director of our Center for the Study of Social Movements (CSSM) at the EHESS, when he compared our research on *Madness and the Social Link* with that of another researcher, Daniel Vidal, author of books on prophets from the Cévennes region and on the writings of mystics: "Vidal, he said, makes the dead talk; and you, the madmen: you can make them say whatever you like." In fact, madmen and prophets of all people are the ones who only say what they want to say: they keep saying the same thing in a disorderly flood that is also an organised sequence. By raising the question of the breakdown of the symbolic Other, who vouches for the given word, and that of the absence of a small other reflected by the mirror, they challenge a ruthless agency whose favourite sport is "attacks on linking," as Bion says, to destroy any form of otherness.

In addition to these three agencies of otherness, the Japanese language has a fourth, according to Augustin Berque, Director of the Center for Studies on Contemporary Japan at the EHESS, which he calls *tanin* – the others with whom one has no relation. The underlying logic is "areolar," progressing by successive extensions from the inner space *uchi*, home, delimited by the raised threshold where people from outside stop and sit. In *The Silent Cry*, the narrator thinks about his own relation to this agency he calls the "absolute other," the same one as in "The Day He Himself Shall Wipe My Tears Away":

> My "new life" in the valley was only a ruse devised by Takahashi to forestall my refusal and clear the way for him to sell the house and land for the sake of whatever obscure purpose was firing him at the moment. From the very outset, the journey to the valley hadn't really existed for me. Since I no longer had any roots there, nor made any attempt to put down new ones, even the house and land were as good as nonexistent; it was no wonder that my brother should have been able to filch them from me with only a minimal exercise of cunning. [...] Now, even if the whole valley should charge me with being a rat, I could retort with hostility, "And who are you, to insult a stranger whose affairs are none of yours?" Now I was just a transient in the valley, a one-eyed passerby too fat for his years, and life there had the power to summon up neither the memory nor the illusion of any other, truer self.
>
> (pp. 134–135)

Another character, a hermit living in the forest – a teacher who has gone mad – plays the role of go-between between the space of wilderness and the space of the village. In Europe, the novels of the Middle Ages call the mountain and the forest "the space of the marvel," where madness meets beings that one never encounters, other than in fairy tales: fairies, ogres, and other monsters or spirits.

The village in *The Silent Cry* is part of such a time-space. For 100 years – since the failure of the revolt led by the great-grandfather's brother – the village has remained outside the social link. The bridge linking it to the rest of the world is broken. It will be rebuilt at the end of the novel, when the stammering of history, brought back into the present by the failure of the rebellion led by Takashi, stops after his self-sacrifice. A new social link emerges on the political front, as the young village priest informs the narrator:

> You remember the spartan young man who worked with Taka? They say he'll get a seat on the council when the first elections since the amalgamation of the village are held. Taka's rising might seem to have been a complete failure, but at least it served to shake the valley out of its rut. [...] I feel that a definite prospect for future development in the valley has opened up at last.
>
> (p. 266)

Madness: a battle against perversion

This does not mean that Ōe advocates suicide. At the end of the novel, he makes a distinction between Mitsaburo's attitude and that of his brother, based on a criterion of good faith. Beyond the looking glass through which pass the phantoms of history, a confrontation takes place between two visions: that of Takashi, who denies what he sees, and that of Mitsusaburo with his blind eye, who perceives intuitively what his brother is hiding. Expecting to die after the raping and killing of the young girl, Takashi wants to redeem himself by giving one of his eyes to his brother: "Then my eyes at least will survive and see lots of things after my death [...]. You'll do it, won't you, Mitsu?" (p. 240).

Mitsu refuses, feeling indignant. He senses the fraudulent nature of this deal that sounds phony, and he tells his brother:

> Taka [...] you're the type who invariably has a way out at the last moment. You acquired the habit on the day that sister's suicide allowed you to go on living without either being punished or put to shame. I'm sure this time, too, you'll work some nasty little dodge to go on living. Then, having so shamefully survived, you'll make your excuses to her ghost: "In fact", you'll say, "I deliberately put myself in a tight corner where I had no choice but to be lynched or executed, but a lot of inter-fering bastards forced me to go on living." [...] but you're expecting somehow to survive. [You] deceive even yourself.
>
> (pp. 240–241)

This refusal to accept the offer is followed by Takashi's suicide; his brother finds him in front of the outline of a target drawn on the wall:

> the outline of a human head and shoulders was drawn in red pencil, with two great eyes carefully marked in on the head. I took another step forward and [...] saw that the pencilled eyes had been blasted full of shot.
>
> (p. 244)

Is he then the cause of Takashi's suicide because he refused to let him play the role of a false hero? Ōe does not answer the question "Why?" but leads us towards another truth cut away from history.

At the end of the novel, the storehouse – sold by Takashi to the "emperor of the supermarkets," owner of a chain of stores and the target of the revolt – is dismantled before being transported to Tokyo to be made into a "folkloric" restaurant. During the dismantling, under the floorboards, a splendid stone cellar with two rooms is discovered. It becomes clear that their great-grandfather's brother had lived there, voluntarily holed up in isolation.

The truth emerging from this cellar destroys the story Takashi had believed about his ancestor's heroic flight to the US, or even Tokyo, under an assumed name, "after the 1860 rising [...] and the tragedy" of his fellow rebels' decapitation (p. 257).

The truth continues to reveal itself in the documents given to the narrator by the young priest of the temple. These documents, written by their grandfather, describe another peasant uprising, in 1871, against the new government officials, after Emperor Meiji abolished the clans. In these accounts, there is mention of a mysterious leader who "disappeared as though wiped off the face of the earth." It is clear that he can be no other than the recluse who came out of his hideout, and then went back again, after the suppression of this second revolt.

Mitsusaburo retreats again, this time into the newly found cellar, where he meditates upon his double refusal: "squatting with my back against the white wall at the far end of the back room, just as the voluntary captive must have done a century earlier." He refuses to understand the man who "had indeed shut himself up here and maintained his identity as leader of the rising to the end of his days." Then he struggles to understand himself, and the fact that he had "refused aid in the face of [Takashi's] pitiful request made when death was already upon him" (pp. 268–269). After this, he "saw another [him] slip free from [his] drooping shoulders [...] and, rising, crawl through the gap in the floorboards." When the phantom "arrived directly below the great wooden beam," he suddenly had the answer, not to the "Why?" but to how to outgrow madness: "I suddenly realized [...] that I still hadn't grasped the 'truth' which, as I hanged myself, I would cry aloud to those who went on living" (p. 269).

Instead of a truth broadcast to attract followers, he finds a truth to pass on, the truth that links him to his ancestors. Now he feels himself to be "meekly beneath the gaze of the same family spirits who earlier had gazed on Takashi at his death" (p. 270). After he and his wife decide to make the journey back, crossing the wild space of the forest and of madness in the opposite direction, never to return, he meets the tatami-maker who has sculpted a mask of Takashi, like a split pomegranate, to be worn by one of the spirits in the nembutsu dance of invocation, that summer. Before leaving, Mitsusaburo gives the tatami-maker the jacket and trousers Takashi had worn when he came back from the US.

The psychoanalysis of trauma is as old as the wars, as Socrates, a veteran of the Peloponnesian War, teaches us. In *Phaedrus*,[9] he evokes the violence of an ancient wrath, *palaiôn meni matôn*, touching someone in a lineage, *en tisi tôn genôn*, from a time no one knows about, which impels that one who is rightly delusional, *tô orthôs manenti*, to find, through ceremonies, *tele tôn*, a way to heal not only himself, but all his relatives. At that point, Socrates invents an etymological fiction: madness, mania, becomes an art of divination, *mantikè*, by adding the letter "t," which comes from the word "history," *istoria.*

In the last pages of *The Silent Cry*, history speaks with the voice of a silenced story, revealed in broad daylight when a cellar is discovered. Time is reset in motion, and the generations assume their proper order. Mitsu's dream at the airport hotel, "I deserted you!" foreshadowed his ultimate decision not to abandon his son. Unexpectedly, his *therapon* – in the Homeric sense of the term, found in the *Iliad*, a second in combat and ritual double responsible for funeral rites – is his wife: "Now you've seen that the ties between your great-grandfather's brother and Taka weren't just an illusion created by Taka, why don't you try to find out what you share with them yourself?" (p. 272).

Tied to the memory of his ancestors who are now relegated to the past, Mitsusaburo can take the risk of asking his wife:

> If we fetch the baby from the institution, do you think we can get him to adapt to life with us? "I was thinking about that for ages last night, Mitsu, and I began to feel that if only we have the courage we can make a start on it at least," she said in a voice pathetic in its obvious physical and spiritual exhaustion. [...] Then [...] I heard a voice inside me reciting quite simply [...] "Now that we don't have Taka, we'll have to manage by ourselves.
>
> (pp. 272–273)

Kenzaburō Ōe is not a clinician, but for his own survival, and ours, he formulates essential concepts for the treatment of psychosis and trauma that we will find in Benedetti's theory, which requires courage to put into practice.

Notes

1 Ōe, K., *Teach Us to Outgrow Our Madness*, Nathan, J. (Trans.), Grove Press, 1977.
2 Ōe, K., *The Silent Cry*, Bester, J. (Trans.), Kodansha International, 1974.
3 See *infra*, Seminar 6 on Pat Barker.
4 Lacan, J., *Transference: The Seminar of Jacques Lacan*, Book VIII, Polity, 2017; *The Seminar of Jacques Lacan*, Book XI, W. W. Norton & Company, 1998.
5 Winnicott, D. W., "Fear of Breakdown," *International Review of Psychoanalysis*, 1 (1974): 103–106.
6 Freud, S., *Delusions and Dreams in Jensen's Gradiva*, S.E. 9, Hogarth Press, 1907, p. 8
7 Warburg, A., "A Lecture on Serpent Ritual," *Journal of the Warburg Institute*, 4 (1939): 277–292.
8 Sophocles, *Oedipus at Colonus*, Dover Publications, 1999.
9 Plato, *Phaedrus*, Focus Philosophical Library, 1998.

2 Seminar 2: 1986–1987
Gaetano Benedetti (1920–2013)
Madness: an exploration of the zones of death

> Gaetano Benedetti, a psychoanalyst in Basel, was a clinician who devoted his life to working with schizophrenia.[1] What is theorised in his work at the limit of rationality resonates with what we find in the work of Kenzaburō Ōe, and of Luigi Pirandello, whom we will discuss in the next seminar.

Structural or psychodynamic approach?

The first point of encounter can be illustrated by a metaphor borrowed from quantum physics. Just as it is not possible to calculate the speed and position of an electron at the same time, it is not possible to describe the structure of a psychosis and to establish its transferential trajectory at the same time. Observing the symptoms prevents the analyst from entering into a psychodynamic relation.

The adjective "psychodynamic" describes movement and its purpose. In *The Silent Cry*, we are shown how madness emerges in the place where a historical catastrophe having found no inscription in a family line is revived 100 years later.[2] Madness is not the consequence of this catastrophe. It is not an archaeological site to be excavated in the psyche of the characters, which would allow some writer or analyst with the talents of a Viollet-le-Duc to reconstitute the original from its ruins. It is not a devastated landscape whose original form has to be restored; it is, rather, a dynamic impetus towards the inscription of erased events.

In that place, history stutters, spinning in mad repetition, in an attempt to create otherness and set up a counter-history. This repetition stumbles over the loss of that which guarantees speech. In Ōe's fiction, there are betrayals of the given word that impel characters to seclude themselves in a storehouse or a cellar. When betrayal becomes the law, a new order prevails in which what could have been otherwise is erased. Madness is a tool for exploring what could have taken place without this erasure. Having escaped from the symbolic chain, surviving images spin endlessly, kept outside of history and away from any "other" able to take responsibility for them.

Benedetti asserts that these clinical manifestations, taking the form of withdrawal, aggressiveness and fragmentation, are not deficiencies in relation to the accepted norm. They exist only in a relation to an "other" to whom they strive to give existence in the singularity of the transference. According to him, the psychotherapeutic setting makes it possible to identify what happened in the place where the "other" has been abolished. Outside of this context, madness is treated like a disease or like an aesthetic object, and betrayal possibly like a miscalculation. But this does not mean that no one is there. Madness deals with a kind of other who is neither a thou nor the Other guaranteeing the symbolic order, in Lacanian terms, but a lawless agency for whom the other does not exist. In the face of such a danger, Benedetti asserts that it is possible to establish a dialogue aiming for what Freud calls "the subject of truth."[3]

"Being with"

Kenzaburō Ōe sets up a dialogue with the reader on the question of how "to outgrow our madness," which manifested its presence by halting time when the atomic bomb was detonated, and when his handicapped child was born. His own answer is to create a literary oeuvre in which he inscribes his truth.

In Chapter 8 of *The Silent Cry*, entitled "Truth Unspeakable," Takashi, the narrator's brother, hints at a truth he will later confess, and which will drive him to suicide. In the meantime, he raises a dilemma impossible to solve:

> If the man who was supposed to have told the truth managed to go on living without [being] killed by others, or [killing] himself, or [going] mad and [turning] into a monster, it would be direct evidence that the truth he was supposed to have told wasn't in fact the sort – the bomb with the fuse lit – that I'm concerned with.

His brother tries to propose a compromise: "What about a writer? Surely there are writers who have told the truth and gone on living?"[4]

Benedetti also uses fiction, pictures created by his patients within the framework of transference. His therapeutic stance can be expressed very simply as "being with." Starting with the negativism characteristic of schizophrenia, he asserts positivity through unconscious interferences with the analyst. The unconscious of which he speaks is not that of repression, formulated by Lacan as the speech of the Other, since the collapse of the given word abolishes all otherness, either big or small. Nor can we say that madness might have a key for unlocking the analyst's toolkit, or his beetle box.[5] About this famous beetle that each of us keeps in a private box, Wittgenstein says: "The thing in the box has no place in the language-game at all, not even as a *something*, for the box might even be empty." Still, this unconscious cut-out of the symbolic chain manifests its presence through interferences and may create a transitional subject "in between" patient and analyst.

Benedetti gives an example of this interference. A patient has a dream that, in its structure, brings to mind a split. Instead of interpreting this as typical of schizophrenia, Benedetti realises that this dream touches upon a split in himself, of which the patient is, of course, unaware. Instead of rummaging through his diagnostic bag, he places something on the side of his patient, where there was nothing. To speak of this, we are always searching for metaphors, since we can't always invoke the unnameable and unimaginable. Lacan turns to the Borromean knot – made up of three linked rings, all of which separate if any one of them is severed – to illustrate the structure of psychosis with the three registers of the Real, the Symbolic and the Imaginary getting loose, instead of staying knotted around the lost object, the cause of desire.[6]

In Benedetti's view, the cut-out unconscious does not fit this metaphor of dispersion. He speaks of a chance encounter, in a fraction of a second, between the narration of a dream by the patient and something similar on the part of the analyst. The dream is not an interpretation of this "something," but it grabs hold of an experience of which it is unaware. If the analyst dismisses this coincidence, the encounter fails. If he thinks that the patient has read his thoughts, he becomes delusional himself, since what happened was coincidental. If the analyst undertakes to interpret by giving explanations, he is tacitly saying: "See how well I am doing? You're not able to do this."

This does not mean that he should say nothing. This is how Benedetti defines "being with": a transformation of the analyst by the irruption of strange impressions, or what he calls "therapeutic dreams," which have to be related to his patient, for they stem from their work together. This, he says, is the anthropological dimension of psychosis.

This overstepping of the characters' limits is constant in Ōe's stories, which do not focus on individuals, and certainly not on the Oedipus complex. This also applies to Benedetti's experience, since his patients' delusions are addressed to "all others." However, he insists that they do not proceed from a collective unconscious, since the frontiers between the individual and the social have disappeared with the shattering of the mirrors and the breaking of the symbolic chain. This "all others" is the plural dimension of madness that speaks through the radio, the television or the Internet, since it cannot say what is excluded from language.

Uncanny coincidences

The psychodynamics of madness force the analyst into strange contradictions, similar to the logical impasses created by Zen *koans*. When Wittgenstein declares, in his "Notes for Lectures on 'Private Experience'": "I cannot choose the mouth with which I say 'I have toothache'," he points out the dissolution of the limits of the subject in cases of madness or trauma, where the affect may be in another person's body.[7] In such cases, invoking the paranormal makes no sense, since this relies on causality when, in fact, what is at work here is mere coincidence. The "calm block fallen here from some dark disaster," evoked by Stéphane Mallarmé in "The Tomb of Edgar Poe," is the only relevant thing in the context of psychosis.[8]

Benedetti calls the work of transference, which admits the relevance of these strange events, "counter-identification." When Freud, in a letter to Jung, in response to the latter's interpretations of the meaning of the cracking noises made by Freud's bookcase, preferred to speak of the "undeniable compliance of chance," he stated the necessity for coincidences to provide otherness where there is nothing.[9]

On this subject, Benedetti's language becomes poetic: "There is no madness other than psychotherapeutic [...]. Psychoanalysis is the anchor that madness has found in this century to be in contact with us." In other centuries, in other regions of the globe, this relation found its place in the theatre of animist healing ceremonies.

Even in secular societies, madness alludes to the dimension of the sacred, *sacer* in Latin, *always* defined as a space outside everyday life. When Voltaire mocks the "sacred poems" of Lefranc Pompignan, he says: "They are sacred because no one will touch them." In *Oedipus at Colonus*, the sacred grove where Oedipus will die is a place known only to Theseus, the king of Athens, a place ultimately tied to political benefits for the city.[10]

Negative existence

Although madness is problematic, it is not unutterable, but a particular place has to be built where it can speak. "Who can talk about me better than I can? – unless there's anyone who knows me better than I know myself!" Erasmus has Folly say in his *Praise*.[11] The major issue is to whom these words are addressed, and this address is not easy to find since madness wages war on perversion. At first, we try to capture delusion in the net of our reasoning and try to fend off attacks on linking, as Bion says. But when we least expect it, this murderous agency succeeds in taking our place and making us responsible for the disaster, despite our efforts to invoke external causes. Yet, these critical moments of transference are the only times when this perverse agency can be confronted and defeated so that a reliable form of otherness can be created from scratch.

Benedetti argues that causal explanations, even applied to structure, are pure illusion when it comes to madness, for they explain nothing when nothingness is at the core of experience. Of course, endless treaties and seminars elaborate on the topic, as if they possessed the answer – the cause of psychosis – whereas Benedetti speaks of "dispossession." Even to speak of analysis is nonsensical, as if it were possible to analyse nothingness – *rien* in French, which comes from *rem* – "the thing" in Latin – and excludes speech. Benedetti gives us tools to "be present" in what he calls "areas of death."

When the identity criteria are destroyed, "I is another," as Arthur Rimbaud wrote, when he was 17, in a letter to Paul Demeny,[12] adding: "I say that one must [...] make oneself a seer. The Poet makes himself a seer by a long, immense, and rational dissoluteness of all the senses." In schizophrenia, Benedetti calls "negative existence" this dissoluteness of all the senses, which reveals the collapse of the symbolic bearings in "areas of death" transmitted through a lineage. This negative existence is impervious to shock treatments and hypotheses, but it reveals the tearing in the social fabric, the foundation of the political. *Oedipus Rex* is anything but a family story. Starting at the point where the enemy brothers confront each other, there are over twenty-five words to signify madness, always used in a context of breaking the law.

We might say the same thing about the stories of patients who don't seem to be mad. Benedetti says: "I met different patients whose mental functioning was normal enough, although their functioning in non-existence was obvious." He presents the example of a young woman who disintegrates under the weight of a past without memories, all the more heavy because it is empty and because it gives her the sensation of nothingness:

> In this state where the Nothing is present, we cannot speak of repression, or even of a healthy and an insane part of the ego. The psychotherapy is only analytical to the extent that the analyst is able to analyse himself in order to find his way to the Nothing.

Psychotherapeutic technique

Psychoanalytic *doxa* asserts that there is no transference in psychosis. Benedetti refutes this statement and contends that in the schizophrenic void, the unconscious manifests itself through communication. The "areas of death" are zones of intense interaction, not only in the "double bind" mode, the paradoxical injunction described by Gregory Bateson, but also in the development of untypical potentialities. When the symbolic sphere collapses, the repressed unconscious, "structured like a language," according to Lacan, remains silent. When the Other's speech cannot respond to the call, "all others" start to speak through "the mouth of the universe." These areas, which are suppressed in a lineage, are like black holes, where the arrow of time changes direction, where one becomes invisible to oneself, and is identified with this area of death. Of course, we could explain this to the patient, but it would be of no use to him whatsoever.

The only possibility is to insert into this compact void the weaving of a dialogue in which the psychotherapeutic exchange may confront psychic death. When Frieda Fromm-Reichmann writes: "Where they say there can be no transference, there is transference to the world at large," she is confirming that where there is no other, the other is summoned with the greatest intensity.[13] Provided she is attentive to impressions arising from similar zones in herself, the analyst can attest to the presence of an otherness. Even when she is destabilised by a remark that is too close to home for her, she is expected to validate a truth. If she does not, and defends herself like a demon, the patient will conclude, like Hamlet when his mother denied his father's murder: "The lady protests too much, methinks."[14]

Hamlet plays the fool when "the time is out of joint."[15] Time becomes unhinged regularly, when the analysis gets stuck. After making some progress, the patient obstinately returns to square one and attacks the murderous agency that took the place of the analyst after he made some blunder. This is when he has to "claim an unclaimed experience," by honestly recognising his mistake.

As Benedetti points out, this situation is described as regression and fragmentation of the patient's self and his world. But in truth, what is taking place is a reconstruction of his world by fragments, starting with a long-ago explosion to which we have no access except in the present of the session. These fragments are not scant traces in a desert, but elements that may hook on to bits of the analyst's history, gradually setting in motion a process that can generate time, provided the analyst validates this interference. Up until then, Benedetti says, the patient had remained transfixed under the petrifying gaze of the Medusa: "Trapped in the reification of his experience, he is dispossessed of any curiosity about the most essential part of himself: his own subjectivity."

Relying on the teachings of mainstream psychoanalysts, we are ill-equipped to face such a rejection. Wittgenstein has better tools when he writes at the beginning of his "Notes for Lectures on 'Private Experience'" that he feels tortured when confronted with "the lost look and toneless voice" of someone is who is unable to tell him what he is feeling. At a loss, he conveys his impressions to the person.[16] Benedetti does the same thing when he tells his patients about his "therapeutic dreams" stemming from a session, through which a "transitional subject" may emerge from the in-between space, voicing as best he can the unspeakable that should stay silent. This is how transference enters the time of psychosis, but without falling into the strict repetition of the hatred towards the one who is dispossessing you of your identity.

Benedetti contends that suppressing the tool of transference in the name of scientific impartiality, or worse still in the name of analytic neutrality, relegates psychiatrists and analysts to the medieval exclusion of the insane from medical discourse. And yet, in the Middle Ages, madness had found refuge in literature, as Jean-Marie Fritz tells us.[17] The very place of madness was the "space of the marvel," where the madman, called "the Wild Man," stepped out of time. There, he encountered fantastical beings and confronted monsters, in a specific transference Bion called "psychotic transference," which elicits the analyst's dreaming, the "alpha function," to connect up the "beta-elements," such as "thoughts without a thinker," that find a thinker to think them when "thoughts are things and things are thoughts," "at the random intersection" between his experiences and those of the patient.[18]

The search for the other

The title of Harry Stack Sullivan's book *Schizophrenia as a Human Process* reminds us that this transference is a life experience and not the observation of a psychopathology.[19] When his colleague and friend Frieda Fromm-Reichmann emphasises that where there appears to be no transference, the transference is to "the world at large," she insists on the intensity of the energy employed in the quest for another with whom what cannot be said or imagined may be testified to. When the other has been destroyed, the dialogical function is everywhere to compel him to appear.

The techniques that can accomplish this task consist in giving all psychotic forms a chance, without any preference. Benedetti observes that "if the language of psychosis is understood with different codes," patients "do not need accumulated knowledge to figure out what is the latest and best treatment," but rather conditions for joint research, which validates suppressed historical truths, big or small, that have been thrown into the garbage bin of history. He gives the example of the transformation of a mother's face into that of a terrifying witch. What must the person do? In order to avoid becoming mad, he creates a myth in his delusion where he is the cause of this sudden change, and by so doing justifies the madness he has to face. In the transference, the delusion found its legitimation when it could respond to the transformations of the analyst's face, and be right to do so.

Thus, what are ordinarily called identity disorders, Benedetti insists, are in fact the places where the identity attempts to emerge in the transference. It is the patient who transforms his interlocutor into an analyst, not the analyst who transforms the patient into an illness or a psychotic structure. Psychotic transference is the only framework in which the vector of illness becomes the vector of therapeutic work. Benedetti gives many examples of the analyst's impressions and dreams, which were triggered by the psychotic experience and reveal elements of which he had no inkling in his own story. As we said earlier, these coincidences happen by chance. Contrary to what young analysts are taught, they are not the trap of "massive transference" to be avoided at all costs. Or perhaps they are .... Still, in such situations, the impossible to say and to imagine may become "the play" Winnicott speaks of, the playing with the "psychotic core" of our dreams, which Freud calls "the umbilicus of dreams" in Chapter 7 of *Traumdeutung*, instead of being relegated to the radical solitude of madness.[20]

Benedetti noticed that the patient looks after the therapist, without interfering in his affairs. But this ability to trigger the analyst's cutaway unconscious is not so much empathy as the faculty of "suffering in the place of the other," a skill acquired from his experience with parental figures. When the analyst recognises this competence, the hierarchy between them disappears, as they confront together what Bion calls "attacks on linking."

Positiveness of psychosis

Benedetti states that in neurosis, the negative is repressed, while in psychosis, it is the positive that is suppressed. By saying this, he overturns the defective image of madness, changing it into a dynamic point of view which contradicts Lacan's position that "it would be premature to speak of transference in psychosis, because it would mean to go 'beyond Freud', and there can be no question of Freud when post-Freudian psychoanalysis has gone back to an earlier stage." But Freud himself did not ask for such precautions. Before going into exile in England, he indicated the path to follow in *Moses and Monotheism*, while his books were being burned in Berlin. I repeat: this annihilation was not a fantasy, but neither was it a threat that psychoanalysis was doomed to disappear under the two totalitarian regimes.

Benedetti follows in the footsteps of Frieda Fromm-Reichmann, William Rivers and Harry Stack Sullivan, who acquired their experience as analysts during World War I. They developed a psychodynamic perspective that analyses what happens "at the intersection of world history and personal history" – a phrase coined by a delusional patient – for the analyst as well. Does this mean, as we often hear in repeated clichés, that treating psychosis is a collective rather than an individual matter? To answer this question, Benedetti refers to the concept of Theodore Lidz on the irrationality transmitted in the families of schizophrenics, and to Franco Basaglia's conception relating madness to the contradictions of society.[21] Both of these authors raise the question of whether psychosis is psychological or social. Benedetti sees no sense in this opposition. Since madness obliterates the limits between the individual and the social, transference is the place where the social link is reinvented on the very site of areas of death and of total solitude, which were bereft of a witness, says Dori Laub.

We used to visit Benedetti every year in Basel, Switzerland, at Carnival season, which opened with *Fasnacht*, when the masks overrun the streets of the city with drums and piccolos. Benedetti was totally unknown in France then. We had met him at the Austen Riggs Center in Massachusetts, at the jubilee in honour of its former director Otto Will. They had both been trained at Chestnut Lodge, another clinic near Washington, where the psychoanalysis of psychosis had been introduced by Frieda Fromm-Reichmann. Benedetti, who was of Sicilian origin, encouraged us to read Pirandello, the subject of my next seminar.

Notes

1 Benedetti, G., *Alenazione e Personazione nella Psicoterapia della malattia mentale* (*Landscapes of Death of the Soul*), Einaudi, 1960; *Paziente e terapeuta nell' esperienza psicotica* (*Patient and Therapist during Psychotic Experience*), Bollati Boringhieri, 1991; *Psychotherapy as Existential Challenge*, Vandenhoecht, 1992.
2 Ōe, K., *The Silent Cry*, Bester, J. (Trans.), Serpent's Tail, 1988.
3 Freud, S., *Moses and Monotheism*, Vintage Books, 1955.

4 Ōe, K., *The Silent Cry*, op. cit., p. 157.
5 Wittgenstein, L., *Philosophical Investigations*, Wiley-Blackwell, 2010, section 293.
6 Lacan, J., *Or Worse*, Book XIX, Polity, 2018.
7 Wittgenstein, L., "Notes for Lectures on 'Private Experience' and 'Sense Data'," in *The Oxford Handbook of Wittgenstein*, Kuusela, O. and McGinn, M. (Eds.), Oxford University Press, 2011.
8 Mallarmé, S., "The Tomb of Edgar Poe," in *Selected Poetry and Prose*, New Directions, 1982.
9 Freud, S. and Jung, C., *The Freud/Jung Letters*, McGuire, W. (Ed.), Princeton University Press, 1994.
10 Sophocles, *Oedipus at Colonus*, Dover Publications, 1999.
11 Erasmus, D., *Praise of Folly*, Clarke, R. (Trans.), Alma Classics, 2008.
12 Rimbaud, A., *I Promise to Be Good*, Mason, W. (Trans.), Modern Library, 2004.
13 Fromm-Reichmann, F., *Principles of Intensive Psychotherapy*, University of Chicago Press, 1960.
14 Shakespeare, W., *Hamlet*, Simon & Schuster, 1992.
15 Ibid., Act I, Scene 5.
16 Wittgenstein, L., "Notes for Lectures on 'Private Experience'," op. cit.
17 Fritz, J.-M.,. *Le discours du fou au Moyen-Âge*, Presses universitaires de France, 1992.
18 Bion, W., *Elements of Psychoanalysis*, Karnac Books, 1989.
19 Sullivan, H. S., *Schizophrenia as a Human Process*, Norton Library, 1974.
20 Winnicott, D. W., *Playing and Reality*, Tavistock Publications, 1971.
21 Foot, J., *The Man Who Closed the Asylums*, Verso, 2015.

3   Seminar 3: 1988–1989
Luigi Pirandello (1867–1936)
Madness in Pirandello's work

Using literature in the analytic process

I could not do without literature in my work as an analyst. Literature acts as a double of mad speech. Literary works drift in my head and connect, in the form of quotes, with mad speech which until then had remained suspended in the air. When I am dealing with someone who is delusional, to whom I appear as a possible other on the horizon of this speech, a particular kind of transference takes place; I catch words and images floating in the air, coming from voices or visions that record, in traumatic memory, unforgettable catastrophes, "at the crossroads of world history and personal history," as the patient quoted in the previous chapter said. These catastrophes wait to be joined up with voices that answer on my side, in the form of literary quotes, for example, so as to be inscribed in the repressed unconscious where they can be forgotten and remembered.

Wilfred Bion said: "Only that which can be forgotten is remembered." Until then, "thoughts without a thinker desperately search for a thinker to think them [and] give them a home."[1] I will develop this idea in a future seminar on Bion,[2] but right now it brings to mind Pirandello's play *Six Characters in Search of an Author*. I will comment on this paradoxical formulation, which also describes psychoanalytic practice.

Inscription of an erasure

Mad speech testifies to catastrophes outside the realm of language whose traces have been erased. It tries to authenticate them with the help of an other who remains to be produced, since otherness has been destroyed on this site of the catastrophe. Indeed, authenticating the catastrophe thanks to the encounter with a double of mad speech, which the analyst brings from literature, leads to the erasure of haunting voices and visions. The paradox consists of fighting against the erasure of traces by erasing the phantoms that emerge in the same place. This second erasure restores their traces thanks to an inscription in the discourse of the Other.

To handle this paradoxical situation, I think of Wittgenstein, who used a technical rather than structural approach: "It is interesting to compare the multiplicity of the tools in language and the ways they are used [...] with what logicians have said about the structure of language (including the author of *Tractus Logico-Philosophicus*)."[3] We can appreciate the difference between his "structural" treatise written on the front line during the Great War, which ends with the phrase: "Whereof one cannot speak, thereof one must be silent," and his second philosophy developed after his return to Cambridge in 1929, in which what cannot be said is shown through an "ostensive definition."[4]

When I am shown by a patient what cannot be said in a case of madness and trauma, I often think of Pirandello's novel *The Notebooks of Serafino Gubbio*[5] or of his play *Six Characters in Search of an Author*. I grasp these stories intuitively, although they suggest no interpretation before I use them with the patient, before he can make use of them.[6] "It is as if we could grasp the whole use of a word in a flash," Wittgenstein says, adding:

> [...] we are led to think that the future development must in some way already be present in the act of grasping the use and yet isn't present. For we say that there isn't any doubt that we understand the word, and on the other hand, its meaning lies in its use.[7]

There follows a sentence reminiscent of Bion's "thoughts without a thinker": "Any interpretation (*Deutung*) still hangs in the air along with what it interprets, and cannot give any support. Interpretations by themselves do not determine meaning (*Bedeuten*)."

Indeed, we can have in mind tons of theories and literary references, but these interpretations have no effect until they find their application through a "language-game" with the patient, in which "the speaker's tone of voice and the look with which the words are uttered"[8] play a major role. Bion and Wittgenstein found themselves in the same traumatised state on either side of the front line after the 1918 Armistice. Both of them experienced the absence of recourse, which they would eventually find: Wittgenstein in philosophy and Bion in psychoanalysis. Wittgenstein abandoned philosophy for ten years, haunted by post-traumatic symptoms until he returned to Cambridge, where he practised philosophy like a therapy of "the bumps that the understanding has got by running its head up against the limits of language."[9] Bion left his first psychoanalyst, whose head was full of ready-made theories, and found John Rickman, a veteran of the recent war like himself, and a disciple of William Rivers, who will be the subject of another seminar.[10]

Both Bion and Wittgenstein had to find a new paradigm for situations where "the tool with the name is broken."[11] The erasure of traces leads to traumatic revivals which show that which cannot be said. The second erasure, in the transference, makes it possible to inscribe what is shown, as long as it can be addressed to another who enables the inscription of a name that "survives the death of its bearer."[12] This is the task Bion calls "psychotic transference," and it is not an easy task.

Later, Lacan would say: "The signifier is the murder of the thing."[13] Yet he refused to address the question of "the use of transference in psychosis" in his "On a Question Preliminary to Any Possible Treatment of Psychosis."[14] But when the murder of the thing threatens to be acted out in a suicide attempt, for lack of someone to address in the transference, "to understand a language means to be master of a technique," as Wittgenstein writes.[15] Because, Freud says,[16] the language of traumatic reviviscences stemming from an unconscious not linked to repression, but to "word-presentations and thing-presentations" of the primary process, requires using a different language, which pioneers of the analysis of psychosis and trauma invented while working in military hospitals during World War I.

To put it another way, let us turn to a book written by France's great jester Raymond Davos, *Sens dessus dessous (Upside Down)*.[17] Speaking of "the protection of empty spaces," those of madness, he advises us to catch butterflies that do not exist and erase them, because otherwise we will have delusional fantasies. These butterflies are the "surviving images" caught by the inventor of this expression, art historian Aby Warburg, during his stay in Ludwig Binswanger's clinic, where he was a patient after World War I, which had driven him mad. He spoke to moths and butterflies that he called "little souls," those of the dead, which helped him survive in "his Hell," until the day he was able to erase them by giving "A Lecture on Serpent Ritual."[18]

I already mentioned the Hopi ceremony that consists of dancers seizing rattlesnakes in their hands and carrying them in their mouths as "the source and substitute of mysterious events." After dancing for half an hour, they release the snakes in the desert, where their lightning-like shape will bring rain, a source of physical and psychic revival. Warburg's lecture, addressed to the clinic's staff and patients, was a revival for him, once he had released in words the mysterious cause of terror that filled his mouth. He left the clinic soon afterwards and resumed his research, as he had been encouraged to do by his disciple Fritz Saxl, who trusted that his intelligence had remained intact, functioning in a psychotic mode, while Freud and Binswanger did not believe he would ever go back to the status quo ante.

In the meantime, interpretations were suspended in the air and spoke through little things, like his butterflies, or through "dreams which have never been dreamed, those created by authors." This is how Freud starts his text on the Gradiva, written by the German author Wilhelm Jensen and entitled *Gradiva: A Pompeian Fancy*. It tells a story of trauma and madness that illustrates psychotic transference between a delusional young man mad about a young girl, the Gradiva – the woman who walks – represented on a bas-relief, and his neighbour, who accepts to enter his delusion on the site of Pompeii. She enacts the death of the Gradiva under the burning ashes of Vesuvius, and is reborn as Zoé – meaning "life" in Greek – out of the death zone they both share, she having lost her mother and the young man both parents, in infancy.

At the time Freud wrote his text on the Gradiva, Pirandello was writing short stories that would become the source of his theatre.

Madness as the stakes of Pirandello's works

Madness is an ever-present element in the works of Pirandello, who witnessed the catastrophes that befell his native Sicily. In 1903, an earthquake destroyed the sulphur mines; revenue from the mines, his wife Antonella's dowry, had been the couple's main income. News of this devastating loss left Antonella paralysed. She slowly recovered physically but developed delusional jealousy, which got worse over time. What role did the madness he lived within his own household play in Pirandello's work?

The play *Right You Are! (If You Think So)*[19] depicts the curiosity of a small town about a strange trio that comes from elsewhere: a man, his wife and his mother-in-law. When they are asked to explain their behaviour, each of them blames it on the madness of the others. The mother, Signora Frola, sees in her son-in-law's wife her daughter, who, according to her, is still his first wife, although she died. Her son-in-law, Signor Ponza, claims his wife is his second spouse and not the living daughter of this woman. In the background, there is an earthquake that destroyed their families and all their records. In the last scene of the play, when the mystery is still unsolved, the daughter, veiled in black, enters to reveal the truth to polite society. She says simply to the curious onlookers:

> The truth? It is only this: that I really am the daughter of Mrs. Frola – and also the second wife of Mr. Ponza. Yes – and for myself, no one! I am no one! For myself, I am what others believe me to be.

The real madness is the earthquake that killed everyone and destroyed all traces of their existence. When Folly speaks, as she does in Erasmus' *Praise*,[20] it is to answer Kenzaburō Ōe's request, *Teach Us to Outgrow Our Madness*,[21] and to testify before curious onlookers about a mode of survival.

In Pirandello's play, interpretations float in the air, unable to ground themselves on certainties, but merely on the coincidence of a similar situation involving someone else that the coincidence was waiting for. I can't help noticing that the play was written in 1917, when whole villages in northern France and Flanders were destroyed by the quakes of bombardments that drove people mad. The solution offered by the play to this madness is coexistence based on the respect each person has for the phantoms of the others.

According to Pirandello, those who have real problems are the observers obsessed with diagnosis. Tormented by the impulse to violate the secret of the one supposed to be crazy, they collect objective proof, of the kind sought nowadays in the folds of the brain or through two-way mirrors. Of course, a sudden and violent event has destroyed the social link, but strangely the play relegates this event to the background.

This brings to mind Lacan's passion for "neologisms" that are reputed to denote psychosis. Unfortunately for him, the one he chose as an example, "galopiner" (to act like a little rascal), had already been used by Maupassant. His presentations of psychotic cases were an attempt to establish the foreclosure of the name-of-the-father and frame it in a psychotic structure, like an insect akin to Wittgenstein's beetle, like a spider on its ceiling, which the philosopher advises us to ignore. Like the French poet Robert Desnos' "18-meter-ant, which speaks French, Latin and Javanese, that doesn't exist, that doesn't exist ... and why not?"[22] For we start to speak using a number of phonemes with which I can make sounds like the "POW" and the "WHAM" in comic strips. Even if people tell me: "That's no way to talk," I only need one person to enter my comic strip and we can play the game. This person has only to catch a slight deviation in the rhythm, and although the new language is unknown to him, he will recognise that one other person speaks it.

In 1931, Lacan published an article entitled "Schizophasia" in *La revue psychiatrique*. In this text, he was asserting that he had uncovered in the writing of a woman patient "something indicating that the source of the writing has been reached." The conclusion of the article speaks of a mental deficit as the foundation of the delusional beliefs. He states that in order to be delusional, "one has to be in a state of frenetic overstimulation, with an egocentric tendency towards hatred and pride." This definitive conclusion was later going to be applied to Artaud:

> Nothing is less inspirational, in the spiritual sense, than this writing she considers inspired. It is when thinking is insufficient and inadequate that this kind of automatic writing takes its place; it is experienced as external because it compensates for a deficit in thinking.

Around the same time, Harry Stack Sullivan and Frieda Fromm-Reichmann were developing the use of transference in psychosis, which they did not consider linked to a deficiency.

The only reference contributing a spark of intelligence to Lacan's discussion relates to the surrealists:

> However, this writing also reveals a playful activity whose intentional and "automatic" components should both be taken into consideration. The experiments conducted by some writers on a type of writing they called surrealist, whose scientific method they described in detail, show the remarkable degree of autonomy that can be reached in automatic writing with no hypnosis involved.

But let us be careful not to associate the nonsense of mental deficit with science-certified surrealism. In 1933, in an article published in *Minotaure* on "problems of style," Lacan seems better informed, after having defended his thesis in psychiatry in 1932. He now sees so-called "morbid" experience as "particularly conducive to symbolic modes of expression." What a relief! The worst has been avoided.

In fact, the new concept of "surrealism," brought back from the front in World War I by Guillaume Apollinaire, with its "objective chance," is not far removed from madness. It is a pity that Nadja,[23] probably traumatised by the war in Lille, a city she left for Paris after the war, ended up in a psychiatric hospital in Perray-Vaucluse, where she died, and where André Breton (1896–1966) never visited her.

In Pirandello's theatre, set in the context of the same catastrophe, the exiled subject is able to find himself.

The theatre of madness as a public place

During the war, Pirandello understood the affinity between theatre and madness. Like psychiatric hospitals – and cafés, like my mother's, where I spent my childhood – theatre is a space with three walls, the red curtain acting as the fourth. Gisela Pankow used to say: "There are no secrets in psychosis." Contrary to Leibniz's monads, "spaces without doors or windows which keep out accidents," these places are completely open and only accidents can happen there.

In a dream recounted by Charlotte Beradt in her book *The Third Reich of Dreams*,[24] a loudspeaker of the Nazi regime is heard ordering the removal of the walls of houses. "One and a hundred thousand people" then become identical and don't recognise themselves in the mirror any more. A person who knew himself inside out discovers that he has never seen himself before. The others pass his strangeness along like the sticky tape in *The Adventures of Tintin*, and the uncanny sensation (*Unheimlich*) keeps running like "the ferret of the pretty woods, my ladies." A public place in which the self disappears makes room for 100,000 strangers, one of whom is the hero of the short story "One, No One, and One Hundred Thousand"[25] – written in 1927 – who goes mad when his wife criticises the shape of his nose. Heinrich von Kleist describes a similar adventure, in his essay *On a Theatre of Marionettes*, involving a young man transformed into a puppet after his mentor refused to recognise, for his own good, the statue of Apollo with a thorn in the pose he struck when they went to the baths together.[26] In his theatre, Pirandello enacted experimentally such disappearances of the self.

The play was staged in Rome in 1921 and caused a scandal, since the spectators entered a dimly lit theatre without a curtain and without stage decor. The head carpenter was nailing something; the stage manager ran up to tell him that the rehearsal was about to start. No one could make out what was going on. The director came in, followed by the actors and the prompter. Rehearsal has barely started when the Six Characters come forward from the back of the house, but they are not real people. They complain that an author created them and then abandoned them so that the play was never written. They embody psychotic energy asking to be inscribed. The director suggests that they play their parts so that, afterwards, the play could be written and the roles given to actors.

The plot concerns a father who has abandoned his wife and legitimate son, pushing her to become the mistress of one of his employees, with whom she has had three more children: the eldest daughter, identified as the Stepdaughter, the Boy, who is now an adolescent, and the youngest girl, the Child. Another public place is mentioned: a brothel run by what was called in the eighteenth century *une marchande à la toilette*, an outfit vendor. The Stepdaughter works there as a prostitute until she finds herself face to face with her father-in-law, in a quasi-incestuous situation. The play impossible to write tries to be written to bring that tale of woe to an end. Two deaths will occur in the wings: the Child drowns in a pool and the Boy commits suicide.

The Six Characters are not people and are not yet roles. To attain the goals pursued by their mad energy, they will enter into conflict with the actors on the questions of their "selves." The father argues with the one who is supposed to play his role:

> As artists [...] you have to create a perfect illusion of reality [...] But we [...] have no other reality. [...] that which is a game of art for you is our sole reality. But not only for us, you know, by the way. (Looking him straight in the eye) Just you think it over well. Can you tell me who you are?

A little later, he addresses the stage managers:

> A character, sir, may always ask a man who he is. Because a character has really a life of his own, marked with his especial characteristics; for which reason he is always "somebody." But a man – I'm not speaking of you now – may very well be "nobody."

The stage manager objects: "I should like to know if anyone has ever heard of a character who gets right out of his part and perorates and speechifies as you do." The father answers: "You have never met such a case, sir, because authors, as a rule, hide the labour of their creations."

This identity problem has to be dealt with by Pirandello, who, in the preface to his play, while his characters intrude on him, introduces his little maidservant Fantasy. She wears the fool's cap and bells that Laurence Sterne tells us he dons in *The Life and Opinions of Tristram Shandy, Gentleman*.[27] She:

> [brings] to his house – since [he] derive[s] stories and novels and plays from them – men, women, children, involved in strange adventures which they can find no way out of [...] with whom it is often very painful to have dealings.

Fantasy often finds them in sundry news stories. The writer gives them an appointment, as he used to do when he wrote short stories taken from Sicilian newspapers.

In his short story "A Character's Tragedy," published in 1911, he grants his characters an audience lasting five hours, on Sundays from 8.00 a.m. to 1.00 p.m.,[28] and he writes:

> I almost always find myself in bad company. [...] I listen to them with infinite forbearing; I take down each one's name and circumstances. [...] Now, it's often the case that at a certain question I pose they jib, they take umbrage, they resist furiously. [...] I do my best to make them see and perceive that my question was perfectly à propos, because it's easy for anyone to *wish* to be one kind of person or another; the real question is whether we *can* be the way we want to be. [...] They can't be convinced of this.

In the story "Conversations with Characters," published in 1915, Pirandello features himself as a character who, on the eve of Italy's entrance into the war, posts this sign on his office door:

> **NOTICE** From this day forward, audiences are suspended with all characters, men and women, of any rank, age and profession, who have applied and submitted credentials to be admitted to a novel or story. NB: Applications and credentials are respectfully held at the disposal of all characters who, not ashamed to display their miserable circumstances, would like to appeal to other writers, provided they find them.[29]

From 1915 on, Pirandello became a prominent playwright whose plays were produced constantly, and characters continued to show up at his door. In 1917, in a letter to his son Stefano, who had been made a prisoner of war in Austria, Pirandello wrote:

> Six characters, caught in a terrible drama, who approach me asking to be put into a novel, it's an obsession. [...] I tell them it's useless, I'm not interested in them, I'm not interested in anything, and here they are showing me all their wounds as here I am sending them away.

These characters were reunited in the 1925 play *Six Characters in Search of an Author*, whose preface reiterates the content of this letter. The play reflects the violent shock of the Great War. Pirandello declared: "My writing for the stage has been war theatre. The war revealed theatre to me."

From trivial events to the theatre of war

Trivial events read in newspapers are not trivial for everyone. They wait for the theatre of short stories, of plays, and of analytic sessions as well, to testify and to bring on stage people to whom catastrophes happened and "with whom it is painful to have dealings," to bring them out of the anonymity in which they were treated like things. One of the Six Characters, the Stepdaughter, driven into prostitution by poverty, comes face to face with her mother's first husband who had repudiated her. On the theatre stage, she shows him attempting to buy her sexual services while she is wearing a black dress to mourn the death of her own father – the employee who had given refuge to her mother.

This scene brings into existence the girls left on the street, the ones that, at the same period, Yvette Guilbert[30] – who called herself *diseuse fin de siècle*, an end-of-century sayer, and was painted by Toulouse Lautrec wearing long, black gloves – was holding up before the old gentlemen in her audience. The abandonment of the girls they had seduced brings to mind that of children who are left to become prey to voyeurs and perverts, and that of young men left without a grave in the theatre of war.

The public space in which they have the good fortune to appear is Pirandello's theatre. On the stage, a monstrosity appears, of which Pirandello learned through trivial events reported in newspapers, just as we do in our work as analysts when we meet with lost souls attempting to mend the social fabric in the face of cowardice. The aim, then, is to help a political self emerge.[31] What does this mean?

The subject of desire emerges from a psychoanalysis by successively dropping his masks, but something terrifying happens when, like the mime Marcel Marceau, he is unable to tear off the last one. An event becomes madness as soon as the sundry incident falls upon – *incidere* – an I that becomes an id, condemned to show the catastrophe on his face until he meets an other who can recognise it. This coincidence brings about the advent of a political self, in a context where an impossible-to-remove diagnosis had been pronounced.

Spaces are unaware, but people know that they feel different than they did before. They have been forced to acquire out of the ordinary knowledge of which they cannot speak. How can this knowledge be reached? "I turn into stone and my pain goes on," says Wittgenstein.[32] Try to get stones to reveal this knowledge! Try to make them speak! They will tell you nothing, unless someone starts to speak to the petrified mask, but this someone can only speak if he is in the place where the other has turned to stone. In his play *At the Exit*,[33] Pirandello lets tombstones speak.

The action takes place at night, in a cemetery. Time and space are inverted since the dead come out at night. They stay in during the day; a tombstone has been thrown over them. They come out at night so that their image may vanish, and work among themselves so that gradually the appearances may fade away: that of the fat man, of the murdered woman, of the man who laughs all the time. Like stones, they have no feelings. In these public spaces where no one lives, although the dead cross paths with the living, there is no need to make them feel anything, but they must account for what happened to them. Horror and pity are not "my" feelings either, but those they ask me to feel.

A reversal takes place – the very dynamics of madness – when the object represented – what is shown – becomes a means of representation, a technique of inscription that occurs coincidentally, when the dead may speak and I am summoned to answer during the sessions, like Pirandello answers anonymous voices in newspapers, the voices of people to whom he gives an appointment every Sunday morning.

As long as no one else comes to stand in this place from where the subject must answer for catastrophes, when, as Wittgenstein says, "the tool with the names is broken," interpretations rush in from everywhere. Radio, television, gossip, the bleating of goats, the sound of the wind in rose bushes try to find a meeting point where at long last it becomes possible to name what has been recorded by the body.[34] For lack of that meeting, a regime of limitless accumulation is instated in rooms filled with objects or trash, since nothing can be thrown away, as if 20 million things had to be shown for one of them to finally be recognised by someone who can answer for what took place.

Recording a catastrophe with no one to answer for it

The novel *The Notebooks of Serafino Gubbio*[35] is centred on "showing" – literally, since it speaks of a camera that films on its own. The four main characters are an actor, an actress, the cameraman who films the scene, and a tigress. The actor is consumed with love and jealousy for the actress, the cameraman films the scene, and the tigress – whom the script intends to be killed by the actor – leaps to devour him after he shoots not at her, but at the actress. The cameraman continues to film, instead of participating in the general hubbub. This is when an incredible thing happens, a thing that could not be written in the script since it was unforeseeable: a scene of horror recorded mechanically by this man who has set his emotions aside. It will be "the last scene" (the Italian title of the novel), because the man goes mad. The scene illustrates traumatic moments when images are imprinted on the retina, which can neither be erased nor recalled as memories. I am thinking of the last look that film director Akira Kurosawa, still an adolescent, exchanged with his older brother just before his brother went off to kill himself.

The cameraman keeps recording while his life recedes and he withdraws from life. His excess of sensitivity has turned into insensitivity, the lethargy of the living dead. Still, he cannot stop writing. The novel, based on posthumous notebooks, is written by a ghost:

> I satisfy, by writing, a need to let off steam which is overpowering. I get rid of my professional impassivity and avenge myself as well; and with myself avenge ever so many others, condemned like myself to be nothing more than a hand that turns a handle.[36]

The Notebooks of Serafino Gubbio is composed of seven notebooks written by the cameraman. The last film sequence, described in the seventh notebook, is the scene of horror in which, finding himself in the place of the inhuman camera that records a random event, the cameraman becomes part of the machine and loses his individuality. He says: "I was not a person, my person was not necessary." He had become "the Thing, *das Ding*," or rather "the representation of a thing," as Freud puts it in his *Project*,[37] whom no one represents because nobody sees him. The cameraman is like a phantom, in a space-time where, in Wittgenstein's words, "language goes on holiday."[38]

The horror and pity felt by the spectator or by the listener to whom this story is told are cathartic, making it possible to forget the tragedy. But first, the spectator must perceive the place in which the cameraman exists when he confuses his eye with that of the camera and gives up his personality. The truth is that he is not a camera and experiences incredible feelings that remain outside any exchange. Normally, when I see a painful scene, I have feelings that I can share with others. But if someone remains unmoved, we say that he has a heart of stone. Does this mean that he has no feelings? Pirandello speaks of relationships with madmen from the vantage point of his thirty years of life with a wife whose delusional jealousy towards him was a constant torment. In Chapter 3 of the fifth book of *The Notebooks of Serafino Gubbio*, this madness makes its entrance.

The cameraman is staying with a family in which the mother is devoured by delusional jealousy towards her husband. The latter, "infected" by his wife's madness, is driven to "eye askance, and [...] touch with a sense of misgiving some object in the room which was for a moment illuminated with the sinister light of a new and terrible meaning by the sick [woman's] hallucinations." Objects really become strange and frightening. "As falcons from their native ayry soar" in De Hérédia's poem,[39] they wait to pounce on the husband and drag him into her delusion, but thanks to the cameraman's presence, he can step back from the brink.

Through his character, Pirandello analyses his own reaction when faced with the "diabolical fury" of his wife and the "bursting of a soul [...] into fragments of life not reflected by the light of reason." He is seized by terror born of recognising "with an appalling clarity, that madness dwells and lurks within each of us and that a mere trifle may let it loose."[40] The cameraman also feels pity for the young girl in the household when he witnesses the "massacre of her heart" by an impossible love. But in the horror scene he would film, no one would feel pity for him.

The cameraman finally shuts himself up in a residence for the aged, where he continues to be a filming machine, the eye of the camera on which all the things of life are imprinted: "What do I know about the mountain, the tree, the sea? [...] I am the mountain, I am the tree, I am the sea. I am also the star, which knows not its own existence."[41] He turned a handle and experienced incredible emotions, but he wondered if he was really needed.

Once the event took place, once the camera recorded the tragedy without knowing it, he could no longer bear the physical proximity of others. Who was he in his indifference to the scene? What will the man do when all the cameras will turn by themselves?

> Do you still retain, gentlemen, a little soul, a little heart and a little mind? Give them, give them over to the greedy machines, which are waiting for them! You shall see and hear the sort of product, the exquisite stupidities they will manage to extract from them.

Who do they belong to, these objects that carry unbelievable feelings, and feel in the places where humans can no longer feel? If the survivors are able to come out of their sideration one day, and to filter what cannot be said when everything breaks down, the ruins may start to speak to someone else, with no need for metaphors. In the meantime, everything has stopped, as if all the relational dials have been turned to zero.

The cameraman has only a public existence, and refuses anyone's help. In his last notebook, he writes:

> No, thank you. Thanks to everybody. I have had enough. I prefer to remain like this. The times are what they are; life is what it is; and in the sense that I give to my profession, I intend to go on as I am – alone, mute and impassive – being the operator. Is the stage set? Are you ready? Shoot ...

This is how the novel ends. The "public" functions as if no relation to another is possible any longer. The last notebook written after the catastrophe, "with a pen and a sheet of paper to communicate with my fellow-men," quotes a sentence he had written elsewhere:

> I suffer from this silence of mine, into which everyone comes, as into a place of certain hospitality. I should like now my silence to close round me altogether. [...] Well, it has closed round me. I could not be better qualified to act as the servant of a machine.[42]

The subject of the novel is nothing other than the medium of a catastrophe, which causes everything to be imprinted on a neutral support. There are no more others since there is nothing but otherness. My intention is to show that in the transference, things can be placed in the space between two people so that they can be heard.

Clinical story

One day, a young man who had been considered retarded as a child came to my office announcing: "I am early!" and adding: "I've come to see you because I have nothing to say. We are very upset because my grandmother died and I don't feel sad at all." He explained that for him, sadness was a sadness-hand that passed over his body. But he experienced it as a film of sadness disconnected from his feelings, which he could not share with anyone. With him, my role could not be limited to that of an analyst curious to see how mourning expresses itself in a feeble-minded youth. He wanted to know my reaction: Did this disconnection frighten me? While everyone was crying, he remained as insensitive as a stone.

In the face of a catastrophe with no other to share it, the dyad individual/collective is broken. The seat of feelings in the body and the soul outruns its limits, and madness waits for someone to see if he feels something. "Prime words," as Marcel Duchamp called them, "words divisible only by themselves and by unity,"[43] which Socrates described as "the primal elements outside of reason (*stoicheia aloga*)"[44] and Bion as "beta elements."[45] They are not transferable to the symbolic level because they are not connected, but simply deposited in public places, waiting for an other to see if he is moved by them.

After a session when I could read the fear on the young man's face, I shook his hand to take leave of him; he made a grimace, as if I had violated a minimal distance. That night I had a dream in which I am travelling and I stop at an inn to have a meal. The hostess brings me a plate with two boiled human hands. I tell myself that people eat pigs' feet after all, and I wake up anxious, holding the plate in my hands. I had a dream in the minimal distance in which I was the hand that can kill at any moment.

This dream was not rooted in repression, but in the unspeakable trauma that happened between us. I tell the young man this dream, connected to the act of shaking a hand not held out, intruding on a margin of safety. In the next session, the two hands that are neither mine nor his were able to connect with us. I find him immersed in a terrible silence, a silence of stone, shattered by unspeakable pain showing on his face. Why? I only know that it is related to what is taking place between us.

I could transfer the responsibility to someone else, like Gavroche did in *Les Misérables* when he fell to the ground under a shower of bullets: "I fell to the ground, the fault is Voltaire's; my face in the dust, the fault is Rousseau's."[46] But we are there together and an intense pain is shown to me like a mask impossible to remove from the face I am seeing. I try to imagine different scenarios; nothing happens. I try not to be simply a spectator who describes what he observes, and finally I offer him my poor, severed hands again. This earns me a smile, twenty seconds of a look I hasten to forget. Before me I see not a young man who is sad, but Sadness itself that slipped between us.

Just then, I hear a piano and I tell him that this happens sometimes in my building. A melody comes to exist in my ears, as if the two hands on the plate have become the two phantom hands playing the piano. Who do they belong to, these things that do not exist, and which are programmed to experience feelings without a subject? If I insist that they should belong to an "I," I open the door to delusion. Indeed, hearing a piano that does not exist is surely a hallucination. Surviving images look for a subject to cling to, to avoid objectification. I play the role of a radio wave receiver, in order to grasp something that exists in a demanding externality, to catch it like a sensation, record it and hold on to it as long as it takes for the incredible feeling to enter an interference in which I am involved.

The young man tells me about a phantom piano, passed on to him by his grandmother who no longer played. The piano became forever silent, because the house was destroyed. I ask him to sing the melody his grandmother used to play, and I hear his voice becoming musical. I hear the piano play through his voice, between the two of us.

Change of vertex

Let us imagine that in geometry, point K is outside a figure and is not part of the statement, so that it has to be constructed. The same is true of madness: the social group that comes across it distances itself from it, and everyone says: "Point K is of no concern to me." Pirandello says this better than anyone in the short story "The Train Whistled,"[47] quoted by his countryman Gaetano Benedetti. The story is about Belluca, a man who is delirious as a result of "cerebral fever."[48] In medical language, "scientific terms" such as "encephalitis" describe what is seen from the outside, without considering the patient's life. But Pirandello constructs point K: "… given the most unusual conditions in which that unhappy man had been living […] his case could […] be considered quite natural."

Nothing is more Cartesian than psychosis: if there is madness, some reason has to be found. Descartes testified to this in his *Discourse on the Method*, in 1797, long after having had nightmares he thought would drive him mad.[49] While he was a soldier in the army of the Duke of Bavaria during the Thirty Years War, and stationed for the winter in Ulm, "alone in a stove-heated room," three nightmares terrified him on St Martin's Eve, in November 1719. In the first dream, wild winds pushed him violently, knocking him down; in the second, he heard a deafening clap of thunder; and in the third, he saw his bedroom full of sparks of light.[50] Eighteen years later, he set out his method of reasoning not as "the method," for he did "not recommend to everyone else to make a similar attempt," but as a method for himself: like a man walking alone in the dark, he "resolved to proceed slowly and with such circumspection, that if I did not advance far, I would at least guard against falling."[51]

Martin Cooperman, another war veteran who fought in the Pacific War, showed us how he constructed point K. At the Austen Riggs Center, a clinic dedicated to the psychoanalysis of psychosis, he told us, pointing to the window in his office:

Suppose that you see a patient gesticulating. Now, move a little to change your angle of observation. You will see that he is fighting an enemy. But the problem is that as soon as you get this glimpse, the enemy occupies your place.

To ignore this is to cancel transference and assert that these symptoms do not send any message, even though the other is ever-present in the form of a lawless, unreasonable agency against which we and the patient must fight. In this context, Wilfred Bion, another veteran of the First World War, speaks of the need for a change of vertex.[52]

Pirandello constructs point K by assuming that Belluca's delusion is "quite natural." As Wittgenstein says, a whole theory is condensed in a bit of grammar – in this case, the use of superlatives:

And it did not occur to anyone that, given the most unusual conditions in which that unhappy man had been living for so many years, his case could even be considered quite natural, and that everything Belluca said which everyone thought was nonsense, a symptom of frenzy, could also be the simplest explanation of his quite natural case.

How does the symptom show the nature of this natural case? By taking into account an external event. To explain nature in *De rerum natura*, Lucretius describes his vision of the falling of atoms, saying that if they never met, nothing would happen.[53] Therefore, a *clinamen* (deviation) must be hypothesised. The trajectory of one of these atoms has to deviate for reasons we cannot know, since this trajectory is outside our system.

Belluca, the narrator of Pirandello's short story, "lived with three blind women: his wife, his mother-in-law, and the latter's sister," who made his life hell (p. 103). As long as he found this normal, he was a model employee. One day, "the train whistled." This is how the *clinamen* intervenes: now, he sees that he is living an "impossible" life, and he becomes the subject of the madness around him.

This deviation from routine plays the role of the uneven paving stone on which Proust tripped in the courtyard of the Guermantes Hotel, on his way to a reception given there just after World War I.[54] Proust writes that in that moment, he had an experience of "time regained," of a fragment of pure time that triggered the writing of *Remembrance of Things Past*. When he entered, he saw the reception as a ball of phantoms, where the guests had been changed into mannequins. A psychiatrist seeing him that evening would have labelled him schizophrenic. He was discovering:

moments of existence cut out of time [...] not a past sensation, but a new truth [...]. As if our most beautiful ideas were airs coming back which we have never heard, but which we endeavor to listen to and to transcribe.

What element transforms Belluca's "delusion" into "the most natural of cases"? There are multiple points of view, one cannot generalise, someone else can always find another point *K*, as in this story Benedetti told us about a patient who lived outside time.

Wherever she went, clocks were not working. He told her that this was not possible. She insisted, and suddenly, in the session, he saw the hands of his office clock spin furiously and then stop. Benedetti, who was not one to miss transference, told her that he had just entered her timeless time. She replied: "You are completely mad, Mr. Benedetti." "What do you think?" he asked me. "Can it be that psychic energy acts directly on matter?" That he asks himself this type of question shows, at the very least, that he participates in the folly he encounters: *Folie à deux*, "foliadiu," as Martin Cooperman, his former colleague at Chestnut Lodge, would call this necessary transference, with his American accent.

It takes energy to construct point *K*, because the train opens the space where the city and what lies beyond it start to exist:

> A moment which ticked for him here in this prison of his, flowed like an electric shiver throughout the whole world, and now that his imagination had suddenly been awakened, he could follow that moment, yes, follow it to known and unknown cities, moors, mountains, forests, seas. This same shiver, this same palpitation of time. While he lived the "impossible life" here, there were millions of men scattered about the entire globe who lived differently [...]. The whole world, all of a sudden within him — a cataclysm. Gradually he would regain his composure. He was still tipsy from having breathed too much air; he could feel it.
>
> (pp. 104–105)

Where was madness located: in the life he used to live or in the sudden existence of the whole world? Pirandello never stops showing the rupture of the limits between fiction and reality.

"I am in a scenario I know nothing about, but I play my role perfectly," a delusional young man used to tell me. The painter Bernard Réquichot jumped out of a window when one of his friends, wanting to be helpful, exposed his paintings entitled *Reliquaires* (*Reliquaries*), in which the artist had taken refuge, in an art gallery. Réquichot used to say: "I don't know what does what to me." When another person is not there to reanimate this "I don't know what" who doesn't know, the exploitation can continue until the victim is killed. Some psychiatrists are not safe themselves from objectification.

Gaëtan Gatiande de Clérambault, Jacques Lacan's master, who theorised "mental automatism," was fascinated with cloth and its folds. He photographed veiled women in North Africa, and he draped cloth around wax mannequins in his house in the suburbs of Paris, where he sat facing a mirror and, surrounded by his dummies, shot at them and then turned the gun on himself.

The core of psychosis is like the eye of the cyclone. All around, it's the end of the world, while at the centre normal life continues its course. To say that the problem is social and historical makes no more sense than to say that it is psychological and individual, because the cyclone abolishes the opposition between collective and singular. The cyclone descends upon the analyst who tries to exist as the other by constructing point *K* not on the basis of a learned professional position, but from a blind point where he relies on the "seismograph of his soul"[55] that records the impressions cut off from the eye of the cyclone. These impressions are the only way to transmit something that cannot be felt or imagined.

"The Man with the Flower in His Mouth"[56] is a story about ordinary people who are not ordinary. One of them asks a stranger who has just missed a train:

> I ask you whether you think it possible that the houses of Messina [...] knowing they were about to be smashed by an earthquake, would have contentedly remained where they were, lined up along the streets and squares [...] No, by God, these houses of wood and stone would some- how have managed to run away!

But in reality, they cannot run away because they don't feel anything. Everyone is surrounded by madness but, like the houses, no one feels anything. Only through a delusion can one express, for instance, that his seismograph tells him that someone will die, as the hero of "The Man with the Flower in His Mouth" explains:

> You're walking down the street and some passer-by suddenly stops you. Carefully, he extends just two fingers of one hand and he says, "Excuse me, may I? You, my dear sir, have death on you!" [...] Many of the people you see walking around happily and indifferently may be carry- ing it on them. No one notices it. And they're calmly and quietly plan- ning what they'll do tomorrow and the day after. Now I ... Look, come over here, under this light ... I'll show you something ... Look here, under the moustache ... There, you see that pretty violet nodule? Know what it's called? Ah, such a soft word – softer than caramel – *epithe- lioma*, it's called. Death, you understand? Death passed my way.[57]

The Pygmies say that "there are three kinds of humans: the not quite dead, the long-time dead and the dead forever." The long-time dead are phantoms that come to life, and that's a problem. In this short story, death is hovering among the living. We who carry it "indifferently," we give it a dissociated position, but this elsewhere is as much our own as everything else. It emerges in the transference with madness, when "the tool with the names is broken," like a language covered with scars in which the subject tries to find himself.

The witness of a catastrophe whom mirrors can't reflect is closeted in the silence of the disappearance of all others, and tries to show it in order to give form to the unimaginable impossible to forget. In the absence of a reliable other, he also addresses himself to the public, which disintegrates into fragments as scattered as his image in the mirror. In this case, the public is not a collective entity, but a collection of small pieces of pulverised others, creating the need for ever-renewed efforts to add more, in hopes that more + more + more will eventually lead to finding a guarantor at the limits of language, in the form of God, the President, the Public Prosecutor or even the Pope. Mathematician Georg Cantor (1845–1918), who was persecuted by his colleagues for inventing set theory, demanded that the supreme authority of the Church, Leo XIII, speak with him directly.

In the meantime, the collection is built stone by stone, letter by letter, and eventually wears away, unless a coincidence occurs in the transference and its linking effect upon these "elements without reason," as Socrates calls them, generates the *logos*, speech and reason.[58] The effort to constitute a symbolic Other mechanically, by collecting bits of the imaginary on the trajectory of a vanishing point, will never lead to anything but a void. The one who dedicates his life to enabling this emergence tries to create time out of space, since in the absence of symbols time does not pass. In the space where there is no forgetting, the present is everything. Nothing is ever lost in the capharnaum of the more + more, which builds up in crowded rooms, and in stuffed cupboards and refrigerators. In these conditions, the clock only serves to carve up, in the present, the repetition of traumatic memory that cannot forget, but without setting time in motion again. As Bion says, in order to remember, one must forget; repression requires that time be in motion.

What makes it impossible to produce the signifiers of the symbolic chain, in this never emptied overflow? To empty an overstuffed space, one must be able to throw something away. But to destroy this or that element of the collection is equivalent to sending oneself into space, for lack of an other with whom to play at destroying the thing, since at this point of catastrophe the limit between inside and outside has been abolished.

But the required play falls outside the framework of traditional psychiatry and psychoanalysis, although the game was invented by a child of wartime, the one who played at "Fort! Da!" with his grandfather Freud,[59] who feared the death of his sons fighting on the front line of World War I.

The play of animistic practices

When dealing with abnormal things, which have destroyed all reliability, abnormal instruments are needed. The short story "Dal naso al cielo" ("From the Nose to the Sky") opposes a senator who supports positive science, and is recuperating from exhaustion in a countryside hotel, where he runs into his former disciple who has taken under his wing a young girl with what appear to be hallucinations. Coming back from a stroll, she heard phantom organ and harp music in the ruins of a nearby convent. The short story ends with the discovery of the senator's body, "nose to the sky," connected to the top of a tree by a spiderweb, in the woods where he had gone off alone, in order to contradict his disciple's superstitions and reaffirm his own diagnosis of the girl's condition: "It is nothing, Gentlemen, a slight passing psychosis, a hysterical crisis, nothing more."[60]

Pirandello raises the question of the limits of what can be known when science is powerless in the face of a phenomenon that cannot be repeated or put to the test. The author relies on the senator's former disciple to develop the subject by discussing the animist world and the mythological universe of legends:

> He [...] began speaking about occultism and mediumship, telepathy and premonitions, and of materializations; and before the eyes of his stunned audience, he populated the earth with wonders and phantoms, this earth that foolish human pride maintains is inhabited only by man and the few animals known to him, which serve him. A serious mistake! Other beings, which through our fault we cannot perceive with our normal faculties, live on earth a natural life like ours, and sometimes reveal themselves in certain abnormal circumstances, and fill us with fear; they are superhuman beings in the sense that they exist beyond our poor humanity and are subject to laws unknown to us, or more precisely, set aside by our consciousness, but which we perhaps obey as well, unconsciously. These non-human inhabitants of the earth, elemental essences, spirits of nature of all kinds, live among us in the mountains and forests, in the air and in the water, in the fire, invisible; but on occasion they are, nevertheless, able to take material shape.

Pirandello accuses short-sighted science, which casts abnormal phenomena into the mire of occultism, and he reanimates the "space of the marvel," which was the scene of madness in the Middle Ages. The contempt in which this space is held today by a doctrine with just as magical a belief in drugs and electroshock carries its own risks. Having declared that the music heard by the young girl "is nothing, a slight psychosis or hysteria," the senator literally took a "path of no return."

During the audiences he starts to give in 1907 in the short story "A Character's Tragedy,"[61] Pirandello portrays himself as an author. These audiences are demanding, because the characters "*wish* to be one kind of person or another," not what he wants them to be. When the characters rebel, the author says, "being basically good-hearted, I'm sorry for them. But is it ever possible to feel sorry for certain misfortunes unless you can laugh at them at the same time?" He gives us some examples from his own experience.

There is the old man who had just returned from the United States, where he was exiled in 1849, after the fall of the Roman Republic, for having set a patriotic hymn to music: "I had him die just as fast as possible in a little story titled 'Old Music'." In the same comic vein, Pirandello rejects a character who finds himself unjustly mistreated by other authors. Yet, his luck is no better with Pirandello, who mocks his special use of Time.

Dr Fileno, the creator of a "philosophy of distance," begs Pirandello to bring to life his "infallible prescription for consoling himself and all men for every public or private calamity." His method consists of "reading history books from morning till night and looking at the present as history – that is, as something already very remote in time." This manipulation of the arrow of time, which prompts many analysts to reject the present tense of traumatic memory by attaching these reviviscences to a causalistic history, was ridiculed by Bion when he returned from the Great War. He nicknamed his first analyst FIP, since he advocated the same solution: "Feel it in the past."

Like the psychoanalysis conducted by FIP, Dr Fileno's prescription consists of an optical illusion that produces a psychological view of history and a historical view of the psyche, both relegated to the past:

> In short, Dr Fileno had made a sort of telescope for himself out of that method of his. He would open it, but now not with the intention of looking toward the future, where he knew he would see nothing. He convinced his mind that it should be contented to look through the larger lens [...] toward the smaller one, which was pointed at the present. And so [...] immediately the present became small and very distant.

This was to be the subject of his book *The Philosophy of Distance*.

The confusion between the repressed unconscious and the cut-out unconscious brought about by the suppression of the symbolic leads to "a psychoanalysis of distance" that points its telescope towards past causality, when in fact the catastrophe in which the analyst has a role to play is occurring in the present.

The in-between position of the transitional subject

When the actor abandons his personality to don the mask of Noh theatre, he prepares to go on stage by crossing the bridge linking the here with the beyond – an in-between space called *ma* or *aida*, shown by an ideogram representing the sun through the opening of a door.[62] His slow entrance, punctuated by music, is that of a phantom wearing a white mask which expresses indifference. Feelings like fear or dread are not hidden under the mask, but produced by an effect of light on the mask in a play of interferences between the stage and the audience.

Like in psychotic transference, something happens at the "crossroads of dreams,"[63] *yume no chimata* – the name of the little stage in Noh theatre –

which may be transmitted to an other – belonging to no one, unrelated to the identity of the actor who brings it to life. In his comedy *Man, Beast, and Virtue*,[64] Pirandello reminds us that the actor was called *upocritès* in Ancient Greece. He is "one who acts because it is his job." The word means "the one who gives an answer through dreams or oracles." In the transference, this function is attributed to the "transitional subject" Benedetti speaks of, who emerges to give an answer when time has stopped and all bearings have collapsed.

Japanese psychiatrist Kimura Bin calls the space where psychotherapy takes place *Hito to hito to no aida*, the in-between man and *ma* (the gods). Anyone prone to "mental illness," he says – that is, divested of any individuality – enters this space called *ma* or *aida*, provided by the theatrical performance and the analytic session. In the Japanese language, personal pronouns facilitate the grasp of this notion, since they indicate social relations, in parenthood as well as in the context of a conversation. Kimura Bin also notes that some words with a double meaning confer positive value to melancholia, the fact that what is lost cannot be recovered – words like *kamashi*: love and sadness; *sabashi*: beauty and solitude; and *hashiki*: beloved and archaic. These words are also addressed to the dead who will never return.

In our work as analysts, when what we do is located in between the two people present, we use a specific grammar. Since the subject's syntax and its object are unavailable, we have to deal with voices that speak from everywhere, which King Midas believed to be the wind in the reeds, telling his secret, that "he has donkey's ears." Could it be that Japanese psychiatrists like Kimura Bin and Takeo Doi[65] have better tools than we do for identifying degrees of distance between people, and degrees of otherness in social situations, especially when ghosts are afoot?

As I am about to close the curtain on this seminar, which started out by transforming private life into a public space, I am no longer asking Pirandello to carry all the weight. I venture to say that, like his theatre, transference, when working with madness, gives access to a particular type of logic. They both try to resolve the paradox of how to build a chain of rationality when reason is irrelevant. How to bring the unprecedented out of a crisis and find the angle from which madness becomes reason. For madness is what exceeds rationality in order to bring this excess back to a point of interference where transference finds support in the relevance of some peculiarities that break the continuity of the sessions.

When he presented his "A Lecture on Serpent Ritual," which allowed him to leave Binswanger's clinic where he was confined, Aby Warburg spoke of the necessity of dealing with beings "saturated with energy" in order to reach the symbolic dimension. We work with an almost-nothing that takes on enormous energy in the setting of the sessions. We work on problems we create by bringing them into the present. The only way for psychic agony to be experienced in the transference, says Winnicott, is "in relation to the analyst's failures and mistakes."[66]

At last, we come to the question of the audience. What is the difference between the audience we are part of when we go to see a play, and the audience we might miss being in the theatre of madness, where speech finds no reflection? The aim of mad speech is to create the fourth wall allowing a performance to emerge, a representation of what is presented by Folly. Until then, she hopes to create it by calling out to the whole world: "Everyone blames me, so everyone must listen to me." When voices come from all sides, like the wind in the rose bushes spreading King Midas' secret – that he has donkey's ears – it's enough for one spectator to change places and, by chance, be able to link up a single element of what is being shown, for the entire space to become a structure that allows reflection.

Still, you will object, it's easier said than done, when your voice blends into the rumble of voices speaking to the patient, when he or she stands in the middle of a public place throwing things in all directions. I will answer your objection by telling you the Japanese story of Satori, a murderous monster coming from the four corners of the Earth. A lumberjack working in a forest sees Satori coming and knows he can't escape, since the monster can read his thoughts and knows what he plans to do. But just then, the unforeseeable happens. Believing his last hour had come, the lumberjack decides to continue cutting down his tree. He raises his axe, its blade flies out and by chance hits the monster, who could not have anticipated such a thing.

This is what happens in the psychoanalysis of madness, when the analyst stays present. Unexpectedly, an improbable contact takes place with traumatic zones, which the murderous agency cannot foresee. Everyone carries a heavy past, and particularly analysts, or else why would they have chosen this job? Our work is to recognise the relation between some detail in our no-longer-private lives and the solitary speech for which madness has been seeking an address for such a long time. This is the subject of Toni Morrison's novel *Beloved*, in which the madness of a runaway slave finally restores her place in the community that had ostracised her.

Notes

1 Bion, W., *A Memoir of the Future*, Karnac Books, 1991, p. 84.
2 See *infra*, Seminar 8 on Wilfred Bion.
3 Wittgenstein, L., *Tractus Logico-Philosophicus*, Psychology Press and Routledge Classic Editions, 2001; *Philosophical Investigations (1945–1949)*, Wiley-Blackwell, 2010.
4 Wittgenstein, L., *Philosophical Investigations*, op. cit., section 28.
5 Pirandello, L., *The Notebooks of Serafino Gubbio*, Simborowski, N. (Trans.), Hippocrene Books, 1990.
6 Pirandello, L., *Six Characters in Search of an Author*, Storer, E. (Trans.), University of Adelaide Press, 1921.
7 Wittgenstein, L., *Philosophical Investigations*, op. cit., section 197.
8 Ibid., section 21.
9 Ibid., sections 133, 119.

10 Barker, P., *Regeneration Trilogy* (based on W. Rivers' clinical notes), Penguin Books, 1998. See *infra*, Seminar 6 on Pat Barker.
11 Wittgenstein, L., *Philosophical Investigations*, op. cit., section 41.
12 Ibid., section 40.
13 Lacan, J., *Écrits*, Tavistock/Routledge, 1977.
14 Ibid.
15 Wittgenstein, L., *Philosophical Investigations*, op. cit., section 199.
16 Freud, S., *Jensen's 'Gradiva'*, S.E. 9; *The Uncanny*, S.E. 17; *Moses and Monotheism*, S.E. 23; *Project for a Scientific Psychology*, S.E. 1, Hogarth Press.
17 Devos, R., *Sens dessus dessous*, Stock, 1976.
18 Warburg, A., "A Lecture on Serpent Ritual," *Journal of Warburg Institute* 2 (1938–1939): 277–292.
19 Pirandello, L., "Right You Are! (If You Think So)," in *Naked Masks: Five Plays*, E. P. Dutton & Co., 1952.
20 Erasmus, D., *In Praise of Folly*, Literary Licensing, 2013.
21 Ōe, K., *Teach Us to Outgrow Our Madness*, Grove Press, 1977.
22 Desnos, R., *Un poète*, Gallimard, 1980.
23 Breton, A., *Nadja*, Grove Press, 1994.
24 Beradt, C., *The Third Reich of Dreams*, Quadrangle Books, 1968.
25 Pirandello, L., *One, No One, and One Hundred Thousand*, Hushion House, 1992.
26 Von Kleist, H., *On a Theatre of Marionettes*, Acorn Press, 1989.
27 Sterne, L., *The Life and Opinions of Tristram Shandy, Gentleman*, Oxford University Press, 2009.
28 Pirandello, L., "A Character's Tragedy," in *Eleven Short Stories*, Applebaum, S. (Trans.), Dover Publications, 1994.
29 Pirandello, L., "Colloquii coi personagii," in *Novelle per un anno*, Vol. III, Mondadori, 1990. Our translation.
30 See *infra*, Seminar 12 on François Rabelais and Yvette Guilbert.
31 Tweedy, R., *The Political Self*, Karnac Books, 2017.
32 Wittgenstein, L., *Philosophical Investigations*, op. cit., section 288.
33 Pirandello, L., "At the Exit," in *Pirandello's One-Act Plays*, HarperCollins, 1970.
34 Van der Kolk, B., *The Body Keeps the Score*, Penguin Books, 2015.
35 Pirandello, L., *The Notebooks of Serafino Gubbio*, op. cit.
36 Ibid., Chapter 2.
37 Freud, S., *Project for a Scientific Psychology*, op. cit.
38 Wittgenstein, L., *Philosophical Investigations*, op. cit., section 38.
39 De Hérédia, J. M., "The Conquerors," in *Sonnets of José-Maria De Heredia. Done into English by Edward Robeson Taylor*, William Doxey, 1897.
40 Pirandello, L., *The Notebooks of Serafino Gubbio*, op. cit., Book V, Chapter 3.
41 Pirandello, L., *The Notebooks of Serafino Gubbio*, op. cit.
42 Pirandello, L., *The Notebooks of Serafino Gubbio*, op. cit., Book VI, Chapter 4.
43 Duchamp, M., *Duchamp du signe*, Flammarion, 1976.
44 Plato, *Theaetetus*, Focus Philosophical Library, 2004.
45 Bion, D. W., *Elements of Psychoanalysis*, Karnac Books, 1963.
46 Hugo, V., *Les Misérables*, Signet Classics, 2010.
47 Pirandello, L., "The Train Whistled," in *Tales of Madness*, Bussino, G. R. (Trans.), Dante University of America Press, 2009.
48 Ibid., p. 98.
49 Descartes, R., *Discourse on Method and Related Writings*, Penguin Classics, 1999.
50 Baillet, A., "Olympica," in *La Vie de Monsieur Descartes*, Books LLC, 2011.
51 Ibid.

52 See *infra*, Seminar 8 on Wilfred Bion.
53 Lucretius, *The Nature of Things*, Penguin Classics, 2007.
54 Proust, M., *Time Regained*, Mayor, A. & Kilmartin, T. (Trans.), Modern Library, 1993.
55 Warburg, A., "A Lecture on Serpent Ritual," op. cit.
56 Pirandello, L., "The Man with the Flower in His Mouth," in *Pirandello's One-Act Plays*, op. cit.
57 Ibid., pp. 227–228.
58 Plato, *Theaetetus*, Liberal Arts Press, 1955.
59 Freud, S., *Beyond the Pleasure Principle*, S.E. 18, Hogarth Press, 1955.
60 Pirandello, L., "Dal naso al cielo," in *Novelle per un anno*, op. cit., pp. 162–163.
61 Pirandello, L., "A Character's Tragedy," in *Eleven Short Stories*, op. cit., p. 145.
62 Bin, K., *Hito to hito to no aida*, Kobudo, 1972.
63 Sieffert, R., *Nô et Kyôgen*, Presses orientales de France, 1979.
64 Bin, K., *Hito to hito to no aida*, op. cit.
65 Bin, K., *L'entre*, Vincent, C. (Trans.), Jérôme Million, 1985.
66 Winnicott, D. W., "Fear of Breakdown," *International Review of Psychoanalysis*, 1 (1974): 103–106.

4 Seminar 4: 1989–1990
Toni Morrison (1931–2019)

Beloved[1] in dialogue with Frieda
Fromm-Reichmann: psychoanalysis
and psychotherapy[2]

Storytellers are valuable allies

Freud's text *Delusions and Dreams in Wilhelm Jensen's Gradiva* starts with
a statement that could serve as a motto for this seminar: "Storytellers are
valuable allies, *bundes genossen*," meaning travelling companions. The German
writer's "A Pompeian Fancy" is a story of trauma and madness that ends with
the healing of the delusional hero thanks to the transference made possible by
his young neighbour Zoe.

We might wonder if the short story, published in 1902, did not prompt
Freud to go back to his "Neurotica," his theory of trauma, which he published
with Breuer in 1895,[3] and then announced to Fliess he was abandoning, in
a letter written in September 1897.[4] Freud himself suggests this possibility
when he writes in 1907: "Everything that is repressed is unconscious, but we
cannot assert that everything unconscious is repressed."[5]

This year's seminar could be called "Delusions and Dreams in Toni
Morrison's novel *Beloved*," which is at once a story of slavery in the
Southern United States and the story of a therapy of madness. To introduce
the novel, I will give you an example taken from my practice.

A clinical story

At the psychiatric hospital, I speak with a woman whose age is impossible
to tell, afflicted with delusions of persecution. She is a recognised expert in
English literature. After she is discharged, I continue to see her at the clinic.
Suddenly, she disappears for eight months, and then returns:

– I couldn't come any more when you started to talk foolishness.
– What foolishness?
– You told me that Beckett was alive.
– It's true, I sometimes see him on the Boulevard du Montparnasse. Have
  you seen any of his plays?
– No, but someone who says things the way he does can only be dead.

For her, Becket is not *a person* someone can brag about meeting on the boulevard, but an author who stands in the "space between two deaths," described by Lacan in his seminar "The Ethics of Psychoanalysis"[6] as in between the moment of death and its symbolic inscription on a grave by a ritual. This intermediary space was familiar to her. Judging that I was not up to the task, she disappeared again and came back two years later to verify scientifically if I had made any progress. Indeed, I had read Toni Morrison's novel where this place is displayed, where the ghosts return, bringing with them a particular way of knowing. *Beloved* is a ghost story as well as a story of Folly – praised by Erasmus, who has her ask at the start: "Who can set me out better than myself?" and say to conclude: "'tis Folly, and a woman, that has spoken."[7]

Beloved

Folly has enigmas to solve. They manifest themselves in the sphere of history, with unknowns and "whys" that prompt a delusional search, as a life-or-death necessity, to look for a co-researcher. If one is not found, out of desperation, she addresses the whole world. We are not able to appreciate this rigorous logic. Only Folly can judge, like the folly of the heroines of *Beloved*: Sethe, a fugitive slave, and her daughter Denver. They live in a house cut off from others, and periodically shaken up by the ghost of a baby that Sethe has named Beloved.

The plot takes place in 1873, after the Civil War, in a haunted house of the outskirts of Cincinnati, Ohio. The character entrusted with the mission of inscribing an impossible history is the ghost of the baby, who says "I."

We are not dealing with an illusion. In fact, this situation is similar to what happens in the psychoanalysis of madness and trauma, where ghosts impose their presence just as forcefully, to say what they have to say, in an exploded time through which the slow and gradual inscription of their stories can be carried out.

At the end of *Beloved*, Sethe and her daughter Denver find their place in the community once again. Yet recovery from "acute psychosis," as Binswanger called it, is often regarded with scepticism by psychoanalysts.

Pioneers in the psychoanalysis of madness and trauma

In regard to the treatment of psychosis, Lacan did not go beyond a "preliminary question,"[8] and did not venture to explore the sphere of transference, on the pretext that "it would be premature to speak of transference in psychosis, because it would be to go 'beyond Freud', and there can be no question of Freud when post-Freud psychoanalysis has gone back to an earlier stage." He does not mention the psychoanalysis of psychosis pioneered during World War I. For the Great War not only drove Freud to go beyond the scope of the "Pleasure Principle,"[9] but prompted his disciples, drafted in military hospitals, to explore the transference specific to madness and trauma. On the brink of the next war, when his books were being burned in Berlin, Freud wrote that what was at stake in psychoanalysis was the subject of "historical truth."[10] I will now list some of the names we will be referring to in this seminar.

Thomas Salmon,[11] psychiatrist at Ellis Island and author of the four principles of "forward psychiatry."

Harry Stack Sullivan,[12] grandson of Irish refugees, first a physician in Chicago, where the immigrants from Ellis Island arrived, and later liaison officer for the St. Elizabeths military hospital in Washington, who invented psychoanalysis with young patients labelled schizophrenic at Sheppard Pratt Hospital in Baltimore.

William Rivers,[13] neurologist, anthropologist and psychoanalyst at Craiglockhart, near Edinburgh, who treated officers returning from the trenches. John Rickman, Bion's second analyst, was his disciple.

Frieda Fromm-Reichmann,[14] neurologist at the same period in a military hospital in Königsberg – where Hanna Arendt grew up – worked with soldiers who had suffered brain injuries. When she fled the Nazi regime and settled in the United States, she introduced the psychoanalysis of psychosis at Chestnut Lodge, in Maryland. I shall have her converse with *Beloved*. In this seminar, both will be our valuable allies in the political fight waged by Folly against perversion.

Speaking of these explorers, let us remember that Proust, their contemporary, wrote *In Search of Lost Time* at the end of his life, closeted in his cork-lined bedroom to cut himself off from the outside world and "regain time,"[15] at an end-of-the-world moment in history, when his era was sinking into war.

I could also mention Daniel Paul Schreber,[16] the judge whose madness emerged at the intersection of his particular history, shaped by the black education – Alice Miller's expression – he received from his father, and by the Franco-Prussian War in which German principalities were abolished, to be replaced by a unified German state. Schreber is in direct contact with this upheaval in his position as magistrate. In Austria, Joseph Roth, author of *The Radetzky March*,[17] witnesses the end of the Austro-Hungarian Empire, described by Robert Musil in his novel *The Man Without Qualities*.[18] On the American continent, Sioux medicine man Black Elk entrusts poet John Neihardt with the book *Black Elk Speaks*,[19] which testifies to the disaster suffered by the Lakota people during the American Indian Wars waged at the end of the nineteenth century.

Folly is rigorous and always proceeds from an absence of text, which prevents transmission. Here, Freud's sentence quoted from the *Gradiva* comes to mind: "Everything that is repressed is unconscious, but we cannot assert that everything unconscious is repressed." We call a cut-out unconscious that which is not repressed and tends towards inscription. The new text to be written has a literary character, since mere information is not enough. The subject of the story has to be born, and be able to bleed, laugh, cry and be affected by connecting with another endowed with the "porosity" Socrates spoke of in *The Symposium*, based on his experiences in battle during the Peloponnesian War. Asked to give his definition of Eros, he quoted a woman, Diotima – "the stranger" – a medicine woman who postponed the outbreak of the plague in Athens. According to her, Eros is the child of *Poros*, the passage – "porosity" – and of *Penia* – "penury" or "poverty."[20]

This kinship links transference to catastrophic situations such as wars, situations familiar to Toni Morrison and Frieda Fromm-Reichmann.

Circumstances in which it is normal to go mad

"The man who does not lose his mind over certain things has no mind to lose," Nietzsche wrote; Frieda Fromm-Reichmann quotes him in her book *Psychoanalysis and Psychotherapy.*[21]

The ghost of the baby who haunts 124 Bluestone Road, where Sethe, the runaway slave, and her daughter Denver are living in seclusion, doesn't prevent life from following its course. When it first came, the enraged ghost cast "a powerful spell." "No more powerful than the way I loved her [when I cut her throat]," Sethe tells Denver.

This event took place after a feast celebrating Sethe's family's freedom with her neighbours, once she arrived at 124 Bluestone Road. Suddenly, Sethe saw three men approaching on horseback; one of them was Schoolteacher, the vicious new owner of the plantation following the death of the previous owner who considered his slaves men. Understanding in a flash that Schoolteacher was coming to retrieve his property, Sethe cuts the throat of her 2-year-old daughter to save her from slavery. Since then, the ghost of the girl Sethe named Beloved on her tombstone has taken possession of the house, which she turns upside down, while her mother and her sister give her every sweet thing of which she was deprived. She doesn't know that she is dead, and therefore cannot know her "birth certificate as a ghost."[22]

The course of life at 124 Bluestone Road is perturbed by the arrival of Paul D, "the last of the plantation men" – a plantation called "Sweet Home." He reappears eighteen years after Sethe escaped, pregnant with Denver, who was born during her mother's flight and was only a baby when she narrowly escaped being slaughtered. By driving the ghost away, Paul D sows discord in the house; his arrival "[left] Denver's world flat," but for Sethe "[e]motions sped to the surface in his company." For the first time, she asks herself if it might be "all right to go ahead and feel? Go ahead and *count on something?*"

How real is the phantom that haunts the house? Boris Vian answers this question in *The Foam of the Daze*, when he introduces his story: "The story is entirely true, because I imagined it from one end to the other."[23] The only thing we can say is that "it" speaks. Not the "it" of the repressed unconscious, but that of a real presence trying to say something, to which all cultures testify. Indeed, I who don't believe in ghosts encounter them every day in my office, where they gather to have their say about the family lines of those who come to see me.

If I adopt a critical position or an anthropological view of beliefs in the Deep South of the nineteenth century, if I leave patients to deal with their ghosts alone while I observe how the situation unfolds, nothing will happen, since ghosts claim their right to exist and to speak. They don't care whether we believe in them or not. What they want is to see to it that the true version of falsified stories is inscribed at last.

In her article "Remarks on the Philosophy of Mental Disorder," Frieda Fromm-Reichmann deplores the fact that:

> most psychiatrists have more respect for the society which pays them their services than for the patients who need their help. [...] Mentally disturbed persons [...] are refreshingly intolerant of all kinds of cultural compromises; hence they inevitably hold the mirror of the hypocritical aspects of the culture in front of society. [...] Considering relationships with mental patients from this viewpoint, it is no overstatement to say that the mentally sick, who allegedly have lost their minds in their interpersonal struggles, may be useful to the mentally healthy in really finding their minds, which are all too frequently lost, as it were, in the distortions, the disassociations, the hypocritical adaptations, and all the painful hide-and-seeks which modern culture forces upon the mind of man.

At the end of *Beloved*, Sethe and her daughter escape the deadly cat-and-mouse game, through a catharsis orchestrated by the novelist, whose ancestors were part of the history she brings to life. Her novel also resonates with the two principles of the psychoanalysis of psychosis: Sullivan's[24] "one-genus postulate: we are much more simply human than otherwise; our differences are of degree and not of kind," and Frieda Fromm-Reichmann's assertion that "when there is no transference, everything is transference." Hence the value of having her converse with Toni Morrison's novel.

Who is Frieda Fromm-Reichmann?

A disciple of neurologist Kurt Goldstein, Frieda Fromm-Reichmann had been in charge of a ward for brain-injured soldiers at the Königsberg military hospital in Germany[25] during World War I. At a 1942 conference held in Baltimore, she remarked:

> War psychotherapy is of rather recent origin. Its use [...] was first initiated during World War I. [...] additional experience [came] with the Spanish Civil War and the present world war. [...] What can we learn from our experience in peacetime psychiatry?[26]

She asserted that psychiatric patients are ready to fight, in the name of freedom and democracy, against totalitarian submission in the domestic and political spheres.

Her discovery of psychoanalysis in the early 1930s was decisive:

> Before I was acquainted with Freud's teachings, I realised, with distress, that something went on in the patient's relations with me, and in my relations with them, which interfered with the psychotherapeutic process. Yet I could not put my finger on it, or investigate it. What a relief it was to become acquainted with the tools furnished by Freud for investigation into the awareness of the doctor–patient relationship.[27]

But she was not in complete agreement with Freud, especially concerning the role of historical events:

> Freud speaks of an objective "reality" of the outside world in contradiction to the private and frequently unreal inner world of the neurotic. While he clearly points out how greatly the person's immediate surroundings are determined by changing environmental influences, he neglects to see that the same holds true for the world at large.

She gives the following example:

> The "reality" to which, for instance, a Vienna girl of the upper middle classes had to adjust in the period before World War I is a long way from the "reality" to which an American salesgirl has to adapt herself in this year of 1941.[28]

Let us note in passing that she does not mention the sexual abuses suffered by young Viennese girls in their protected environment, just as Freud chose to ignore the subject when he set aside his "Neurotica," to avoid "incriminating the father, not excluding my own." Yet eight months earlier he had written to Fliess that "my own father was one of those perverts, and is responsible for the hysteria of my brother and several [...] younger sisters."[29]

Frieda herself was raped as a young girl, in Königsberg, by a man on the street. Her mother considered that such a thing happening to a young Jewish girl from a good family, and before marriage, was an abomination; she simply washed and mended her daughter's underwear and ordered her to put it on. Nothing had ever been said about the traumatic event again, and it remained a secret from then on.[30]

Fromm-Reichmann's second disagreement with Freud, just like Ferenczi's, concerned the analyst's neutrality:

Freud taught us that, ideally, the analyst, as nearly as it is possible, must be a blank to the patient. [...] [The analyst's] aloofness [could] also become a means of protection against his patient's legitimate reactions to him [...] whether resentment if he blundered or appreciation when he struck the right chord [...]. Of course, the analyst will [not] talk about his personal life [...]. He will [...] not use the patient to serve his own needs. But he should make use of his emotional counter reactions for the purposes of the treatment.

Frieda Fromm-Reichmann protests against stereotyped interpretations and jargon: "Freud warned us to bear in mind that analysis is a procedure designed to cure the patient, not to show him how clever his analyst's interpretations are." For instance, sexual feelings towards the analyst do not always originate in the Oedipus complex: "They may be an expression of insecurity." When Beloved asks Paul D to have sex with her, it is to sweep him up and drive him away from her mother. Indeed, he leaves the house to live outside like a tramp.

According to Frieda:

Another advance in analysis comes from the change in the choice of patients. During the last fifteen years [since the beginning of World War I] attempts have been made to adjust the analytic method to the needs of psychotic patients.

In 1924, tired of wasting energy on people who did not interest her, she decided to devote herself to those who really needed psychoanalysis. She made this decision after the death of her father. Like her mother, he had become deaf and was threatened with losing his job; he fell into an elevator pit, an accident she took to be disguised suicide.

In 1926, Frieda married Erich Fromm, who had been in analysis with her, and who soon left her for Karen Horney. She remained alone and had no children. Encouraged by the revival of the Jewish culture in the Weimar Republic, she opened a psychoanalytic clinic in Heidelberg, near her friend Groddeck's sanatorium in Baden-Baden. She often exchanged ideas with Groddeck, as well as with members of the Frankfurt School.

When Hitler came to power, and Jewish doctors, teachers and lawyers were forbidden to practise, kidnapped and shot, she realised that a male nurse had her under surveillance. After telling her patients that she would not return, she left Heidelberg for good in 1933, on the pretext of a weekend in Strasburg. After trying to go to Palestine, she immigrated to the United States, from where Erich Fromm, who was already there, sent her the necessary papers. Once in the United States, she was offered a summer job in Dexter Bullard's Chestnut Lodge clinic near Washington. Soon, impressed with her experience, Dexter Bullard decided to dedicate his institution to the psychoanalysis of psychoses under her direction, and built a cottage for her on its grounds, where she lived until her death in 1957. At Chestnut Lodge, she developed the new paradigm for intensive psychotherapy of psychosis[31] with Harry Stack Sullivan, who gave seminars at Chestnut Lodge on a regular basis. It was there that the future analysts of psychosis, Harold Searles, Otto Will, Martin Cooperman, Gaetano Benedetti and many others, received their training.

During a 1942 conference organised under the auspices of the William Alanson White Institute, which she contributed to create with Sullivan, Fromm-Reichmann analysed an article by British psychiatrist George Brown, which presented the positive results obtained by psychoanalytic psychotherapy for civilian victims of air raids in London during the Blitz. This psychotherapy was probably influenced by William Rivers' experience during World War I, as well as by Thomas Salmon's four principles[32] developed during his military mission in England in 1917, before the United States entered the war.

Frieda Fromm-Reichmann's work was based on the principle that everything patients experience exists in a cancelled place, which is the opposite of nowhere, and remains invisible until they find elements to which they can bind, on the side of the analyst. Her other principle, as we already mentioned, concerns the role of historical events. When men, women and children are treated like things, their emotional and sensory experience cannot fade away. Traumatic memory persists, literally "outside" the subject. Hence, the necessity for "proximity" with the therapist – one of Salmon's principles – who becomes "a passionate witness," as Dori Laub[33] says, of "events without a witness," bringing them back from dissociation – a dissociation maintained today by "therapies" such as shock treatments that prevent the subjective appropriation of the events in question.

Beloved: the subjective appropriation of a mass crime

The therapist must fill in the missing details, with the feelings awakened in him, so as to bring the erased scene into existence, between the patient and himself. Likewise, Toni Morrison's novel unfolds the subjective appropriation of particulars that are usually lost in general discourses. These specific elements never disappear, since they are not filtered through the symbolic chain; they come back into the present through sensorial images saturated with energy.

One day Denver sees her mother kneeling in prayer, embraced by a white dress. This tender embrace reminds her of the details of her birth, of the miraculous encounter of two women helping each other so that she might come into the world. The midwife Amy is a young white girl on her way to Boston. The account of Sethe's exhaustion, labour and delivery on the banks of the Ohio River, before she reaches freedom on the other side, ends with Amy telling her, while she rubs her wounded feet: "It's gonna hurt now. Anything dead coming back to life hurts."

After her vision, Denver thinks: "Maybe the white dress was in pain. If so, it could mean the baby ghost had plans." Entering the room, she tells her mother what she saw and asks what she was praying for. Sethe answers: "I don't pray anymore. I just talk."

This is where Toni Morrison provides us with a formidable analysis of the workings of madness and trauma:

– "I was talking about time. It's so hard for me to believe in it. Some things go. Pass on. Some things just stay. I used to think it was my memory. [...] But it's not. Places, places are still there. If a house burns down, it's gone, but the place – the picture of it – stays [...]. What I remember is a picture floating around out there outside my head. I mean, even if I don't think of it, even if I die, the picture of what I did, or knew, or saw is still out there. Right in the place where it happened."
– "Can other people see it?" asked Denver.
– "Oh, yes. Oh, yes, yes, yes. Someday you will be walking down the road and you hear something or see something going on. So clear. And you think it's you thinking it up. A thought picture. But no. It's when you bump into a memory that belongs to somebody else. Where I was before I came here, that place is real. [...] It's going to always be there waiting for you. That's how come I had to get all my children out. No matter what."
– "If it's still there, waiting, that must mean that nothing ever dies."
  Sethe looked right in Denver's face.
– "Nothing ever does," she said.

Then she told her about the arrival, after the death of Mr Garner, of the new master Schoolteacher, whose cruelty replaced the kindness of the previous couple. At the end of their conversation, both of them agree that "the ghost baby could have plans."

Harry Stack Sullivan's interpersonal approach

In 1949, the year when Sullivan died in Paris, Frieda Fromm-Reichmann insisted on his interpersonal approach. Personality can only be understood in terms of relationships, real or imagined, through transference that places the catastrophe at its centre and brings back out-of-reach emotional experiences, in a collaboration between equals: "Due to the dangers they faced early in life," says Sullivan:

> psychotic patients are driven into a state of continuous vigilance, so that they become highly efficient eavesdroppers [...] who may know or sense character traits or emotional problems in their doctor [...] of which he himself is unaware, and which he is asked to validate.
>
> In his view, "patients are participant-observers" in the collaborative endeavour. This is what allows many schizophrenics and people with other

schizoid disorders to recover. The therapist must know that adherence to conventionalities should never be used as a measuring rod for mental health.[34]

Remaining outside conventionalities includes, among other things, the freedom to ask oneself how ghosts come into being. For, not knowing that they are dead, they must wander, waiting for a space between two beings from which they could be called. This in-between space is created at the end of *Beloved* thanks to the spontaneous reaction of a neighbour named Ella. She is the one who opens the space of transference.

The ghost has become increasingly tyrannical. Sethe no longer has the strength to go and cook at the restaurant where she works, and so can no longer bring food from there. Starving, Denver decides to do something: "she had stepped out the door, asked for the help she needed and wanted work."

Ella had been repeatedly raped in puberty by a father and son who owned another plantation. When she heard that:

> 124 was occupied by something-or-other beating up Sethe, it infuriated her. [...] There was also something very personal in her fury. [...] Ella didn't like the idea of past errors taking possession of the present. Sethe's crime was staggering and her pride outstripped even that; but she could not countenance the possibility of sin moving on in the house, unleashed and sassy.

For her, "the future was sunset" and the past was something to leave behind. "And if it didn't stay behind, well, you might have to stomp it out."

Denver's decision to leave the house and ask for help for the first time touches Ella: it resonates with the deep wounds of her own adolescence, and prompts her to gather the other women in the neighbourhood, to bring Sethe's house out of isolation. Enough is enough! "As long as the ghost showed out from its ghostly place – shaking stuff, crying, smashing and such – Ella respected it. But if it took flesh and came in her world, well [...] this was an invasion."

The ghost has no name. The seven letters in "Beloved," etched on the tombstone, do not make up its first name, which is absent from the novel. The string of letters is not inscribed in a chain of signifiers. "Ten minutes for seven letters," spelled out for the engraver, enough:

> to answer one more preacher, one more abolitionist and a town full of disgust. [...] she had forgotten [...] the soul of her baby girl. Who would have thought that a little old baby could harbour so much rage? [...] Not only did she have to live out her years in a house palsied by the baby's fury at having its throat cut, but those ten minutes she spent [...] her knees wide open as the grave, were longer than life, more alive, more pulsating than the baby blood that soaked her fingers like oil.

The origin of the name Beloved emerges when the "tool with the name is broken." It comes from a passage in the Bible, quoted as an epigraph in the novel: "I will call them my people, which were not my people; and her beloved, which was not loved."

This contradiction is the space in which the tragedy seeking catharsis is played out, creating terror and inspiring pity for a mother who kills her child in the name of liberty. Caught in the dilemma "live free or die," she cannot pronounce her baby's name. The seven letters of "Beloved" carved on the grave have a negative meaning: "the one not loved."

In a sense, this is not an inscription. Indeed, Sethe shows not the slightest annoyance when the ghost turns the house upside down. When a tragic time-space opens, with edges that will not come together, sculptors may etch stones tirelessly, writers may fill endless pages, nothing is inscribed, though everything tends towards inscription.

Frieda Fromm-Reichmann warns that if therapists cling to stereotyped interpretations, encouraging patients to write without involving themselves, they will miss "meeting them on an equal footing, and not in the spirit of any pre-established authority." And she goes on to say that this encounter requires – in the words of a young military psychiatrist working with soldiers during the war – "that the doctor possess tact to a superlative degree."

When, at the end of the novel, the two edges – impossible to join – of freedom and maternal love come together, the book becomes the monument on which a plural memory is inscribed. Toni Morrison needed 400 pages to arrive at the point where Sethe is reintegrated into the community at the end of a story that unfolds over fifteen years.

No psychotic structure can tell such a story. In this space between two deaths where nothing makes sense and everything makes sense, the analyst's puns are futile syllables thrown at the patients. On the other hand, when history finds a Toni Morrison, a Kenzaburō Ōe or a Pirandello, the works they create are the crucible where ghosts emerging from the disasters of History may carry out their plans.

The plans of a ghost

One of the expressions of madness in *Beloved* takes the form of a house that cries like a person, which sighs and screams, a colourless house in which two orange patches in a quilt "looked wild – like life in the raw." The second form is the white dress with its arm around Sethe, which makes Denver say: "Maybe the white dress was in pain." The mother's relation to suffering is disconnected. Things suffer on her behalf. The plan of the ghost is to raise the subject of this pain. For the role of ghosts is not only to trouble us, but to make that trouble stop. The fate of a ghost, we are told at the end of the story, is to be forgotten.

In every culture, ghosts return from the beyond, as if their one-way journey was from there to here. But this viewpoint is too simplistic.

Although we don't always see them, they walk alongside us towards the future. A ghost can come from a future that has not taken place. Sethe is not surprised by the presence of the ghost actively interacting with them as a young girl. For her, the image of the crime is wavering; it belongs to another temporality. She is "wrapped in a timeless present" without any tomorrow.

It is possible to make contact through things, or clustered words that are not symbols. They exist rather than not existing; they are something rather than nothing. At the start of the novel, the reader is bombarded with a myriad of sensations, which Sethe eliminates one after the other:

> All her effort was directed not on avoiding pain but on getting through it as quickly as possible. [...] Unfortunately her brain was devious [...] and suddenly there was Sweet Home rolling, rolling, rolling out before her eyes [...] in shameless beauty. Boys hanging from the most beautiful sycamores in the world [...]. It shamed her – remembering the wonderful soughing trees rather than the boys.

This memory belonging to no one, bringing back the disasters of History, is not a collective memory, nor a storehouse of signifiers, but an active place in motion, a poem that looks back at you. When you are nothing, a certain word thinks of you, a certain rhythm stirs you, a nursery rhyme, a circle dance, a song. Psychosis and trauma are to be explored by moving backwards, in search of another who has run away, as Freud did, in September 1897, the day he revealed to Fliess "the great secret: I no longer believe in my Neurotica,"[35] his psychoanalysis of trauma.

Frieda Fromm-Reichmann's debt to Freud

Frieda Fromm-Reichmann did not hold this against him. On the contrary, she thanks him for having changed his mind, and for anticipating "modifications and changes in [his] technique" so that it would become applicable to the psychoses, in which mental and emotional content is "barred from awareness," rather than repressed.[36]

Her controversial article attacks his disciples' indiscriminate adoration: "Marx countered [this] with his famous statement: 'I am not a Marxist'." Let us remember that Freud also said in spirit, time and again: "I am not a Freudist." Far from not daring, like Lacan, "to go beyond Freud," she recognises him to be a pioneer of the psychodynamic psychotherapy of psychoses, which remained unknown in France for many years, while in the United States it was refused the name of "psychoanalysis." She claims that name for her approach, as it is founded on the principles below.

First, exclude all those who attempt to be more Freudian than Freud by generalising the sexual causality of trauma. Second, abandon the structural approach in favour of a dynamic perspective. Freud's formula "*Wo Es war, soll Ich werden*" – "Where 'Id' was, 'I', the subject, must become" – induces the future, in the sense of an induced current. Where the id imposes the past on the present, – since an affirmation, *Bejahung*, of what took place has been denied – there, in the actual context of the sessions, what has been barred entry to any relationship must be transferred to the analytic interaction. Finally, she objects to the couch and to the analyst's neutrality, which reinforce the absence of otherness, when we know that cut-out elements are only accessible through interferences.

This barred content is embedded in a permanent anxiety, revealed not so much by the patient's unintelligible discourse as by his total helplessness, comparable to that of the soldiers with brain injuries in the Königsberg military hospital during World War I. Recalling her experience there, she refers to the words used by her teacher Kurt Goldstein to describe this "abject feeling" he calls "nothingness," when the soldiers were faced with a task which they [...] could not accomplish for reasons unknown to them. Goldstein calls this deep anxiety a "catastrophic reaction," which makes them say: "I am an imbecile, my brain doesn't work anymore, I'm done for." From that point on, anxiety is not so much a psychological reaction as the symptom of a threat to the subject's existence. Hence the paradox that defines catatonia as the impossibility of transference, when in fact "everything is transference."

In the presence of a threat to existence, the only thing that remains is the relation to others, and this is what is frightening, since others are not available – like in a play when insensitive monsters come on stage – except that here theatre is daily reality. Frieda does not mince words in her criticism of psychoanalysts who, instead of climbing on the stage, are content to comment on the situation, deploring their patients' fragility. The patient's purported fragility, she says, is as solid as that of the Glass Graduate in Cervantes' short story.[37]

In her article "Transference Problems in Schizophrenics,"[38] Frieda Fromm-Reichmann contradicts another psychoanalytic dogma which holds that schizophrenic patients are too narcissistic to develop an interpersonal relationship with their therapist. Therefore, they are unsuited for transference and psychoanalytic treatment. Yet the new technique invented during World War I by Freud's disciples, such as Ferenczi, Rivers, Karl Menninger in his clinic, Sullivan, herself and many others, led to the conclusion that the problem was not the patient's inability to form a personal relation, but his very intense transference reactions that re-enact severely traumatic experiences.

Like the pearl in an oyster, transference often crystallises around an impurity, a blunder made by the analyst, foreseeable in its unpredictability, given that "our access to the schizophrenic's means of expression is blocked by [...] our own adjustment to a world [he] has relinquished." In reality, what is seen as a symptom denotes particular knowledge of a landscape of destruction. It is an end of the world that mixes together "yes" and "no,"

"I" and "others," "here" and "elsewhere," "yesterday" and "today." The symptoms attempt to inscribe this indescribable state, always imminent, prophesised by Cassandras and enacted in the sessions by the analyst's slip-ups:

> If the schizophrenic's reactions are stormier and seemingly more unpredictable than those of the psychoneurotic, I believe it is due to the inevitable errors in the analyst's approach to the schizophrenic, of which he himself may be unaware, rather than to the unreliability of the patient's emotional response.

And she goes on to say: "If the analyst is not able to accept the possibility of misunderstanding the reactions of his schizophrenic patient and, in turn, of being misunderstood by him, it may shake his security with the patient." A little further, she adds:

> If the analyst deals unadroitly with the transference reactions of a [patient], it is bad enough, though as rule not irreparable. [...] To summarise: [...] successful psychotherapy with schizophrenics depends upon whether the analyst understands the significance of these transference phenomena and meets them appropriately.[39]

She answers critics by saying:

> Other analysts may feel that treatment as we have outlined it is not psychoanalysis. The patient is not instructed to lie on a couch, he is not asked to give free associations (although frequently he does), and his productions are seldom interpreted other than by understanding acceptance.

Then she turns to Freud to support her argument:

> Freud says that every science and therapy that accepts his teachings about the unconscious, about transference and resistance, and about infantile sexuality may be called psychoanalysis. According to this definition, we believe we are practicing psychoanalysis with our schizophrenic patients.

Le parti pris des choses

This title, translated into English as *The Voice of Things*, was given by the French poet Francis Ponge to a collection of 32 prose poems published in 1942. When words fail, things begin to speak.

One of Frieda Fromm-Reichmann's catatonic patients would repeatedly stroke his blanket with a tender expression that would light his rigid face:

When he felt that I had noticed these mechanical movements, his expression would simultaneously become withdrawn, if not actually hostile. After a while I discovered that he strokes the blanket as disguised evidence of his tenderness until he was sure of being understood.

After giving other examples, she concludes: "The stereotyped actions of schizophrenics serve to screen the appropriate emotional reactions which are at their bottom."[40]

The emotional significance of gestures that seem ridiculous can only be understood in an interpersonal context, as enacting the repeated rebuffs that forced the patient to hide behind "a screen," to remain invisible. When communication is re-established, he can again express himself clearly. This screen will appear in the novel.

In *Beloved*, we also encounter evidence of a screen when the ghost asks her sister to tell the story of how she was born. "Tell me how Sethe made you in the boat." Denver now revealed the details to the alert and hungry face, which took in every word. Up to that point, she appeared psychotic to the reader, but in the telling she gradually becomes the subject of her own birth. In that narrative, the white girl Amy, whom she calls the midwife, is suddenly there to help Sethe, who can't walk any longer, deliver her baby.

We know how Sethe recounted these events when Denver questioned her after seeing the white dress with its arm around her. We've heard about the bank of the Ohio River, facing the land where freedom starts, about the boat in which Sethe lay exhausted, her feet bloody, and about Amy, the white girl in rags who suddenly appeared, with "arms like cane stalks," which later, "as it turned out, were as strong as iron." We know that the runaway girl lost her mother soon after her birth, and that she is on her way to Boston, her mother's home town, intent on finding carmine velvet in a shop called Wilson, where her mother used to work.

When Denver told the story to Beloved, she "began to see what she was saying" and not just hear it. She saw the 19-year-old slave girl, a year older than herself. She was feeling, through Beloved, in minute details what her mother must have felt. Her monologue became a duet, allowing them "to create what really happened." Denver now feels Amy's "tender-hearted mouth," as the girl looked after Sethe's feet, treated her whipped back with spiderwebs, and sang her a song while she delivered her baby.

When chance brought her this vagrant girl, Sethe briefly saw the future open for her. When their work together was done, just before continuing on her way, Amy tells Sethe her name: "You better tell her. You hear? Say Miss Amy Denver of Boston." This reveals the origin of Denver's name. Moreover, in the retelling, Denver becomes aware of the hidden meaning behind "the screen" of velvet.

In the story Sethe told her daughter, the runaway girl is identified with velvet: its colour, its feel, its texture, which she tirelessly describes to the exhausted slave. Amy got hold of velvet and used it to soften the ravaged landscape, on the other bank of the river, of the history of slavery. Had it not been for velvet, she might have gone past Sethe without seeing her. Velvet takes the place of what Folly can transfer to another, as a promise for the future. With Amy's arrival, Sethe receives strange things that have no meaning in her usual language, but are the language of a new world without slavery: "What's it like, velvet?" Sethe asks. "Well [...] velvet is like the world was just born. Clean and new and so smooth," Amy answers. About to continue on her way, she changes her mind. Still speaking of velvet and Boston, she helps Sethe walk to a cabin and makes her feel that "maybe she wasn't, after all, just a crawling graveyard for a six-month baby's last hours."

Velvet is the screen through which Sethe receives the message of life beyond death and slavery, which is the fabric of the novel. Velvet is an object allowing love – Eros, son of *Poros*, the passage, and *Penia*, poverty – to bring Denver into the world. A strange soft thing like Amy's velvet speaks to other awful things like Sethe's ravaged feet and the tree-shaped scars on her back, which she can't see, for life to be set in motion again.

At Chestnut Lodge – when people still smoked in psychiatric hospitals – one of Frieda's patients lost his right to have matches because he was in the habit of setting fires. To show that she trusted him, Frieda gave him her matches and stayed with him. He took a cigarette from a red package, which he "put [...] close to the red trimming of his pyjamas and said: 'Look how it matches, don't you like that?'" And he added that he felt like setting a fire that day, but that "it had nothing to do with them both, for they [other people on the ward] don't understand what it means."

This is how words act like things. The word "match," a singular noun until then, has entered into the language-game of an agreement, "to match," and showed that the part of himself that had set fires everywhere until then becomes an in-between which "matches," thanks to a new convention. Similarly, velvet turns into a brand-new word for "two lawless [women] [...] wrapping a ten-minute-old baby in the rags they wore."

Sometimes, though, word-things regain their power instead of entering a language-game. At the end of the novel, a choir is formed to bring Sethe and Denver out of their reclusion. But the path to healing is blocked by the return of the scene of murder.

The choir

In Greek tragedies, people who think of themselves as individuals become a plural entity. The choir, with its singing and dancing, draws everyone – people like you and me – into a dynamic where there is no longer an "I" and a "we," but only a rhythm going back farther than words.

At the very end of *Beloved*, the choir of freed slaves gathers around the haunted house where Sethe is starving in order to feed her ghost. For the first time, Denver has gone out to look for help and brings 124 Bluestone Road into existence for those who pretended it did not exist. The choir is the opposite of the ghost, which is like a hole in the universe that people ignored, until it entered this world and forced them to take it into consideration.

When Denver tells the neighbours what is happening in the house, the women divide into three groups: those who believe the worst, those who don't believe her at all, and those who think. From then on, the women who form the choir are no longer themselves. Just like the analyst when, losing his bearings after a blunder, he is transformed into a choir: he must think or give up.

Thirty women set out and come together in front of number 124, as if keeping an appointment. The dynamic driving the choir towards the haunted house has a religious dimension. The women mumble prayers, and fall to their knees as if for an exorcism. The abolition of slavery is not a self-evident matter; hundreds of years cannot simply be erased.

What happens when the choir approaches number 124? The first thing it sees is itself. The women remember the celebration, twenty years earlier, just before Sethe killed her baby. It was a wild party, to celebrate her daring escape. *Ubris* – Greek for "excess" – usually ends in tragedy, for the gods punish humans who try to surpass them.

Seeing this mother reduced to a shrunken shell by the ghost which tyrannises both of them after having made them love it madly, the black women tell themselves that they have been racist. They are moving towards the house driven by an unconscious force, in a joint gesture, a common rhythm and a voice that has lost contact with the words it utters.

This choir, as I already said, could also be the analyst when he loses his head and becomes the screen on which *unclaimed experiences*, as Cathy Caruth calls them,[41] are recorded, waiting for an answer. The expected messages are unrelated to the understanding of what happened, or to the reconstitution of a past drama. They are more like trifles without value, like those sifted through by archeologists, except that in this instance they belong to the present.

In the present, Sethe is breaking a lump of ice into chunks when she sees not only the choir of women, but also a white man in a horse-drawn cart, holding a whip, a wide-brimmed hat hiding his face. Everyone knows him. He is the owner of the house at 124, an abolitionist who saved Sethe from being hanged 20 years ago. But she feels her eyes burning, she hears, as she did then, the wings of hummingbirds that stick their beaks into her head, and she rushes at him to strike him with an ice pick. Denver and the other women take hold of her and drag her back. The traumatic revival brought together the same people, in the same place, and voiced Sethe's mute cry: "No, no. Nonono!"

But the choir acted like a screen on her path, when she was ready to destroy everything. It became the social link, illustrating precisely what Sullivan calls "interpersonal relatedness." But to do so, one must be willing to lose one's identity, that is, go through an interval of temporary madness. The women had become nameless and did not even form a group. This allowed Sethe and Denver to inscribe their story in History at last, thanks to support from the plural mouths and hands of those who saw them, and not only heard them.

By extending the psychoanalytic approach to traumas produced by the catastrophes of history, Frieda Fromm-Reichmann acknowledges her debt to Freud once again:

> Through our experiences with psychotic patients, we have been compelled to discover zones that escape sexual repression. But we must not forget that it was only when the taboo concerning sexuality was lifted that Freud's teachings made this discovery possible.[42]

The paradoxes of dissociation

In 1948, Frieda Fromm-Reichmann referred once again to Freud's abandonment of his "Neurotica," confirmed by his 1925 article "On Narcissism: An Introduction":[43]

> The reluctance to apply psychoanalytic knowledge and technique to the psychoses stems from Freud's paper on narcissism. This concept of the narcissistic origin [...] of schizophrenic disorders excluded, according to him, the possibility of establishing a workable relationship between the schizophrenic and the psychoanalyst. It is true that the schizophrenic is hit by initial traumatic warp and thwarting experiences at a very early period of life when he has not yet developed a [...] stable degree of relatedness to other people. It is also true that the final outbreak of schizophrenic disorder will be characterized by regressive tendencies in the direction of this original early period of [...] traumatisation.[44]

Still, Freud hopes that the analytic technique might be modified in that case.

She answered his expectancy: "The goal of interpersonal relatedness is not to try to 'interpret' content, and translate the manifestations of that which is barred from awareness. The schizophrenic is swamped by unconscious material which breaks through the barriers of dissociation." As a matter of fact, "the neurotic and the healthy person have succeeded in keeping this material dissociated, whereas most of the time this material is within the schizophrenic's awareness. He knows the meaning of his psychotic productions."

Then what should the analyst do? Certainly not fight them, for his problem is to be able to convey this production to another person. But when this other tries to discourage his irrational attitude by making meaningful interpretations, his is only encouraging the patient to continue to cut out, as he has been doing, what he tries to show, for lack of words to say it. "At times 'acting out' is the only way of communicating available to the inarticulate schizophrenic. The acting out, per se, has to be accepted."

Not only do psychotic patients know what they are doing, but they know that they use showing devices. We might ask what good it is to use such complicated devices to obtain such modest results. Still, the problem is not the devices, but rather the absence of someone who can witness what they show.

The end of *Beloved* is a meditation on interpretation. Its refrain – "It was not a story to pass on" – is contradicted by the story we are reading, written for us, the readers. Toni Morrison quilted a text by sewing together pieces of material of different textures. The ghost is the instrument that "typed" the text. The story not to pass on is transmitted regardless, and circulates through the symptoms of a mother and her daughter. The story cannot be lost since no one is looking for it. Still, the ghost claims it, but it remains unclaimed until the choir confirms its reception. After this, Beloved can be forgotten "like a bad dream" and her story can be made into myth.

Before commencing the ritual leading to the forgetting of the one who was "disremembered and unaccounted for," Beloved speaks in epic terms that allow the passage from images to words for us, the readers, since in a context of catastrophe images need such a rhythm to be told. They need what Jean-Jacques Rousseau calls "the social link," which means – when all is well, that is to say never – "what holds individuals together." This link is usually a matter of political management, except when it breaks and when it explodes.

Then identity criteria are abolished, the space between individuals is erased: "I am Beloved, and she is mine," says the ghost daughter about her mother:

> how can I say things that are pictures I am not separate from her there is no place where I stop I am not dead her face is my own All of it is now it is always now it is the face I lost she is my face smiling at me.

The ghost asks questions, like children do, in the form of statements, which are both ethical and political. Sethe's statement "If I hadn't killed her she would have died" takes us to a totalitarian space where freedom is conquered at the price of death.

When Schoolteacher took over the plantation, his nephew stole Sethe's milk with his "mossy teeth," while another man held her down. Reproduction was organised so as to prevent children from knowing their fathers, and breastfeeding was ended quickly to prevent maternal attachment. Sethe barely knew her mother, who was hanged for trying to run away. For her, being separated from her children is out of the question, although her two sons fled from the haunted house and were later killed in the Civil War, fighting on opposite sides.

Don't take my symptoms away

Sethe's aporia, death or death, can only be resolved by showing "things that are pictures," and by "acting out" in the sense of staging a play – if the analyst is able to climb on the stage, like Ella, the neighbour who gathered the choir together, dared to do.

Frieda Fromm-Reichmann writes:

> An insecure psychiatrist will be made anxious by being exposed to the schizophrenic's empathic capacity tosense some of the psychotherapist's liabilities. Some analysts have misevaluated the significance of the meaningfulness of schizophrenic communications by operating on the faulty conclusion that they can, for example, try to "talk" the patient "out" of a delusional system.[45]

However, "[as] Freud demonstrated most convincingly in *The Problems of Anxiety*,[46] mental symptoms can be understood in their bipolarity as *uno acto*, an expression of anxiety and a means of warding it off."

At the prospect of being dispossessed of her symptoms, a patient at Chestnut Lodge shouted at her therapist: "You'll take my gut-pains, and my trance, and my withdrawal states away from me! And where will I be then?" We all know that when delusion loses its hold, the risk of suicide is the greatest. After having identified with her symptom, the patient now has no place in which to exist. One of my patients at the psychiatric hospital used to say: "When I am ill I am cured, and when I am cured, that's when I am ill." The therapist must reassure her that he will not take her symptoms away, nor interpret their content, but rather find, with her, the place of the subject who is shouting, while they both participate in "the vicissitudes of the doctor–patient relationship."

Sometimes the place is that of a feeling without object which overwhelms one of them in the transference, like in Charles Trenet's song: "Il y a de la joie" ("There is joy, there is love!"). There can also be fear or hate. When the feeling is love, erotomania which shouts "I am loved" and tries to attach this love without an object to causal reasoning: "There is love because of me," it may be that one is invaded by cut-out impressions which make themselves known that way. Likewise, voices and visions may be the intrusions into the body and mind by cut-out perceptions, which in this fashion find a way to be acknowledged. Here, psychic and physiological systems function backwards, in order to produce the sensation by projecting it through voices and visions that invade the ears and eyes, and nevertheless preserve their truth.

In *Beloved*, the ghost is truly born when Sethe "empties out her eyes" to revive the unnameable and unrepresentable sensation of the child she killed. The ghost wants to know where her place is:

> Tell me the truth. You rememory me? You never forgot me? Why did she do that when she was just about to smile at me? I will not lose her again. You are my face; I am you. I will never leave you again.

Telling a patient that her visions come from her inner world is stupid. Above all, don't fake anything. To say: "You see pink elephants and I see them too" is to underestimate the patient's acute ability to spot anything fake. A hypocritical attitude is quickly identified, after years of facing denial, cognitive dissonances and contempt for her intelligence. This is why she built a barrier against the stupidities thrown at her, and refuses to talk. What's the use?

The analyst should admit his mistakes quickly, rather than trust the patient's polite acceptance of useless comments, while showing his disagreement through his posture or facial expression. By talking instead of staying silent, the analyst "wants to say," not in the sense of "to mean," as Wittgenstein points out,[47] but in the sense of "wanting to tell" what he experiences in the transference.

Just before the choir sets out for 124 Bluestone Road, Denver speaks, to express a feeling of terror:

> Beloved is my sister. I swallowed her blood right along with my mother's milk. [...] All the time, I'm afraid the thing that happened [...] could happen again. [...] Whatever it is, it comes from outside this house. [...] I shouldn't be afraid of the ghost. [...] I just [have] to watch out for it because it [is] a greedy ghost and [needs] a lot of love. And I love her. I do. She's mine.

She uses the present tense in the arrested time of the catastrophe. Time is a major actor in the novel.

Continuity

It is quite difficult to read *Beloved* without interruption, because of Toni Morrison's use of flashbacks throughout. The reader is puzzled, but gradually pieces the puzzle together. We are constantly forced to go back and forth, creating a rhythm that breaks up time, like Laurence Sterne does in *Tristram Shandy*.[48]

Three years before she died, Frieda Fromm-Reichmann published a text on continuity,[49] discussing transference with her traumatised and psychotic patients, who regularly go back to square one and give a false impression of relapse: "From the experience with these patients we learned [to advocate] the same type of psychoanalytic approach through all phases: during a psychotic illness and after recovery." This confirms that there is "continuity between the person in the psychosis and the one he is after his recovery."

This is illustrated by a patient who used to mutilate herself during her two-year stay in the disturbed patient ward at Chestnut Lodge. After her release from the hospital, she continued her analysis with Frieda, while enrolled in college. But one symptom persisted, resisting the effects of analysis: by pulling the skin off her heels, she continued to injure herself. A positive comment made by the analyst about her transformation was followed by a state of great anxiety. This is when she had the following insight: "I am [so] surprised [...] about the change which I have undergone, and [I am] maintaining the continuity and the identity between the girl who had to stay locked up, and the successful college girl of today."

Frieda concluded: "She could be well and ill at the same time, and preserve her continuity." She then took the opportunity to condemn severely the attitude of some psychiatrists and psychoanalysts "who hold that recovering patients should learn to detest and eject their psychotic symptomology, like a foreign body, from their memory."

As we already mentioned, she also disagreed with prevalent views on schizophrenic withdrawal and catatonic stupor, seen as abandonment of all external investment, saying:

> These patients are, more frequently than not, keen observers of what is going on. This comes about not only in response to the threat of rejection by others but much more for fear of their own hostility or violence in response to actual or assumed acts of rejection from other people.

Once again, the problem stems from interpersonal relations that were severely warped in a past that does not stay in the past.

"We could even say," she added, "that in these cases investment in the external world is greater than usual. Fear of dependency is increased, since dependency has condemned the subject to death." At the psychiatric hospital where we worked as analysts, Françoise and I, a patient calling herself Sissi, the Austro-Hungarian empress, used to say: "The babies work. They work day and night. One night, there was a full moon, the wand of history turned everything to stone." The hand holding the wand was an abusive father.

When time is petrified, modes of communication are filtered in a different way. Frieda Fromm-Reichmann observed that she was tempted to make her presentations more dramatic than academic protocol required. But she accepted to do this in order to illustrate that she felt:

> inclined to duplicate [in the sessions] tone and inflections of the patient's and my voices, the concomitant gestures, changes in facial expression, etc.

> This comes about because the doctor's non-verbal concomitants of the therapeutic exchange [...] are equally, if not at times more, important than the verbal contents of our therapeutic communication.

She created a first reflection when all mirrors were shattered.

In a presentation she gave in Boston, at a conference of the International Society for Psychological and Social Approaches to Psychosis (ISPS) – founded by Gaetano Benedetti in the 1950s to foster the psychoanalysis of psychosis – Frieda's patient Joanne Greenberg, who describes her psychoanalysis in her best-selling book *I Never Promised You a Rose Garden*[50] – was asked about her analyst. She remembered the extreme mobility of Frieda's face, and her bursts of laughter: "she laughed her head off." Fortunately, she added, she was "a virgin" in regard to chemical treatments, which had not been invented yet. By expressing her reactions, and by revealing bits of her own history, in the mayhem of their sessions, Frieda provided continuity in their relationship through the relational distortions – anti-Semitism, exile – that had taken place during her lifetime and before her birth. The therapy, says Frieda, addresses time frames which become superposed in a process that "depends on coincidences which vary according to the clinical experience and personality of the therapist."

Beloved opens with a coincidence: the arrival of Paul D, "the last of the Sweet Home men." He tells Sethe what happened while she was being tortured, when her milk was stolen, when her back was being whipped while Schoolteacher took notes. The father of her children saw everything from a loft, could do nothing, covered his face with butter and disappeared. Paul D went mad, wanted to kill, was imprisoned, with an iron bit in his mouth, in Alfred, Georgia, where he kept trembling until he escaped during a hurricane. He came to the camp of Cherokee Indians suffering from a disease. They told him to follow the flowering trees going north: "You will be where you want to be when the tree flowers are gone."

The eavesdroppers of history

This expression, in *Beloved*, replaces the predictive inadequacy of diagnoses. The epigraph of the book, which we have already quoted, is taken from Romans 9:25. The words are those of the prophet Hosea: "Those who were not my people I will call 'my people' and her who was not beloved I will call 'beloved'." Israel has betrayed God – like a prostitute. But intercession is possible. Those who were cursed, who were not beloved, do not have to remain unloved. Hosea speaks of a time of political upheaval, of a timeless present with no tomorrow. "Today is always here, tomorrow, never," Sethe says. In moments of catastrophe, such words describe the annulment of time and people. Still, the double negation opens the future.

Psychotic transference functions like this grammar, in which speech acquires coherence by acting out catastrophes that cannot be inscribed in the social link. The choir of voices that gathers in front of the house meets the thoughts of the two women at 124 Bluestone Road: unspeakable and unspoken thoughts. Their grammar, different from that of ordinary speech, functions in a poetic mode, omitting logical links and making a particular use of negation.

In his commentary on Freud's text *Negation*,[51] the philosopher Jean Hyppolite refers to the "negativism displayed by some psychotics." Still, Hosea's prophetic discourse transforms this negativity through the double negation that is rooted in otherness: "I will call them my people which were not my people and her beloved who was not beloved." The negativism alluded to is not the devastating description of a field of ruins, but a construction site, in which the prophet eavesdropping at the doors of History becomes its spokesman.

In *Beloved*, negativism aims at pushing back the ghost into a memory that can forget, which then replaces traumatic memory, which never forgets: "So they forgot her. Like an unpleasant dream during a troubling sleep."

Harry Stack Sullivan's phrase "We are much more simply human than otherwise" leaves open the possibility that man can be inhuman. There is God's wrath that Hosea speaks of, and there are terror and hate without a subject. Patients are extremely vigilant regarding their analyst's ability to face inhumanity. Instead of avoiding it by means of humanitarian slogans, we would be better advised to think of Virgil's verse, quoted by Freud in *The Interpretation of Dreams*.

Flectere si nequeo superos, Acheronta movebo

Following the example of Freud's *Gradiva*, Frieda Fromm-Reichmann begins her article on intensive psychotherapy with manic-depressive patients by stressing the use of literature, legends and folklore to understand psychotic productions.[52]

When Freud cannot move the heavens and sets out to stir the Acheron in Chapter 7 of *The Interpretation of Dreams*,[53] he does not tell us that line 312 of Book VII of the *Aeneid*[54] is spoken by Juno, enraged when she learns that seven ships of Aeneas' fleet found a safe harbour. Aeneas is about to marry the daughter of the king of Latium; Juno summons Allecto, "the grief-bringer, a monster hated by her own father Pluto, since she brings the scourge and the funeral torch into the houses." The inhuman enters the scene.

Allecto has cut off all access to the symbolic chain. Therefore, it is impossible to carry out the substitutions and displacements that require an empty space to make metaphors and metonymies. In the place of the unconscious defined by Lacan as the speech of the Other, where inscription is possible, a foreclosure, *Verwerfung*, which he first translated by "*retranchement*, cutting off," makes it impossible for any signifier "to represent the subject for another signifier." At the level of the structure, the

Real is silent. This does not mean that nothing is possible in that situation. The analyst may manifest his presence, saying: "I know, I am here," as Frieda Fromm-Reichmann did with patients withdrawn into loneliness, the topic of a text written when she became deaf, just before she died in 1957.

In *Beloved*, this loneliness happens to Denver, and takes the form of sudden deafness at school – where she liked to go – after Nelson Lord, a boy as smart as she was, asked her a question about her mother out of curiosity, meaning no harm: "But the thing that leapt up in her [...] was a thing that had been lying there all along." She never went back to school; she felt terrified: "For two years she walked in silence too solid for penetration. For two years she heard nothing at all." Then her brothers left.

The cutting out of history, through several generations of slavery, cuts off Denver's hearing. It will only be restored when the ghost, who until then had signalled her presence by wreaking havoc, speaks only words from beyond the grave, with the successfully realised intention of bringing back unspeakable stories of slavery.

Beloved shows that ghosts come out of diagnostic categories, to return from Acheron with a mission. When the social link is in danger, enormous energy is mobilised to stir the Acheron. Living myth is needed, not of the stereotype: "My son didn't get over his Oedipus complex," but myth in the making, in which Oedipus who slept with his mother becomes Oedipus at Colonus,[55] arriving at the sacred place where "invariable, untrod; goddesses, Dread brood of Earth and Darkness [...] abide." Oedipus' death in that sacred place, in the suburb of Athens, will be a political asset for the city.

The gods have fallen on their heads

Juno's rage against the Trojan fleet is translated in Greek by the word *menis*. The Indo-European root "mn" is found in the Greek words *mania*: madness, *mainomai*: I am mad, *menô*: I desire, and *mimneskô*: I remember, as well as in the Latin *mens*: mind and the Sanskrit word *mana*: life force.

Plato has Socrates speak these words to Phaedrus, his disciple, in praise of folly.[56] These words resonate with *Beloved* and Frieda Fromm-Reichmann: "In reality, the greatest of blessings come to us through madness" (section 244a). In support of his argument, Plato refers to the delirium of prophetesses who "conferred many splendid benefits upon Greece both in private and in public affairs, but few or none when they have been in their right minds" (section 244b).

More precisely, he gives us a lesson in psychoanalysis based on etymology:

> And it is worthwhile to adduce also the fact that those men of old who invented names thought that madness was neither shameful nor disgraceful; otherwise they would not have connected the very word *mania* with the noblest arts, that which foretells the future, by calling it the mantic art, t inserting a T in the word.

(section 244c)

In fact, says Socrates, this added letter comes from the name of history: *historia*.

Socrates then goes on teaching us about the psychoanalysis of madness, through different stages:

> Moreover, when diseases and the greatest troubles have been visited upon certain family lines through some ancient guilt, *mania* [...] has found a way of release for those in need [...] and so, by purifications and sacred rites, he who has this madness is made safe for the present and the after time.

(section 244e)

The stages of analysis are represented by the myth of the souls, *psychai*, circling around the Real, *to on*, in a chariot pulled by two winged horses, following a procession of gods: "In the revolution, Psyche beholds [...] knowledge, not such knowledge as has a beginning and varies" (section 247d), "[but] the colorless, formless, and intangible truly existing being with which all true knowledge is concerned" (section 247c). Still, the situation is far from ideal, and there is turmoil in this celestial revolution.

Some souls, which have grown heavy with forgetfulness and perversion, see nothing and fall to the earth (section 248c). Others keep the memory, *anamnesis*, of what they have seen, *kateidos*, when they looked for what was truly real, by gathering a multitude of sensations into a unity through an act of reflection. But, says Socrates, it is precisely when a man uses judiciously the recollection of what he has seen that he can be accused of being mad: "Since he separates himself from human interests and turns his attention toward the divine, he is rebuked by the vulgar, who consider him mad and do not know that he is inspired" (section 249d).

Socrates talks to himself when his *daimôn* visits him and keeps him stalled for hours in the middle of the road. Alcibiades tells this story when he arrives, completely drunk, at the end of *The Symposium*,[57] and is asked to praise Socrates. He describes his unusual habit to stand in the same spot, listening to his *daimôn*, an aptitude that made him an exceptional therapist during the Peloponnesian War, when he fought under his command as a hoplite, helping his companions and his general, Alcibiades himself, when he was wounded.

In the *Phaedrus*, Socrates describes how he tries to be worthy of this therapeutic gift; his ideas are not unlike those of Frieda Fromm-Reichmann:

> it is not easy for all souls to gain from earthly things a recollection of those realities. [Many], after falling to earth [...] do not understand their condition, because they do not clearly perceive. So, they have to analyse themselves, *dia nistha nestai*."

(section 250a)

This is the knowledge brought into play in transference involving delusions and trauma, which Socrates calls prophetic and poetic.

The word for divination, *mantis*, is linked to the verb for knowing, *manthanô*, which means "to learn." They contain the root "mn," also present in the word *Mânes*, the souls of the dead to whom ghosts urge us to speak words of anger, madness and recollection, to "become such as we are." This injunction, *Genoi oios essi*, taken by Nietzsche from Pindar's *Pythian II*, leaves out the word *mathôn*; "*Genoi oios essi mathôn*: Become such as you are, having learned to know yourself" (verse 131).

Learning what "you" are, in the animist societies of Ancient Greece and in Native American societies, does not limit the "you" to an individual, but expands it to include "all my relatives," everything to which I am connected, as is repeated in the ceremonies of the Sioux Lakota American Indians of South Dakota, which we attended.

At the end of *Beloved*, the reader attends such a ceremony. Every Saturday afternoon, Baby Suggs, Sethe's mother-in-law, in whose house she has found refuge, takes "her great heart" to a clearing in the forest, "followed by every black man, woman and child who could make it through." Sitting on a huge flat rock, she prayed silently. Then she called all of them, in turn: "Let the children come! Let your mothers hear you laugh [...]. Let the grown men come [...]. Let your wives and your children see you dance." Then she told them all to cry for the living and the dead. She told them that the only grace they could have was the grace they could imagine. If they couldn't see it, they wouldn't have it: "O my people [...] they do not love your flesh. *You* got to love it, *you*!"

Freedom tries to be admitted into the circle of the ancient gods. The novel tells the story of winning this place. Throughout the story, something strives towards the impossible inscription that the choir makes possible when it starts to reflect on its own madness. It came together once more after the forest ceremony ended in the aftermath of Sethe's incarceration and her hospitalisation in an asylum, which forced the grandmother into seclusion in the haunted house. Now the baby ghost can rejoin the souls of the dead, from which slavery had cut them off.

Beloved also provides an analysis of Denver, the schizophrenic, as psychiatry would call her, who, when she was a baby, almost died as well. She went to prison with her mother and lived as a recluse for about ten years. Her life, after the cutting of her sister's throat and the family's exclusion from the community, takes on a dynamic spurred forward by the ghost's plans. It is Beloved's ferociousness that impels Denver to seek help by visiting the teacher who taught at the school she had left; now, Denver becomes who she is by taking another road than the old familiar anger, after having learned some things from Paul D as well.

No, foreclosure is not irreversible. It triggers a process of striving for the freedom of a "political self," a process we will see at work by following the Swedish author August Strindberg as his delusions guide him through the streets of Paris.

Notes

1 Morrison, T., *Beloved*, Alma Classics, 2017.
2 Fromm-Reichmann, F., *Psychoanalysis and Psychotherapy*, University of Chicago Press, 1959.
3 Freud, S. and Breuer, J., *Studies on Hysteria*, Basic Books Classics, 2000.
4 Masson, J. M. (Ed.), *The Complete Letters of Sigmund Freud to Wilhelm Fliess, 1887–1904*, Harvard University Press, 1985.
5 Freud, S., *Delusions and Dreams in Jensen's Gradiva*, S.E. 9, Hogarth Press, 1907, Chapter 2.
6 Lacan, J., "Antigone between Two Deaths," in *The Seminar of Jacques Lacan*, Book VII, Porter, D. (Trans.), W. W. Norton & Company, 1997.
7 Erasmus, D., *The Praise of Folly*, Aeterna Press, 2010.
8 Lacan, J., "On a Question Preliminary to Any Possible Treatment of Psychosis," in *Écrits: A Selection*, Sheridan, A. (Trans.), Tavistock/Routledge, 1977.
9 Freud, S., *Beyond the Pleasure Principle*, S.E. 18, Hogarth Press, 1955, pp. 44–61.
10 Freud, S., *Moses and Monotheism*, Vintage Books, 1955.
11 Davoine, F. and Gaudillière, J.-M., *History Beyond Trauma*, Other Press, 2004.
12 Sullivan, H. S., *Schizophrenia as a Human Process*, W. W. Norton & Company, 1974.
13 Barker, P., *Trilogy*, Penguin Books, 1994–1998.
14 Fromm-Reichmann, F., *Principles of Intensive Psychotherapy*, University of Chicago Press, 1960.
15 Proust, M., *Time Regained*, Modern Library, 1993.
16 Schreber, D. P., *Memoirs of My Nervous Illness*, Macmillan, 2000.
17 Roth, J., *The Radetzky March*, The Overlook Press, 2002.
18 See *infra*, Seminar 11 on Robert Musil.
19 Neihardt, J., *Black Elk Speaks*, Bison Books, 2014.
20 Plato, *The Symposium*, Penguin Classics, 2003.
21 Fromm-Reichmann, F., "Remarks on the Philosophy of Mental Disorder," in *Psychoanalysis and Psychotherapy*, op. cit.
22 Davoine, F. "El acta de nacimiento de los fantasmas," Seminar July 2008, Cordoba, Argentina. Ediciones Fundacio Mannoni, Argentina, 2010.
23 Vian, B., *The Foam of the Daze*, Tam Tam Books, 2003, p. 3.
24 Sullivan, H. S., *Schizophrenia as a Human Process*, W. W. Norton & Company, 1974.
25 Hornstein, G., *To Redeem One Person Is to Redeem the World: The Life of Frieda Fromm-Reichmann*, Free Press, 2000.
26 Fromm-Reichmann, F., "Insight into Psychotic Mechanisms and Emergency Psychotherapy," in *Psychoanalysis and Psychotherapy*, op. cit., p. 55.
27 Fromm-Reichmann, F., "Notes on Personal and Professional Requirements of a Psychotherapist," in *Psychoanalysis and Psychotherapy*, op. cit., p. 63.
28 Fromm-Reichmann, F., "Recent Advances in Psychoanalytic Psychotherapy," in *Psychoanalysis and Psychotherapy*, op. cit., p. 51.
29 Masson, J. M., *The Complete Letters of Sigmund Freud to Wilhelm Fliess*, op. cit., letters February 11 and September 21, 1897).
30 Hornstein, G., *To Redeem One Person Is to Redeem the World*, op. cit.
31 Fromm-Reichmann, F., *Principles of Intensive Psychotherapy*, op. cit.
32 Davoine, F. and Gaudillière, J.-M., *History Beyond Trauma*, op. cit.

33 Laub, D., *Une clinique de l'extrême* (*Treating Extreme Trauma*), Le Coq Héron, 2015, no. 220.
34 Fromm-Reichmann, F., "Personality of the Psychotherapist and the Doctor-Patient Relationship," in *Psychoanalysis and Psychotherapy*, op. cit.
35 Masson, J. M., *The Complete Letters of Sigmund Freud to Wilhelm Fliess*, op. cit.
36 Fromm-Reichmann, F., "Psychoanalytic and General Dynamic Conceptions of Theory and Therapy: Differences and Similarities," in *Psychoanalysis and Psychotherapy*, op. cit., Chapter 8.
37 De Cervantes, M., *Exemplary Stories*, Lipton, L. (Trans.), Oxford World's Classics, 2008.
38 Fromm-Reichmann, F., "Transference Problems in Schizophrenics," in *Psychoanalysis and Psychotherapy*, op. cit., p. 117.
39 Ibid., pp. 119–126.
40 Fromm-Reichmann, F., "A Preliminary Note on the Emotional Significance of Stereotypes in Schizophrenics," in *Psychoanalysis and Psychotherapy*, op. cit., pp. 129–131.
41 Caruth, C., *Unclaimed Experience*, Johns Hopkins University Press, 1996.
42 Fromm-Reichmann, F., "Psychoanalytic Psychotherapy with Psychotics: The Influence of Modifications in Technique on Trends in Psychoanalysis," in *Psychoanalysis and Psychotherapy*, op. cit., p. 135.
43 Freud, S., "On Narcissism: An Introduction," 1925.
44 Fromm-Reichmann, F., "Notes on the Development of Treatment of Schizophrenics by Psychoanalytic Therapy," in *Psychoanalysis and Psychotherapy*, op. cit.
45 Fromm-Reichmann, F., "Some Aspects of Psychoanalytic Psychotherapy with Schizophrenics," in *Psychoanalysis and Psychotherapy*, op. cit., p. 175 and p. 168.
46 Freud, S., *New Introductory Lectures on Psychoanalysis*, S.E. 22, Hogarth Press, 1932.
47 Wittgenstein, L., *Philosophical Investigations (1945–1949)*, Wiley-Blackwell, 2010.
48 Sterne, L., *The Life and Opinions of Tristram Shandy, Gentleman*, Alma Classics, 2017.
49 Fromm-Reichmann, F., "Psychotherapy of Schizophrenia," in *Psychotherapy and Psychoanalysis*, op. cit.
50 Greenberg, J., *I Never Promised You a Rose Garden*, St. Martin's Paperbacks, 2008.
51 Lacan, J., *Écrits*, Fink, B. (Trans.), W. W. Norton & Company, 2007.
52 Fromm-Reichmann, F., "Intensive Psychotherapy of Manic-Depressives," in *Psychoanalysis and Psychotherapy*, op. cit., p. 221.
53 Freud, S. *The Interpretation of Dreams*, S.E. 5, Hogarth Press, pp. 509–625.
54 Virgil, *The Aeneid*, Fagles, R. (Trans.), Penguin Classics, 2008.
55 Sophocles, *Oedipus at Colonus*, Dover Publications, 1999.
56 Plato, *Phaedrus*, Focus Publishing/R. Pullins Co., 2003.
57 Plato, *The Symposium*, op. cit.

5 Seminar 5: 1991–1992
August Strindberg (1849–1912) and Martii Siirala (1922–2008)

The Inferno and *From Transference to Transference*[1]

Two Scandinavian practitioners of psychotic transference

Martti Siirala is a Finnish psychoanalyst, a colleague of Gaetano Benedetti,[2] whom he met when he was young, at the Burghölsli Hospital in Zürich. Siirala's book *From Transfer to Transference* is about the prophetic abilities of schizophrenic patients. These patients are trying to pass on their prophecies to a co-researcher who cannot remain simply an observer.

The book begins with the delusion of a patient, involving an Egyptologist in the year 2000 BC who discovers the secret hidden in a pyramid: a prisoner buried alive. The Egyptologist, henceforth called "the helper," is able to pass food and drink to the prisoner through an aeration vent but is unable to free him. The prisoner finally rebels against his helper and wounds him with an arrow, causing him to fall into his prison. Only then does the helper turn into a therapist, after accepting to be treated by the prisoner.

This story touches Siirala deeply. His patient's delusion brings to light, through this timeless tale, the humiliations inflicted on his own family of peasant origin during the Finnish Civil War that followed World War I, humiliations locked away in secrecy once the family acquired a certain social status. After the next war, the Winter War against Russia, the young Finnish Republic proclaimed in 1919 was amputated of a part of Karelia. The loss of this legendary region, where the Finnish epic *The Kalevala* takes place,[3] was felt as a profound injury by the psychoanalyst, who participated regularly in demonstrations demanding its return. In Helsinki, we saw this old gentleman disguised to personify the lost region, wearing the traditional costume of a young Karelian girl.

For Siirala, his patient's delusion is illustrative of transference in the treatment of psychotic patients: "Less the repetition of affects directed towards the analyst, than a shared investigation of historical situations" (p. 30). Situations buried alive, carried by the patient beyond any temporal limits, are transferred to analogous zones in the analyst, who is also healed in that process.

The gods must not be excluded from this story either, Siirala says. After all, Hippocrates, born around 460 BC, was said to be a descendant of the famous Asclepiades family – who claimed to be descendants of the god Asclepius – on the island of Kos, where there stands a temple to this deity. In the Epidaurus Sanctuary, honouring the same god, several buildings were dedicated to therapy. One was the famous theatre where tragedies and comedies intended to produce catharsis were presented. Another was the *thalos*, a round white marble building, dwelling of the sacred serpents so dear to Aby Warburg. In Ouidah, in Benin, we saw such a circular building housing serpents, in the sanctuary dedicated to Python, the god of medicine. At a third site, the *Abaton* brings psychoanalysis to mind. It is a hall where patients lay during the night while Asclepius' serpents roamed free among them. In the morning, priests interpreted their dreams, to which inscriptions carved in the stone testify.

Michel Foucault[4] states that scientific clinical practice, born in the eighteenth century, transformed madness into an illness by eliminating the divinities.[5] Later, historian Jean Marie Fritz showed that in the Middle Ages, madness was already subject to organicist medicine, and treated with shock treatments and pharmacological drugs. But the real place of madness was literature, "the space of the marvel," where knights ventured to meet fairies and fight monsters, losing all sense of time.[6] In those days, the madman was called "the wild man," who can still be seen parading during the Basel Carnival, in Benedetti's home town. Another space assigned to madness during the Renaissance was that of the Sotties, where fools came on stage called by Mother Folly – who was praised by Erasmus – for a mock trial of political abuses. This seminar testifies to the fact that today, madness still has its place in literature, as evidenced by August Strindberg's work, the topic of our seminar this year.

Inferno:[7] a delusional experience in Montparnasse

The *Inferno*, written in French in 1897, focuses on the analysis of Strindberg's delusions during the three years when he wandered through the streets of Montparnasse. He was assailed by the same social humiliations buried in his family's past as those of Siirala's patient. No doctor understood his condition. The Finnish analyst points out that in a psychotic transference, the subject cannot exclude himself from his investigation. While psychoanalysts try in vain to pass this hot potato to each other, madness ceaselessly tests their own story, so that it becomes unclear whose hot potato they are dealing with.

"Being sick can serve the purpose of making those who are well come out of their stubborn denial," Siirala says. "The prophecies of schizophrenics reveal illnesses and murders left untold in our societies for generations" (p. 16). This is the conclusion Strindberg comes to at the end of *Inferno*, after he discovers, in his own analysis, the works of Swedenborg. Up until then, writing had not been enough to allow for the inscription of that which was cut out of his family history.

In his works, where fiction and life are intertwined, Strindberg gives literary form to a narrative in the present tense, for it is not inscribed in the past. The first chapter of *The Son of a Servant*,[8] entitled "Fear and Hunger," reveals that madness possesses the skill of a historian: In Sweden:

> the 1840s were over. The Third State, which had gained a number of human rights through the 1792 revolution, had just been reminded that a fourth and fifth state were also aspiring to their place in the sun [...]. After the turbulent events of 1848, the movement was taken in hand by the enlightened despot Oscar I, who gained the sympathy of the bourgeoisie by granting it economic freedom and free trade, discovered the power of women, and allowed daughters the same inheritance rights as those assigned to sons.
>
> (p. 25)

After this flashback, he exposes the rift between social classes on the different stories of the house where he was born, and in his parents' marriage. His father, from a bourgeois family, begets eight children – August being the fourth – with the servant-maid, before marrying her. When August was 13, she died of tuberculosis, and was quickly replaced by the governess, who became his father's second wife. After going to an extremely severe school, August took refuge in Pietism and studied chemistry, which he later abandoned to study journalism and literature.

His writing, refused at first by publishers, eventually made him famous. In his plays – *The Father, Miss Julie, Creditors*[9] – he depicted social and political violence, masked by hypocritical conventions. He was considered a spokesman of socialist ideology with Rousseauist overtones and had connections to anarchist circles, but he was criticised for his anti-feminist views. Despite these controversies, Hjalmar Branting, the founder of the Swedish Social Democratic Party, remained his lifelong friend.

His delusions of persecution in Paris were not so delirious, since he had really been persecuted and forced to leave his country in 1883, on account of his writings, which attacked the monarchy, the army and religion. In Switzerland, he wrote his pamphlet "A Catechism for Workers,"[10] reminiscent of Livy's "Apologue on the Limbs and the Stomach," written during unrest in the Roman Empire, when the people gathered on the Aventine Hill. This allegory, taken up by Jean de La Fontaine[11] centuries later, raises the question of who is crazy, of the two parties involved. Is it not society that claims to be sane when it rejects the part of madness in itself? Strindberg's solution goes beyond the duality of the apologue: "I am crazy so others can be sane," or: "I am in the dark so that social sunlight can shine on others."

In 1991, he divorced his first wife and was separated from his three children. He went to live in Paris and travelled to Denmark and to Berlin, where he befriended Norwegian painter Edvard Munch, met a young Austrian woman and married her. The couple returned to her native mansion in Lower Austria, where she gave birth to a little girl. But once they were back in Paris, they quickly separated.

The English translation of the *Inferno*[12] begins with the hatchet blow of this separation:

> With a savage joy I walked away from the Gare du Nord, having parted there from my sweet little wife as she set off to rejoin our child who had fallen sick in a distant country. The sacrifice of my heart's love – finished! Our last words to each other – "When shall I see you again?" "Soon." – still echoed in my ears like one of those lies whose true nature one won't admit even to oneself, although something told me that we had parted forever. And those farewells exchanged in November of 1894 were indeed the last, since up till this moment, in May 1897, I have not seen my beloved wife again.

The Inferno, a reference to Dante's *Inferno*, ends with Strindberg's reunion with "Beatrice," his little daughter, who brings him back to the world of the living. In the meantime, he has delusions. We can't help but think of his mother's last farewell, when she was the living-dead prisoner of the lies told by the paternal side of the family, which tried to refuse her a tomb in the family vault, and falsified her testament.[13] But this explanation did not stop his madness from trying to inscribe the persecution inflicted by visible or invisible enemies, until he finally met some therapists worthy of the name at the end of the book.

Madness takes hold when double-talk pushes your speech back into your throat, when erased events come back to say: "But we are the real history," when a cancer eats away the place that guarantees the truth. For Strindberg, God is an insurrection, because nothing guarantees God. The task of the madman is to warn of this deficiency. He tries to repair the absence of the Other who guarantees the given word, by filling the hole with patches, in an impossible attempt at totalisation. "When mysteries are beyond us, let's pretend we're organising them," Jean Cocteau says in *The Eiffel Tower Wedding Party*. Strindberg asserts that it is logical for him to be persecuted by a sick society, but invoking social madness means losing oneself in generalities. Strindberg's delusion is much more specific. After his wife's train leaves the station, he decides to give up literature, go back to the study of natural sciences and make gold in his "poor student's room in the Latin Quarter." His aim is to find the touchstone of values falsified by lies. His burned hands testify to the physical struggle in which he engages daily, in his fight against perversion.

Taking the same stance, the analyst Gisela Pankow (1914–1998) used to tell her psychotic patients: "Bring me monsters. I am a monster monger," insisting on the catastrophes that had occurred in family lineages. Having herself been persecuted in Germany at the end of the 1930s for her family's anti-Nazi views, she was familiar with the work of Frieda Fromm-Reichmann,[14] and participated in the first congresses of the International Symposium for the Psychotherapy of Schizophrenia (ISPS), founded in the

1950s by analysts treating psychosis: Christian Muller in Lausanne and Gaetano Benedetti in Basel.

The main features of this new paradigm of psychoanalysis, to be reinvented each time, are all present in *Inferno*, carefully laid out by Strindberg chapter after chapter.

Madness is addressed to a lawless agency, which can be personified by the Devil. Like *Faust*,[15] the *Inferno* starts with a prologue in Heaven, in which the Lord is conversing with Lucifer about the latter's new plan to create a world of madness, the world of the *Inferno*. Written in French between 1894 and 1896, the story is set in the Montparnasse quarter, where Strindberg wanders in a delusional compression of time and space, about which he writes day after day.

"The style is the man himself," said Count de Buffon – in this case, the style of a narrator to whom madness imposes its dynamics and its uneven tempo. The text proceeds very quickly. Its speed and ubiquity are a response to the break which has occurred in the symbolic chain, and strive to ensure that space has the least possible void to fill, because the signifying play through which the repressed unconscious can be heard is ineffectual now that the symbolic chain is broken. Strindberg creates a text that takes over the entire space. The intensity of psychic, social and historical phenomena spills onto the streets and ends up turning Paris into a space too small for him. Finally, his delusion extends to Europe, by contiguity, in the present from which he is unable to escape or create the least distance. The more he says about it, the greater his impression that he is saying nothing.

Of course, the foreclosure of the name of the mother's father is interesting to note, but it is powerless in the face of the exhausting dynamics of his delusions that gradually open, in this compactness, a zone where otherness finally emerges, where affect appears behind the fortifications built to keep it out, and where "the tiniest flower is a thought." His eyes fall on this quote when he opens Balzac's *Séraphîta*[16] at random – a book inspired by Swedenborg, an unforeseen other encountered at the end of his hell.

The heuristic influence of delusions[17]

Strindberg begins by sketching the voluntary loss of his identity. After savouring the "worthless victory" of having one of his plays presented in a Parisian theatre, he abandons literature to return to his first subject of study: chemistry, or alchemy to be more exact, which he practised in his "poor student's room in the Latin Quarter." The rest of the time, he roamed aimlessly, like a Don Quixote, in search of small adventures.

Alone, he walks on "dreadful Rue de la Gaieté," turns onto rue Delambre, "more conducive to despair than any other street of the [Montparnasse] quarter," reaches the Boulevard du Montparnasse and "lets himself fall on a seat, on the terrace of the [...] Lilas," where "driven [away] by furies," he leaves his glass of absinthe and hastens "to seek for another in the Café François Premier on the Boulevard St. Michel," and finally flees home (p. 35).

The first encounter that breaks through his solitude is therapeutic both physically and psychically. The burns to his hands caused by his experiments force him to seek medical assistance at St Louis Hospital, where he can call "mother," a nun who, in turn, calls him "my child." The veil surrounding the affects associated with these words is lifted: "It does me good to be able to say this word 'mother', which has not passed my lips for thirty years." An "Invisible Hand" has intervened. "Must I be humbled in order to be lifted up [...]? Providence is planning something with [me], and this is the beginning of education." He pursues his mission in the quixotic style of wandering, which drives him into the streets of his neighbourhood, where seemingly "insignificant" things attract his attention and he says: "my nightly dreams assume the form of premonitions." The absence of an ego is not such a negative thing as traditional descriptions might suggest. On the contrary, it opens new, potential spaces for him: "I am born into another world [...] and the consciousness that the unknown powers are on my side lends me an energy and confidence which impel me to unwonted efforts of which I was formerly incapable." This energy, not filtered by the ego, brings him in contact with the beyond:

> The Unknown has become for me a personal acquaintance with whom I speak, whom I thank, whom I consult. Very often I compare Him in my mind with the "demon" of Socrates [...]. A bankrupt as regards society, I am born into another world where no one can follow me.[18]

As these improbable encounters continue, another name surfaces, that of the chemist and toxicologist Orfila, which he happens upon in a bookshop on the Boulevard Saint-Michel, and again on a white marble medallion in the Montparnasse Cemetery, and yet again a week later on Rue d'Assas, on the wall of "a house which looks like a convent, Hôtel Orfila." Today, a plaque on the façade of this building commemorates the illustrious resident. When he discovered his name, Strindberg felt him to be his "friend and protector who [...] often guided me through the labyrinth of chemical experiments." He now senses that the future is opening before him:

> Can it be [...] that [St Louis] is my patron, my guardian angel, who drove me to the hospital, so that I [...] should win (glory) again [...]? Was it he who directed me to Blanchard's book-shop and hither also?

He promises to tell us in the next chapters what happened in this old house, "when the Invisible Hand chastised me, taught me and, why not, enlightened me."

Having no one else to talk to, he pursues his enlightenment by conversing with the dead and with nature. In the Montparnasse Cemetery, where he goes every morning, the tombstones predict that henceforth he shall have neither love, nor money, nor honour, but shall follow "the Way of the cross, the only path leading to wisdom" (p. 54). This path requires renouncing the principle of objectivation of the subject of knowledge:

> Dead to the world, as I have renounced the vain delights of Paris, I remain in my quarter [...] and thence descend to the Luxembourg Garden to greet my flowers. [...] a kind of religion has been forming in me.
>
> (p. 55)

His "conversion" brings to mind that of Auguste Comte, after his attack of madness, which he called his "cerebral episode," in the spring of 1826. He was hospitalised in Dr Esquirol's clinic, from which he escaped, to invent his "subjective method," as a pact with madness:

> Wisely given over to its spontaneous course, this crisis would undoubtedly soon have reestablished the normal state. But thanks to the disastrous intervention of an empirical medication, in the establishment of the famous Esquirol, the most absurd treatment led me rapidly to a very pronounced alienation.

He goes on to say that after medicine "fortunately, declared [him] incurable," he continued his research and condemned the "materialistic and doctrinal vertigo of the objective."[19]

Seventy years later, Strindberg salutes in the same manner "the call to arms raised by the critic Brunetière about the bankruptcy of science." He announces his change of perspective:

> I had been well acquainted with the natural sciences since my childhood and had tended towards Darwinism. But I had discovered how unsatisfying can be the scientific approach that recognizes the exquisite mechanism of the world but denies the existence of a mechanic. [...] I went further [...] and eliminated the boundaries between matter and what was called the spirit.
>
> (p. 57)

The fundamental power of delusion

In 1897, Strindberg published a treatise entitled "Purgatory or *Sylva Sylvarum*." In it, he describes how the "soul of plants" was revealed to him when, like Dante:

> in the middle of my life's journey, I sat down to reflect. Everything I had audaciously desired and dreamed had been granted. Satiated with shame and honour, pleasure and suffering, I asked myself: to what end? [...] A generation that had the courage to eliminate God, to demolish the State, society and customs, was still bowing to science. Where freedom

> should reign, the watchword was: believe in authority or die. […] I heard an old woman's voice telling me: Come, child, don't believe a word of it.

After this injunction, he in turn addresses the reader, and invites us to accompany him on the path where plants converse with each other through mimicry: "Passer-by, if you want to follow me, you shall breathe freely, for in my universe disorder reigns, and disorder is freedom." We think of Paracelsus' doctrine of signatures, of Baudelaire's poem "Correspondences": "Nature is a temple in which living pillars / Sometimes give voice to confused words,"[20] and of Nerval's sonnet "Golden Verses": "Each budding flower is a soul."[21] Both poets were inspired by Emanuel Swedenborg's *Doctrine of Correspondences and Representations*, whose author would soon play a major part in Strindberg's life, through the intermediary of two old women conjured up prophetically by his madness, as Siirala pointed out.

The poetic language-game between beings opens communication between the dead and the living. A moth called "death's-head hawkmoth" – like those Aby Warburg called "little souls" when he was a patient in Binswanger's clinic – incites Strindberg, whose soul is in a state of chaos, to meditate on phantoms: "What, then, are life and death? The same thing? What if the dead are not dead and the indestructible nature of energy is immortality?" He would find the answer at the Montparnasse Cemetery:

> The din of the streets dies away, and is replaced by the peace of the dead. As I am always alone here at this early hour, I have grown accustomed to regarding this public place of refuge as my pleasure garden […]. The dead and I! […] Yes, I know how to revive the dead, but I don't try it again, because the dead have foul breath, like revelers after a night on the town.
>
> (p. 75)

In other words, he is done with spiritism. He prefers to analyse his impressions, making him rethink his earlier convictions: "During this whole year I have not brought a single friend here; no man or woman who would, perhaps, have left some memory behind to intrude upon my personal impressions." These impressions lead to a path of spirituality:

> I became an atheist ten years ago! Why? I don't know exactly! I was bored with life, and I had to do something, above all something new. Now, when all that is old, my wish is not to know anything, to leave questions unresolved, and wait.
>
> (p. 77)

His quest is clear. Like Siirala's patient, Strindberg is trying to free the prisoner buried under the dead without tombs: his shabbily buried mother and a murdered child, who will be evoked in the next chapter.

As we read this diary, we realise that Strindberg's dialogue with the dead brings him into contact with the cutaway part of himself. As a result, traumatic memory emerges. The scene takes place on the Right Bank, near the de la Madeleine Church, Rue Chauveau-Lagarde, where "the mysterious murder of an old lady occurred [...] and the two murderers were never discovered!" Strindberg continues his self-analysis:

> Accustomed to observing everything that happens in my soul, I remember having been seized with familiar terror while the images crowded in one upon another, helter-skelter, like the imaginings of a madman. [...] What was all that? I've no idea! A tempest of memories, of dreams, conjured up by a tombstone, dispelled by cowardice.
>
> (p. 78)

This renewed dialogue with the "inner thou," to use Dori Laub's expression,[22] allows Strindberg to set aside political generalities, and become aware of the particular distress of a young woman who:

> seemed to be waiting for someone [...]. Each morning she was there, ever paler; sorrow had brought refinement to her plain features [...]. She waits here all day and every day. A madwoman? Yes, someone who has been struck by the great madness of love!

He speaks to the clouds, to children, to birds. A blackbird looked at him and flew off, then:

> returned from its excursion and calls to me with his harsh cry. [...] When I approach, the bird flies off leaving his prey behind on the top of the railing. It is the chrysalis of a butterfly [...]. A terrifying picture, a monster, a goblin's hood, which is neither animal, vegetable, or mineral. A shroud, a tomb, a mummy [...]. And this splendour is endowed with life, with the instinct of self-preservation [...]. A living corpse, which will assuredly rise again!
>
> (p. 87)

The poetry of surviving images, as Aby Warburg calls them, moves through the zones of death to bring back life.

Back to the beginning in search of unsymbolised elements

This crucial period follows any progress made in an analysis of madness and trauma, which strives to gather new elements "without reason – *aloga*," as Socrates said,[23] elements outside of language:

For four days I had let a nut germinate, and now detached the germ. This had the shape of a heart [...]. One may imagine my surprise when I saw on the glass-slide of the microscope two tiny hands, white as alabaster, folded as if in prayer. Was it a vision, an hallucination? Oh, no! It was crushing reality which made me shudder. [...] immovable, as if adjuring me. I could count the five fingers [...] – real woman's or child's hands. [...] The fall has happened. I feel the mercilessness of the unknown powers weigh heavily upon me. The hand of the invisible is lifted and the blows fall thickly upon my head.

(p. 90)

Per Olov Enquist's biography of Strindberg[24] comes back several times to the death, when she was 3 days old, of Strindberg's first child, a baby he had with his first wife Siri; the baby was killed by an "angel maker," paid for her services. The terror provoked by the little ghost caused Strindberg to leave his lodgings: "Weary of struggle, I bid farewell to the hotel and restaurant, and depart, plundered to my last shirt, leaving behind my books and other things. On February 21st, 1896, I entered the hotel Orfila" (p. 92). The crisis was brought to an end by this new solution, entitled "Purgatory," to escape the *Inferno*.[25]

The invention of Purgatory in the second half of the twelfth century, according to historian Jacques Le Goff, paralleled authorisation by the Church of dialogue with the deceased, a practice previously condemned as being pagan. It seems as if Strindberg also discovered the forbidden road to "the souls of Purgatory," whom one can now appease by soothing oneself. The future is hopeful, because contrary to Dante's inscription at the entrance to Hell: "Abandon hope all ye who enter here," Le Goff defines Purgatory as a transitional hell, "a hell for a period of time."[26]

"That which never ceases not to be inscribed," the Real, according to Lacan, emerges in the process of an inscription, thanks to the encounter with an other who can be addressed, in the shape of an American painter: "He becomes my sole companion." This man, as lost as Strindberg himself, prefigures a possible therapist – the *therapon*, in *The Iliad*, second in combat, and "ritual double" in charge of funeral duties. But contrary to the narrator, the painter leads a double life: "after he has spent the evening in half-philosophic, half-religious discussions with me, he is always seen late at night in Bullier's dancing-saloon." The two men finally separate, dissolving "the partnership we had entered on for mutual help" (p. 104).

At that point, the Sunday before Easter, by coincidence, the encounter with Swedenborg takes place – Swedenborg, who will be a reliable other for him. When the symbolic chain is broken, precluding any recourse to causality, the only way to create a link in the midst of what Bion called "attacks on linking"[27] is the "undeniable compliance of chance," as Freud once wrote in a letter to Jung.[28]

After crossing the Luxembourg Gardens and reaching the arcades of the Odeon, Strindberg came across "an edition of Balzac in a blue binding, and by chance picked up the novel *Séraphîta*."[29] The novel tells the story of the love of a young man and a young girl for an androgynous being, Séraphitüs-Séraphîta, whose parents were disciples of Swedenborg. "Why just that [novel]?" Strindberg asks himself, analysing his spontaneous gesture in the most Freudian fashion. "Perhaps it was an unconscious recollection of reading a criticism of my book *Sylva Sylvarum* in [a] periodical, in which I was called 'a countryman of Swedenborg'" (p. 105).

Henceforth, other coincidences pop up from all sides:

> When I got home I opened the book, which was almost entirely unknown to me, for so many years had passed [...]. It was like a new work to me, and now my mind was prepared for it, I swallowed down the contents of this extraordinary book wholesale. I had never read anything of Swedenborg, for in his own native land and mine he passed for a charlatan, dreamer and quack. But now I was seized with enthusiasm and admiration, as I heard this heavenly giant of the last century speak by the mouth of such a genial French interpreter. I read now with religious attention, and found on page 16 the 29th of March given as the day on which Swedenborg died; I stopped, considered, and consulted the almanac; it was exactly the 29th of March, and also Palm Sunday.
>
> (p. 105)

Here, the past encounters the present.

Now, the past encounters the present. This is a turning point in *The Inferno*, where thanks to the psychodynamic analysis of his delusional experiences, Strindberg turns his life in a new direction, owing to his encounter with the exceptional character who will act as analyst for him: "Swedenborg [...] was to play [...] a great part [in my life] as judge and master, and on the anniversary of his death he brought me the palm, whether of the victor or the martyr – who could say?" A little later, Strindberg reconfirms the names of those who opened the door to his exit from madness: Orfila and Swedenborg, and of course Balzac: "*Séraphîta* became my gospel, and caused me to enter into such a close connection with the other world." Hope is reborn. He felt deliverance was near, and wrote: "The spirits had become positivist, like the times, which were no longer content with visions" (p. 107). Indeed, the inventor of positivism, who had suffered the same torments, confirmed the "positivity of madness."

The house known as that of Auguste Comte (1798–1857) was the site of our research centre at the EHESS, before we moved to the Maison des sciences de l'homme; Alain Touraine's sociology laboratory was located there, at number 10, Rue Monsieur-le-Prince, near the Luxembourg Gardens, on the itinerary of Strindberg's daily walks. The intuitions triggered by the "cerebral episode" of the man who invented the words "sociology" and "positivism" were to be developed up to the 1850s through a critique of the objectivist interpretation of his theory. Auguste Comte's "subjective positivism" considers madness to be an "excess of subjectivity" that perceives upheavals in history (a view that agrees with Strindberg's): the 1848 Republican crisis, the 1850 dictatorial crisis, and of course the French Revolution, just before he was born. These ruptures of the social link endanger the subject who is part of them.

In Comte's view, madness renews "the link between the dead and the living by blurring the boundaries between outside and inside, through the intensity of memories and images competing with present perceptions." Instead of reducing the subject to a debilitating diagnosis, "these images, which evoke the past and suggest the future strengthen his consistency and place him in a continuity." According to Paul Arbousse-Bastide, Comte's originality consists in the fact that he stopped focusing on structure and equated the course of madness with that of history.

From this point of view, the brain is more than the encephalon: "It is a device by which the dead act upon the living;" it is what allows us to fight the "Western disease" described as "a continuous insurrection of the living against the dead." This is what constitutes the "positivity" of madness: it allows access to astonishing resources of knowledge and sensitivity, best exemplified by Don Quixote, according to Auguste Comte:[30] "Cervantes' admirable work describes in-depth how our emotions alter our sensations, sketching the true theory of madness before any biologist." And he adds, as Strindberg did after reading Balzac's novel: "The only effective theory should resemble a conversion process, in order to make a pact with time."

Positive subjectivity

In neurosis, Benedetti explains, the negative is repressed, but in psychosis the positive is cut away, a fact that causes analysts to become fascinated by horror and emphasise the negative instead of seizing upon small details which make it possible to reverse the perspective. The "positive subjectivity" of Strindberg's experience is made possible by "small daily occurrences" accumulated in the vicissitudes of life. One of these occurrences took place in the Observatory Garden at the foot of the Carpeaux fountain, when he found two pieces of cardboard with the numbers 207 and 28, the atomic weights of lead and silicon. A year later, a sculptor in Lund gave him "some glaze composed of lead and silicon." In the world of false pretences that drove him into solitude, chance encounters were veritable gifts. To the question "Is one to call it 'accident' or 'coincidence', this sign of an irrefutable logic?" Strindberg replies: "I repeat that I have never been plagued by visions, but actual objects sometimes seem to me to assume a human shape in a grandiose style. [...] The old gods return." And with them, "thoughts without a thinker," as Bion called them, find a thinker to think them:[31]

> When I came home last evening the pansies – *pensées* in French also means thoughts – in my window-box looked at me like so many human faces. I thought it was a hallucination of my overexcited nerves. And here are these pictures drawn a long time ago. It is then a fact and no illusion, for this unknown artist has made the same discovery before me.

And he concludes: "We make progress in the art of vision" (p. 110), echoing Rimbaud's sentiments in his 1871 letter to Paul Demeny: "I say that one must be a seer, make oneself a seer." But let us not rejoice too quickly, for we know by now that every advance is followed by a renewed intrusion of catastrophe:

> Why am I here? Because loneliness compels me to seek human society and to hear human voices. Just as my mental suffering reaches its highest pitch, I discover some pansies blooming in the tiny flower-bed. They shake their heads as though they wished to warn me of a danger [...] "Go away!"

Strindberg feels the hatred of a Polish pianist he met in Berlin, who wants to kill him. The feeling tortures him: "I had sinned through conceit, the one sin which the gods do not forgive" (p. 150).[32]

The psychoanalysis of psychosis teaches us the hard way not to cry victory too soon. The Tarpeian Rock is not far from the Capitoline Hill. To name a thing requires that "the object be destroyed," according to Winnicott, Wittgenstein and Lacan. Attaining otherness is a gradual process that alternates destruction with construction, in a back and forth resembling the "Fort! Da!" game of Freud's grandson. In 1915, when facing not only the absence of his mother, but also the anxiety of his grandfather whose two sons are away at the front, the baby plays at throwing a bobbin out of his crib. Freud is intrigued by the fact that the baby's excitement is visibly greater when he casts the bobbin away, shouting: "Oh – *fort* – gone!" than when he retrieves it, saying: "Ah – *da* – there." This observation led Freud to conclude that "The unpleasurable nature of an experience does not always unsuit it for play"[33] or theatrical performance. It is clear that the grandson alleviates his grandfather's distress by helping him to think in the middle of this zone of death that was to last another three years.

Once again, Strindberg throws his identity overboard:

> Everything *i.e.*, the little which I know, goes back to the Ego as its central point. Not the cultus, indeed, but the culture of this Ego seems, therefore, the highest and ultimate aim of existence. [...] To combat for

the preservation of my ego, against all influence which a sect or party, from love of ruling, may bring to bear upon me, *that* is my duty enjoined on me by conscience; the guide which the grace of my divine protector has given me.

(p. 132)

In the urgency of his new combat, Strindberg confesses a secret, in spite of his fear of calling down upon himself the wrath of Nemesis. For the first time, he links the fluctuations of his ego, as Auguste Comte would have done, to the political upheavals to which he had lent his voice:

It was ten years before this time, during the most stormy period of my literary life, when I was raging against the feminist movement, which, with the exception of myself, everyone in Scandinavia supported. The heat of the conflict hurried me on, so that I so far overstepped the bounds of propriety that my countrymen considered me mad.

(p. 133)

But this anamnesis does not provide an answer, because for him this past is present: "At the beginning of July the [hotel] is empty, [and] the students have gone for their holidays." For the first time, he loses faith in his scientific experiments. The loss of the security he thought he would find in them leaves him naked, feeling like a forsaken child, with the sensation of electric currents going through his body. Unable to take any more, he packs his belongings and tells a coachman to drive him to Rue de la Clef, near the Jardin des Plantes, where he plans to "complete [his] studies incognito," before going back to Sweden, where the Pole Star and the Great Bear have been calling him, from above the roofs of the Rue d'Assas and the Rue Madame: "To the North, then! I take the omen!" Having left, he feels momentarily appeased. He meditates in the Jardin des Plantes – "This wonder of Paris, unknown to the Parisians themselves, has become my park" – where he spends hours there looking at the flowers, especially the hollyhocks, the flowers of his youth, while reflecting on the past: "At length a pause ensues in my sufferings." But the calm is broken when, abandoning the shelter of his incognito, he informs the Hotel Orfila of his new address: "At the moment that I write this, I do not know what was the real nature of the events of that July night when death threatened me, but I will not forget that lesson as long as I live."

At last, it has become possible for him to look back on the distress of his childhood, and understand how it has shaped his life:

Born with a heavenly homesickness, I wept as a child over the filthiness of life, and felt strange and homeless among relations and friends. [...] I have wandered through a thousand hells, without trembling, and have experienced enough of them to feel an intense desire to depart from the vanities and false joys of this world, which I always despised.

For the first time, he dares to ask for help, and leaves for Dieppe "to find shelter with some friends, whom I have neglected as I have all others, but who are considerate and generous towards the fallen and shipwrecked." But the boundless hospitality of his friends' beautiful home does not suffice to allay his distress: "The idea that I am being persecuted by means of electricity again takes possession of me."

Telling himself that he probably has a "nervous illness," he wants to seek medical help and leaves Dieppe for Sweden, to stay with a friend who is a physician. This man wants to hear everything that happened to him. The answer is foreseeable, resembling what happens in a first session when the patient checks if his analyst is worth talking to: "But I tell him nothing special, for my first thought is one of suspicion. He is prejudiced against me, has made inquiries about me in some quarter, and wants to have me confined."

Since the physician does not venture out of his neutrality, the transference turns sour, until a frightful night when Strindberg knocks on his friend's door: "What is the matter? – I begin my report by giving an account of the attack in the Rue de la Clef." The diagnosis is prompt and unforgiving: "Stop, unhappy man! Your mind is affected." Strindberg tries to fend off the diagnosis that attacks his mental faculties: "Test my intelligence, read what I write daily and what is printed. – Stop!" the doctor orders. "These stories of electricity are frequent in asylum reports. Treaties on mental illness have described them in detail." The official argument reduced his intelligence to zero, as Antonin Artaud found out through personal experience.

Strindberg and Antonin Artaud: the same combat

Artaud (1896–1948) was examined by Jacques Lacan at the Sainte-Anne Hospital in 1938 and was given the same diagnosis: "Unable to continue his literary activities." The difference was that by then, electricity had made progress. Artaud was transferred to Rodez psychiatric hospital, to be treated by Dr Ferdière; there, he escaped the famine that devastated psychiatric hospitals during the war, but could not escape 50 electroshocks, recently imported to France by German doctors, who had first conducted experiments on pigs: "It provoked the loss of my memory, numbed my mind and body, turned me into an absence aware of this absence, into a dead man next to the living man who is no longer himself."

"Doctor L" (Lacan)'s diagnosis, on the brink of World War II, which Artaud had predicted in his Theatre of Cruelty, echoed the diagnosis Freud and Binswanger gave Aby Warburg, whom they judged "unable to pursue his scientific activities."[34] History contradicted this judgement, showing that the intelligence at work in a delusion is not incompatible with literature and scientific research. Aby Warburg proved this, when he published *The Mnemosyne Atlas*,[35] assembled after he left the psychiatric clinic. Antonin Artaud proved it again, when he published *Van Gogh: The Man Suicided by Society* in 1947. In this book, he settles the score with Doctor L and "his grotesque terminology" with a violence of which Strindberg would have approved: "This is why a tainted society has invented psychiatry to defend itself against the investigations of certain superior intellects whose faculties of divination would be troublesome."[36]

Like Strindberg, Artaud was also plagued by "stories of electricity." As a child, he suffered from migraines, and at the age of 4 was treated with an electric machine whose electrodes were applied to his head. A little later, he lost his 7-month-old baby sister, killed by the "unfortunate action of a servant." Artaud's version of events eliminates the euphemism:

> Germaine Artaud, strangled at seven months, watched me from the St Peter's Cemetery in Marseille, until the day in 1931 when, in the middle of the Dôme [café] in Montparnasse, I had the impression she was [right there] watching me.

The affinity between Strindberg and Artaud was confirmed when Artaud directed Strindberg's *A Dream Play* in 1927 at the Theatre Alfred Jarry, which he founded with Robert Aron after he broke away from the surrealists. His refusal to adhere to communism as they did, "kneeling before fetishes in human form," caused him to be called a "rotten bastard" by surrealist luminaries. The two authors had this in common too.

Strindberg's transference to his doctor had been similar, when he saw the latter as both the cause and target of his madness, as is often the case in critical moments in the transference, when the perverse agency takes our place, giving us the opportunity to identify it by recognising in ourselves the flaw through which it got in: "Grant that I am suffering from persecution-mania, but what smith forges the links of these hellish syllogisms? The discoverer would have to be killed." Once the true goal of his combat has been stated, sleep overtakes him before sunrise.

The doctor tries one thing after another. His transference goes from showing neutrality to being comforting, and then authoritative. His patient watches him closely and identifies his superiority complex:

> The doctor seems to me to be struggling with conflicting emotions. At one time he seems prejudiced against me, looks at me contemptuously, and treats me with humiliating rudeness; at another he seems himself unhappy, and soothes and comforts me as though I were a sick child. But then again, it seems to give him pleasure to be able to trample under his feet a man of worth for whom he has formerly had a high regard. Then he lectures me like a pitiless tormentor. I am to work [...] I am to fulfill my duties ...

In fact, madness has attained its goal, as it does each time when the analyst, pushed to the limit, commits the blunder that projects him into the place of the perverse agency for whom the other does not exist. Through his madness, Strindberg notices the shift in his doctor's attitude: "I forcibly suppress the growing hatred which I feel towards this unexpected tormentor." There is proof. His eyes fall upon a whole panoply of torture devices: axes, saws, hammers, guns and poisons, and he exclaims: "Druggist! Are they slowly poisoning me with alkaloids such as hyoscyamin, hashish, digitalis ...?" But he changes his mind:

> They do not dare to murder me, but they are trying to drive me mad by artificial means, in order to make me disappear in an asylum. [...] Everything which he says contradicts itself the next moment, and when confronted by a liar my imagination takes the bit between its teeth and rushes beyond all reasonable bounds.

Strindberg is aware of the psychotic transference involved in "the effort to drive the other person crazy,"[37] and analyses it as a phenomenon of traumatic revival: "There occur in life such terrible incidents that the mind refuses to retain the memory of them [at the] moment, but the impression remains and becomes irresistibly alive again."

He is in a state of heightened vigilance, sensing that "a turning-point in my destiny is at hand." Indeed, critical moments always usher in something new, provided the analyst can analyse and tell the patient what is taking place between them, as far as he is concerned as well. As is usual in such a case, the doctor remains silent. Fortunately, a letter from Strindberg's wife invites him to come and see his little daughter, in her family's ancestral house on the banks of the Danube. This call from afar creates another place in which speaking, above all with his child who has just learned to speak, becomes possible: "I part from my friend – my executioner – without bitterness."

Achieving alterity

Beatrice is the name given to the child Strindberg thought he had lost. He had left a 6-month-old baby and is reunited with a little girl of two and a half: "She turned on me a searching look [...] as though she wished to find out whether I had come for her own or her mother's sake. After she had assured herself of the former, she let herself be embraced." The child tested him, before granting him her trust, just as he had tested his doctor. As a matter of fact, during the Middle Ages, fools were celebrated on a day called the Feast of the Holy Innocents.

The Feast of Fools, which opens Victor Hugo's *Hunchback of Notre Dame*,[38] was also the Feast of Children. For an undisclosed reason, the mother of Strindberg's mother-in-law puts him out of her house after a few months, and sends him to live with her other daughter, in the next village. In spite of their mother's orders, the two elderly women, his mother-in-law and her twin sister, are going to act as therapists, in a way he could not have expected.

In his first conversation with the two sisters, thanks to the confidence his little girl gave him, he confides in the two women. They react with immediate sympathy and are eager to help. Strindberg is astonished. No one had ever talked to him like this before: "You are where we have already been": sleepless nights, mysterious accidents, terrible fears, attacks of madness and indifference to religion, before they encountered Swedenborg. Surprised that he does not know the writings of his countryman, they give him an old volume in German: "Take it, read, and don't be afraid." He opens the book at random and comes upon a description of hell to which the Swedish philosopher likens life on earth.

What he reads gives him access to his first years of life:

> When I go over my past, my childhood already appears to me like a prison house or torture chamber. In order to explain the sufferings inflicted upon innocent children, one has only to suppose an earlier existence, out of which we have been cast down in order to bear the consequences of forgotten sins.

The transgenerational transmission of traumas that occurred before his birth is written there in black and white, and triggers the usual blocking of his affects: "With a docile mind, which is my chief weakness, I receive a deep and sombre impression from my reading of Swedenborg. And the powers let me rest no more. [...] The image of Dante's hell [...] rises before me." Don Quixote's hell comes back also, as it is staged by Cervantes in the episode of the treading hammers. The noise of a waterfall, a mill, a smithy or a waterwheel frighten Strindberg as much as it frightened the knight and Sancho Panza when they heard at night the rhythm of deafening blows stricken by the Devil, which in the morning turned out to be treading hammers.[39]

The gift of the two sisters provokes a powerful transference:

> The reading of Swedenborg occupies me during the day and depresses me by the realism of its descriptions. All my observations, feelings, and thoughts are so vividly reflected there, that his visions seem to me like experiences and real "human documents."

His mother-in-law confirms the documentary value of the text when she relates to him, in the evenings, the history of the district:

> What a monstrous collection of domestic and other tragedies, consisting of adulteries, divorces, lawsuits between relatives, murders, thefts, violations, incests, slanders. [...] I cannot take my walks without thinking of Swedenborg's hells. Beggars, imbeciles of both sexes, sick persons and cripples line the high roads.

The positive truth conveyed by the appearance of madness, as Auguste Comte would say, is validated.

Strindberg confides in his mother-in-law, who confirms his discovery: "Certainly, you must be doing penance, for sins which you committed before your birth" (p. 183). From then on, "restored to self-respect by Swedenborg," he sees himself as a worthy man. Witnesses have appeared, to testify to the hellish agonies passed down to him.

Swedenborg (1688–1772) had also "already been there" after he suddenly abandoned his scientific research. He was considered one of the most learned men of his time, known all over Europe for his encyclopaedic knowledge, for which he was ennobled and given a seat in the Swedish Parliament. Like Strindberg, he experienced humiliation through the disdain of his colleagues for his newly acquired nobility. At 53, he went through a mystical crisis period, and developed a passionate interest in dreams, angels, spirits and visions. Once, while in Gothenburg, he saw a fire threatening his home in Stockholm, hundreds of kilometres away. Accused of being a madman and a heretic, he was forced to go into exile in England, where the number of his disciples grew, although he never considered himself the leader of a sect. After his death, he was buried in his native land, among the kings of Sweden, at the Uppsala Cathedral.

The emergence of a subject

The awareness of himself as a subject, which emerges from Strindberg's readings and the mirror lent him by the two women, in a place where he saw nothing reflected before, is consciously transmitted to his little girl, as he himself recounts: "From my early days I am accustomed to plan out the day's work during my morning walk. No one, not even my wife, has ever been allowed to accompany me on it." The child says she wants to go with him on his walk. He refuses, she cries. "I have not the heart to sadden her today, but make a firm resolve not to allow her again to misuse her rights."

His daughter tries to attract his attention. He becomes paranoid, seeing her "as jealous as a lover about my thoughts; she seems to watch for the exact opportunity to destroy a carefully-woven web of thought with her prattle." Ready to accuse the innocent child of this dark design, he starts to think. The ability to reflect was given back to him literally and figuratively: "I go on with slow steps [...] my brain [is] exhausted by the effort of continually having to descend to a child's level."

The place of the other, which Swedenborg's writing and the presence of the two elderly sisters bring into existence for him, is transferred to the child. He can see her feelings in the way she looks at him, with reproach, and notices that she retreats little by little, "because she thinks I find her a nuisance, and imagines that I love her no longer." Contrary to the silence in which his own withdrawal was buried when he was a child, and from which no one came to free him, now he is touched by their shared sorrow:

"I feel myself bereft of the light which this child had brought into my dark soul." He kisses her, carries her in his arms, gathers flowers and pebbles for her, and plays with her.

The unrelenting unhappy fate transmitted for generations is outwitted through these simple gestures more eloquent than a seminar on psychosis. Besides, he analyses the mechanism of projection:

> I have sacrificed my morning hour. So do I atone for the evil which in a moment of madness I had wished to conjure down on this angel's head. […] Truly the powers are not so cruel as we are!

A cruel agency can be defeated by replacing it with the presence of an other, vulnerable and trustworthy, and able to play. But this happy interlude was not to last, because ghosts now seized the opportunity to return.

A dialogue takes place between Strindberg and his mother's ghost, who reproaches him for his divorces. After all, she had to wait a long time to become a wife, and was not recognised by her in-laws the way he is now. He blames her, in turn, for his own woes, and calls her a devil. This is enough to provoke the Furies to invade the present scene: "The spirits of discord are abroad and despite the fact that we are quite aware of their game and our freedom from blame in the matter, our repeated misunderstandings leave a bitter wish for revenge behind them" (p. 194).

Awareness is no protection:

> The wrath of ancient memories Socrates spoke about in the *Phaedrus* attacks those who "are rightly mad" in a lineage. But they also make it possible to transform madness, *mania*, into *mantike*, the prophetic art, by inserting the "t" of history, provided one "gives a correct analysis of the self."[40]

But Strindberg is fighting another battle. The Erinyes are chasing him. The house is haunted: "The black window opening gapes at me." Only the birds and ladybugs speak to him: "I curse the ever-present, unavoidable 'chance' which persecutes me with the obvious purpose of making me fall a victim to persecution-mania." The delirium reaches a pitch. Feeling condemned to die, he prepares to leave and waits for a sign. On this November day, a "ray of light abides in my heart like a happy smile […]. Then suddenly there is a single thunder-clap over my head. […] The Eternal has spoken!"[41] But he is not appeased.

In Chapter 16, "Hell Let Loose," he recognises that his little daughter is able to heal him. She follows him to his room, forces him to draw with her and, when an organ grinder is heard playing outside, he improvises a dance for all the neighbourhood children: "This goes on for an hour, and my sadness is dispelled." His mother-in-law tells him that just then, in the village, an old woman gone mad dances without stopping, to avert death. Like in Swedenborg's *Treaties*, the phenomenon defies scientific explanation:

> Explain that [to] me, O doctors, psychiatrists, psychologists, or acknowledge the bankruptcy of science! My little daughter has exorcised the evil spirit who, driven out by her innocence, has entered into an old lady who used to boast of being a free thinker.

Socrates would say that *mania* has been transformed into *mantike* through its extension to the history of the country, and freed him from the trap of negativity.

On the eve of his departure, Strindberg climbs to the summit of a mountain, which offers a splendid view of the valley of the Danube and the Styrian Alps. There, he can finally recall the most beautiful moments of his life. The sound of a bridal march sung by triumphant voices reaches him: "Childish enough and unhappy enough to give a poetical colouring to the most ordinary occurrences, I take this as a good omen."[42] He comes down into the valley with a piece of mistletoe for his Beatrice. Little things, like "My Favourite Things" sung by Julie Andrews in *The Sound of Music*,[43] set in the Austrian Alps, help to lighten the imminent separation from his daughter.

Back in Sweden after a six-year absence, Strindberg starts by visiting doctors. Each one gives him a different diagnosis: "The first speaks of neurasthenia, the second of angina pectoris, the third of paranoia, a mental disease, the fourth of emphysema. This is enough to ensure me against being put into a lunatic asylum." But a sense of humour doesn't protect him from noise, which pursues him everywhere, in his hotel room and in the restaurant. In Lund, he is reunited with an old friend from his student days, who appears very demoralised. The members of their former student association (called the Young Old) are "dead, [downtrodden], turned into Philistines and steady members of society. [...] they complain of nightmares, constrictions of the breast and heart."

His friend is melancholy until Strindberg mentions Swedenborg. The friend's mother has the writer's books: "I thank Providence which has sent me into this small despised town to expiate my sin and to be delivered." Once again, this name produces a rallying effect, "when the tool with the name [was] broken," as Wittgenstein[44] says, saving both of them from depression by prompting a new language-game.

All of Strindberg's torments are described in Swedenborg's works, and resumed by the word "devastation." But his redemptor Swedenborg, instead of resigning himself to the sheer repetition of misfortune, brings about a sacrificial catharsis, like in Greek tragedies, where "the flesh is destroyed, so that the spirit might be saved." Swedenborg considers that dead spirits are survivors who continue their relationships with the living. Therefore, evil spirits are not so evil and their intention is good; he proposes calling them "corrective spirits," for they eliminate fear and despair. Strindberg expresses his relief: "Be comforted, and be proud of the grace bestowed upon you, all ye who suffer from sleeplessness, nightmares, apparitions, palpitations, and fears of death! *Numen adest!* God is seeking for you!" Now, the place of the symbolic Other is assured and signals a turning point in his analysis. Time measured by symbols is set in motion again, allowing him to analyse his past: "I engage in the terrible fight against my worst enemy – myself." Let us review the various stances he adopted throughout his life: first he was pious, then a freethinker, then an atheist, and finally he was inspired by humanitarian ideas. But he admits he was disillusioned: "I have been a herald of socialism. Five years later you have shown me the absurdity of socialism; you have made all my prophecies futile." After the collapse of his illusions, he may become the subject of his life. He has gained enough hindsight to be able to say:

> Ah, what a game the gods play with us poor mortals! And therefore, in the most tormented moments of life, we too can laugh with self-conscious raillery. How is it that you wish to take earnestly what is nothing but a huge bad joke?

Medicine is also a joke: "Go to the asylum, and ask the doctor; he will talk to you about neurasthenia, paranoia, angina pectoris, and stories of that kind, but will never heal you." Still, he is not tempted by nihilism: "But when night, silence and loneliness reign, the heart beats, and the breast suffers from constriction, then [...] seek someone to share the sleeping chamber" (p. 234). The function of the *therapon* is now exerting its effect. From this perspective, which offers the possibility of an exchange, traumatic revivals can be seen as a dynamic able to "grind" terrible things into words, those, precisely, that we read in *The Inferno*:

> Have you in the solitude of night or in broad daylight observed how memories of the past stir and arise, singly or in groups? Memories of all your faults, crimes and follies which make your ears tingle, your brows perspire, your spine shudder? You re-live your life from birth to the present day, you suffer over again all the sorrows you have endured, you empty again all the cups which you have drunk to the dregs so often; you crucify your skeleton when there is no more flesh left to crucify; you consume your soul when your heart is reduced to ashes! You know all that? Those are the "mills of God" which grind slowly but exceedingly small!

At the very same time, Freud was writing *Project for a Scientific Psychology*, in which the colossal energy of the Real goes through a succession of filters that reduce it to signifiers.[45]

Swedenborg does not deny the aporias madness comes up against: "To seek out the demons in their dens within myself, and there to slay them," including when they wear the mask of love for humanity:

> I try to love mankind in the mass; I shut my eyes to their faults, and within exhaustible patience endure their meannesses and slanders, and one fine day I find myself a sharer of their crimes. Whenever I withdraw from society which I consider injurious, the demons of solitude attack me, and when I look for better friends, I come on the track of the worst.

The solution to this dilemma, particular to the enquiries of madness, will be given in the last chapter, which solves the aporia: "How is one to explain the fact that every step of progress in virtue gives rise to a fresh sin?" The answer to this question is given in the last chapter of the book, entitled "Whither?"

Strindberg the therapist

Delusions return, as they do each time there is progress:

> a wintry sadness still weighs upon our spirits, for so many weird and inexplicable things have happened, that even the most incredulous waver. The general sleeplessness increases, nervous breakdowns are common, apparitions are matters of every day, and real miracles happen. People are expecting something.

In his case, the expectation is answered by a visit.

This time, a young man knocks on his door. For once, he does not turn him out as an enemy. The visitor asks: "What must one do in order to sleep quietly at night?" Instead of pondering over his neurosis, Strindberg voices the simple question that must be asked: "What happened?" The young man answers that when he opened the door of his room at night, someone seized his arm and shook it. But there was no one in the room. Again, instead of thinking that this is psychosis, Strindberg enters his visitor's delusion and asserts: "It is the invisible." And he tells the young man his story:

> Listen, young man, I am neither a physician nor a prophet. I am an old sinner, who does penance. Demand therefore neither preaching nor prophecy from an old gallow-bird, who wants all his leisure time to preach to himself. I have also suffered from sleeplessness and paralysis of the arms; I have wrestled eye to eye with the invisible, and finally recovered sleep and health. Do you know how? Guess! The young man guesses my meaning, and casts his eyes down. – You guess it! Go in peace, and sleep well!

After his departure, Strindberg ponders over the session that just took place: "Yes! I must be silent and let my meaning be guessed, for if I began to play the preaching monk, they would turn their backs on me at once." He knows this by experience? (p. 240). Indeed, silence had allowed the young man to regain his grip on himself, but only after his therapist recounted his own experience. Without fearing the loss of his neutrality, or claiming a false brotherhood, he took on the role of second in combat – the *therapon* in the *Iliad* – against the invisible. The young man was no longer alone on his journey towards the unknown. He has learned that his symptoms are not an illness, but rather an investigation he has shared with a co-researcher.

In the epilogue of the book, he concludes: "Such then is my life, a sign, an example to serve for the betterment of others," like a toy in a child's play, to demonstrate the nothingness of fame and of celebrity, and show the younger generation how they should not live. Anticipating Winnicott, Strindberg concludes in a playful tone: "Here you have, my brothers, the picture of a human destiny, one among so many, and now confess that a man's life may seem – a bad joke!"

The mad teach us to write history

This is Martti Siirala's way of saying that madness is not reasonable, since it insists on validating and putting back into circulation voices and visions testifying to what was cut out of history. *Le parti pris des choses* (*The Nature of Things*) – the title of Francis Ponge's collection of prose poems[46] – offers a poetic space needing no objectivation, when words break down.

Sharing this viewpoint, Boris Vian, who translated Strindberg's *Miss Julie*, ridicules – in his own book *Foam of the Daze*[47] – Sartre's *Nausée*,[48] presented as the chronicle of madness. He calls Sartre: "Jean Sol Partre, the author of *Spew* (*Dégueulis*)." Sartre intended to give a scientific description of everyday events, by objectifying the things around him without any emotion, until nausea set in at the end of 150 pages. Published in 1938, the text is not a narrative, and excludes any irrational effects and any references to history, so that it culminates in the absurd. Boris Vian, on the contrary, wants to force nausea to stop; to this end, he turns to fiction, where events set the plot in motion.

Martti Siirala also speaks of a malignant violence that the social order gets rid of through "vicarious transference" onto people diagnosed mad. This is attested to by Louis Althusser (1918–1990) in his book *The Future Lasts Forever*,[49] which exposes the historical stakes involved in his tragedy. As soon as he met his future wife Hélène Rytmann in 1947, Althusser was hospitalised and given, like Artaud in the same period, a series of electroshocks. At the end of a long analysis in parallel with hospitalisation, sleep therapies and heavy medication, he strangled his wife in 1980 in their living quarters at the École normale supérieure (ENS). Another episode in the life of the couple brings Artaud to mind. In 1948, Hélène was excluded from the Communist Party by a tribunal whose members were to become celebrities. The wording of their edict advised Althusser to leave her. Is it possible that, as was the case for Strindberg, the writing of his book was a search for catharsis?

I do not know, but I remember clearly the impression he made on us at the Hotel PLM on the Boulevard Saint-Jacques, on March 16, 1980. The members of the École freudienne were gathered there to hear Jacques Lacan announce the dissolution of his School. Just as Lacan finished saying, in a weary voice: "*Je dis solution: dissolution!*" ("My solution: dissolution!"), Louis Althusser entered the room like a ghost. This is how he himself describes the scene:

> Conspicuously, coming down the wide aisle that divided the silent audience, I was advancing very slowly, my pipe in my mouth. I stopped and, with a deliberate gesture, I knocked my pipe against the heel of my boot, filled it and lighted it, then walked towards Lacan and shook his hand warmly. He was clearly exhausted after his long presentation. I endeavoured to show by my attitude all the respect I had for this great, elderly man dressed like a Pierrot. Then I spoke "in the name of analysands, reproaching strongly the audience for its silence. I don't remember what I said, but I remember the silent commotion that followed my speech." I remembered too. None of the 500 people present reacted, except to voice inane witticisms such as: "*La colle de l'école doit être dissoute*" ("The glue of the school has to be unglued").

Two members of the audience escorted Althusser to the back of the room, like an uninvited guest at a family reunion, gathered to tacitly assess an inheritance before the anticipated death occurs.

Back in the days when we threw snowballs from the rooftop terrace of the ENS on fur-clad ladies and elegant gentlemen who came to hear Lacan's seminars, we didn't know that Althusser had been the one who put at his disposal the Dussane lecture hall. It looked out on Rue d'Ulm, "which, says Althusser in his book, quickly became cluttered, every Wednesday, with expensive English cars encroaching on the sidewalks, causing outrage among the residents of the neighbourhood." But this time, fifteen years later, the outrage was the deathly silence that ostracised him: "I wanted to continue the discussion after Lacan's speech, but everyone left." Indeed, they rose and left to have a drink, leaving Althusser standing there, completely alone. We went up to him to try to say something, but he was speaking aloud to himself, in his flawless rhetoric. It was impossible to get a word in! Eight months later, on November 16, he strangled his wife while giving her a massage. A year later, on September 9, 1981, Lacan died.

In his book, Althusser, like Strindberg, examines the trials of his family . He was born in Algeria. His mother too was the daughter of poor peasants.

His father's father came from Alsace, and had to emigrate to Algeria after the annexation of Alsace-Lorraine by Germany, following the Franco-Prussian War. His father fought during World War I and came back traumatised. His brother, Althusser's uncle Louis, whose name he was given, had been his mother's first love, and was killed in combat. His father succeeded in rising to a high position in a bank, but he could not express himself in public because of his Alsatian accent. He had nightmares every night. In 1939, Louis Althusser passed the competitive entrance exams to the ENS, after having been drafted and spending five years as a prisoner in Germany. He finally came back in 1945, to start his studies at the school where he had passed the entrance exams six years earlier.

Our next seminar will focus on the discovery by William Rivers, neurologist and anthropologist, of the psychoanalysis of trauma, during World War I.

Notes

1 Siirala, M., *From Transfer to Transference*, Therapeia, 1983.
2 See *infra*, Seminar 2 on Gaetano Benedetti.
3 Lönnrot, E., *The Kalevala*, Bosley, K. (Trans.), Oxford Paperbacks, 2008.
4 Foucault, M., *The Birth of the Clinic*, Routledge, 2003.
5 Fritz, J. M., *Le discours du fou au Moyen-Âge*, Presses universitaires de France, 1992.
6 De Cervantes, M., *Don Quixote*, Canterbury Classics/Baker & Taylor, 2013.
7 Strindberg, A., *Inferno*, Mercure de France, 1966.
8 Strindberg, A., "Le fils de la servant," in *Œuvres autobiographiques*, Vol. I, Mercure de France, 1990.
9 Strindberg, A., *Twelve Plays by Strindberg*, Constable, 1955.
10 Strindberg, A., "A Catechism for Workers," in Sinclair, U. (Ed.), *The Cry for Justice: An Anthology of the Literature of Social Protest*, Sinclair, 1915.
11 De La Fontaine, J., "The Limbs and the Stomach," in *The Complete Fables of Jean de La Fontaine*, University of Illinois Press, 2007, p. 57.
12 Strindberg, A., *Inferno, Alone and Other Writings*, Coltman, D. and Sprinchorn, E. (Trans.), Anchor Books, 1968.
13 Enquist, P. O., *Strindberg, une vie*, Flammarion, 1985.
14 See *infra*, Seminar 4 on Toni Morrison and Frieda Fromm-Reichmann.
15 Von Goethe, J. W., *Faust*, Oxford Paperbacks, 2008.
16 De Balzac, H., *Séraphîta*, Kessinger Publishing, 1997.
17 Subsequent quotes from Strindberg, A., *The Inferno*, Field, C. (Trans.), G.P. Putnam's Sons, 1913.
18 Strindberg, A., *The Inferno*, op. cit., p. 45.
19 Comte, A., *Course in Positive Philosophy*, Vol. 6, Cambridge Library Collection, 1842, Personal Preface.
20 Baudelaire, C., *The Flowers of Evil*, CreateSpace, 2009.
21 De Nerval, G., *The Chimeras*, Black Swan Books, 1985.
22 Laub, D., "Rétablir le 'tu' intérieur dans le témoignage du trauma" ("Re-Establishing the Inner Thou in Testimony of Trauma"), in *Une clinique de l'extrême* (*Treating Severe Trauma*), Le Coq Héron, 2015, No. 220, érès.
23 Plato, *Theaetetus*, Liberal Arts Press, 1955.
24 Enquist, P. O., *Strindberg, une vie*, op. cit.

25 Strindberg, A., "La chute du paradis perdu," in *Inferno*, op. cit., Chapter 8.
26 Le Goff, J., *The Birth of Purgatory*, University of Chicago Press, 1986.
27 Bion, W., "Attacks on Linking," in *Second Thoughts*, Karnac Books, 1993.
28 Freud, S. and Jung, C., *The Freud/Jung Letters*, McGuire, W. (Ed.), Princeton University Press, 1994.
29 De Balzac, H., *Séraphîta*, op. cit.
30 Comte, A., *The Positive Philosophy*, Calvin Blanchard, 1855.
31 Bion, W., *A Memoir of the Future*, Karnac Books, 1991.
32 Strindberg, A., "Extracts from the Diary of a Damned Soul," in *The Inferno*, op. cit., Chapter 9.
33 Freud, S., *Beyond the Pleasure Principle*, S.E. 18, Hogarth Press, 1920.
34 Freud, S. and Binswanger, L., *The Freud-Binswanger Letters*, Fichtner, G. (Ed.), Open Gate Press, 2000.
35 Warburg, A., *L'Atlas Mnémosyne*, L'Écarquillé, 2012.
36 Artaud, A., "Van Gogh: The Man Suicided by Society," in *Antonin Artaud: Selected Writings*, University of California Press, 1988.
37 Searles, H. F., "The Effort to Drive the Other Person Crazy," *British Journal of Medical Psychology*, 32 (1959): 1–18.
38 Hugo, V., *The Hunchback of Notre Dame*, Wordsworth, 1998.
39 De Cervantes, M., *Don Quixote*, op. cit., Vol. I, Chapter 20.
40 Plato, *Phaedrus*, Focus Publishing/R. Pullins Co., 2003.
41 Strindberg, A., "The Eternal Has Spoken," in *The Inferno*, op. cit., Chapter 10.
42 Strindberg, A., "Hell Let Loose," in *The Inferno*, op. cit., Chapter 11.
43 Wise, R. (Dir.), *The Sound of Music*, 1965.
44 Wittgenstein, L., *Philosophical Investigations*, Wiley-Blackwell, 2010.
45 Freud, S., *Project for a Scientific Psychology*, S.E. 1, Hogarth Press, 1895, pp. 283–397.
46 Ponge, F., *The Nature of Things*, Fahnestock, L. (Trans.), Red Dust, 1995.
47 Vian, B., *Foam of the Daze*, TamTam Books, 2012.
48 Sartre, J.-P., *Nausea*, Penguin Books, 2000.
49 Althusser, L., *The Future Lasts Forever*, The New Press, 1995.

6 Seminar 6: 1997–1998
Pat Barker

The Regeneration Trilogy:[1] objectivity degree zero[2]

A subjective story

Pat Barker's *Trilogy* deals with the psychoanalysis of war traumas, as it was practised by William Rivers in England during World War I. This practice is in stark contrast to the absence of such an approach in France, where the dominant practice was traditional psychiatry, according to historians Stephane Tison and Hervé Villemain in their recent book *Du front à l'asile, 1914–1918* (*From the Front to the Asylum, 1914–1918*).[3]

How did we come across the *Trilogy*? In 1977, we were invited by the Appalachian Psychoanalytic Society in Knoxville, Tennessee, to speak about Faulkner's *Absalom, Absalom!*[4] which starts with an old maid, Miss Coldfield, who has a "rapport with the [...] cradle of events," summoning a young man, Quentin Compson, about to go off to Harvard, to listen to the tragic story of her family, caught in the Civil War, which she has recorded since childhood by "eavesdropping at the door of History." Faulkner's novel brought to mind the wars fought by our fathers and grandfathers, of which we and our patients were contemporaries in the arrested time of the madness of wars. After our presentation, Bill MacGillivray, a member of the Society, suggested that we read Pat Barker's books, which had to do with the things we were talking about.

At the same time, I read Jean-Baptiste Duroselle's work about World War I, entitled *La grande guerre des francais, 1914–1918* (*The Great War of the French, 1914–1918*).[5] In the preface, the historian explains the subjective nature of this book: his father had been wounded in Verdun, and his professor, historian Pierre Renouvin, came back from the war with one arm missing, as well as three fingers on his other hand. Duroselle's vocation as a historian was inextricably linked with the history of war traumas. More recently, Stéphane Audoin-Rouzeau, a World War I specialist, made the same admission when, as a historian, he told the story of his paternal grandfather, who had met with contempt when he came back from the front traumatised. His book *Quelle histoire* (*What a Story*)[6] was published on the occasion of the centenary of the Great War.

The Sassoon case

The first book of the *Trilogy, Regeneration*, starts with the diagnosis that William Rivers, neurologist, experimental psychologist, anthropologist and psychoanalyst, must make in the case of the poet Siegfried Sassoon, who left his army unit in 1917 and published a sensational anti-war Declaration.

Too old to be sent to France during the war, Rivers was recruited as a military doctor and assigned to work at the Craiglockhart Hospital, near Edinburgh, where shell-shocked officers were treated. Sassoon was brought to him by his friend Robert Graves – future writer of *Good-Bye to All That*[7] – in the hope that Rivers could help him. Rivers is caught in a double bind – which Americans will call a "catch-22" after the next war, from the title of Joseph Heller's novel.[8] The patient does not seem shell-shocked, and the military expect an answer: Is he mad or not? One answer is as problematic as the other. Graves has chosen Rivers knowing that he does not consider war trauma a pathology, but rather the greatest catastrophe that could befall the social link.

Sassoon is a poet[9] and a hero who had been awarded the Victoria Cross for having saved wounded men at the risk of his own life. His problem started when he tore off his medal and threw it in the river. A ship sailed past; Sassoon reflected that throwing the cross in the water to stop the war was like trying to stop the ship with his bare hands. Then he devised a new strategy: he wrote a letter addressed to the House of Commons. Dated July 1917, it is entitled "Finished with War: A Soldier's Declaration." The text reads as follows:

> I am making the statement as an act of willful defiance of military authority because I believe that the war is being deliberately prolonged by those who have the power to end it. I am a soldier, convinced that I am acting on behalf of soldiers. I believe that the war upon which I entered as a war of defence and liberation has now become a war of aggression and conquest. [...] I have endured the sufferings of the troops and I can no longer be a party to prolong these sufferings for ends which I believe to be evil and unjust. I am not protesting against the conduct of the war, but against the political errors and insincerities for which the fighting men are sacrificed. On behalf of those who are suffering now, I make this protest against the deception which is being practised upon them; also I believe it may help to destroy the callous complacency with which the majority of those at home regard the continuance of agonies which they do not share and which they have not enough imagination to realise.[10]

Thus, Rivers is faced with a dilemma: either he judges Sassoon to be mad and invalidates his act, or he judges him to be sane and sends him to face court martial. Since Rivers does not like the usual tests, his first neurological exam is a tea party session, which goes quite well – the patient presents no tics or trembling. The second test is political. Rivers reads to him, from his medical file, his military citations and the support he received from pacifists like Bertrand Russell and Lady Ottoline. Sassoon rejects any political uses to which they might be put. Rivers concludes: "the Declaration is logical and coherent."

Now a psychiatric exam has to be performed: Is this a case of war neurosis diagnosed just recently? Not really. Sassoon's last nightmare occurred in April, when a friend died in a useless mission. He even hallucinated piles of corpses, on whose faces people were walking in Piccadilly. But there had been no nightmares or hallucinations since: "Sometimes a dream seems to go on after I've woken up [...]. I don't know whether that's abnormal." – "I hope not," Rivers answered. "It happens to me all the time" (R, p. 13).

Psychoanalysis of traumas

Sassoon: the analyst's "I"

Rivers reads Freud, but differs from him because he remains personally involved with patients. Of course, their clinical practices are radically different. The Craiglockhart Hospital is filled with catatonic men, silent or delirious, who scream during the night. From a window of this loony bin comparable to Dante's *Inferno*, we see Rivers watching Sassoon arrive with his friend. He perceives the poet's fear: "After paying the driver, Sassoon lingered for a moment, looking up at the building. [...] Sassoon [...] took a deep breath, squared his shoulders, and ran up the steps." River's sensitive "seismograph" is also recording his own impressions: "Rivers turned away from the window, feeling almost ashamed of having witnessed that small, private victory over fear" (R, p. 9).

His shame disqualifies him at once from representing the figure of the traditional psychiatrist, who is personified at the end of the book by Lewis Yealland, the "great dissector of the brain,"[11] advocate of electroshock, the British equivalent of France's Vincent Clovis, who considered the soldiers' symptoms malingering and cowardice. Rivers did not believe that objectivity was the golden rule in psychiatry.

The *Trilogy* is dedicated in great part to the conflict between subjectivity and objectivity, centring around a signifier inscribed in the title of the second book, *The Eye in the Door*. This signifier plays on the homonymy of the words "eye" and "I," depending on whether Rivers observes through the door, like a voyeur looking through a peephole, or is involved as a subject, "I," at their side. Pat Barker based her story on Rivers' clinical notes and the ethnographic journal he kept in Melanesia. The interplay between the researcher and his field of enquiry, and later his patients, is the main focus of his interest, and of our seminars.

Not only does Rivers trust his subjective impressions, but he shares his questioning with his patients: "Do you think you were shell-shocked?" Sassoon doubts it, because he has been writing poems he considers good. "Would it be possible for me to see them?" his future analyst asks. Sassoon agrees and enquires about his diagnosis:

> You said [...] you didn't think I was mad? – The point is you hate civilians, don't you? [...] You seem to have a very powerful anti-war neurosis. You realize [...] that it's my duty to ... to try to change that? I can't pretend to be neutral. Sassoon's glance took in both their uniforms. No, of course not.

End of the first session (R, p. 15).

The approach to this complex situation is described by Harry Stack Sullivan – their contemporary, liaison officer at the St. Elizabeths Hospital in Washington, and later psychoanalyst of young schizophrenic patients at the Sheppard Pratt Hospital in Baltimore – as a "twosome laboratory" that brings together "all the elements of the social sciences"[12] and takes into account the lineage of analysts, as we shall see. From the start, Sassoon points out the break in the social link between civilians, on the one hand, who exclaim indignantly that war is horrible and deplore the losses while they sip their beer, and, on the other, those who have seen men die in a shell-hole (R, p. 14).

Bryce, Rivers' colleague, asks him what he thinks of the newcomer: "I found him ... much more impressive than I expected," Rivers answers. Contrary to other patients, Sassoon's efforts are not directed at forgetting, as families and doctors often advise, but rather at remembering and inscribing. He has agreed to spend a little time each day speaking to Rivers about that.

The analyst's standpoint

In one of his poems, Sassoon expresses his desire to remember:

> I am back again from hell ...
> That shall not be unsaid, ...
> And the wounds in my heart are red
> For I have watched them die.

Rivers, who is not well versed in poetry, doesn't know what to say. But these verses are addressed to a therapist, not to a literary critic. He understands that writing the poems was therapeutic, just as writing the Declaration had been; both sprang from the same source. Yet he has taken a stand, which he made clear to his patient, and at the same time he worries that Sassoon's return to the Front would be a "risky business [...] and might well precipitate a relapse."

Their second meeting is more eventful, since Rivers does not intend to let the patient unfold his family history without saying anything. Sassoon begins to recount his life from the beginning, as he thinks he is expected to do: his father's death when he was 8, his loneliness, not going to the funeral. The army was the first place where he felt he belonged: "And yet you've cut yourself off from it," his analyst cuts in. – Yes, because ... Rivers interrupts him again, knowing from experience that in the field of trauma, causality does not apply:

> I am not interested in the reasons [...]. I'm more interested in the result. The effect on you. – Isolation, I suppose. I can't talk to anybody. – You talk to me. Or at least I think you do. – You don't say stupid things.

Rivers turned his head away: "I'm pleased about that."

The transference has been established. Sassoon has found someone to talk to, as it becomes clear when the analyst challenges him again:

> You can't bear to be safe, can you? [...] If you go on refusing to serve, you'll [...] spend the remainder of the war in [...] Complete Personal Safety. You don't think you might find being safe while other people die rather difficult?

Sassoon is enraged: "Nobody else in this stinking country seems to find it difficult. [...] I'll just learn to live with it. Like everybody else." Rivers takes the risk of jeopardising a positive transference and frustrating the patient's desire for their relationship to continue this way. Revealing his own shame at "having witnessed" Sassoon's "small victory over fear," he introduces Shame into the session.

But other patients don't allow him the time to reflect at length on this heated exchange. Campbell, Sassoon's room-mate, is convinced that Sassoon is a German spy, since his first name is Siegfried. Rivers assures him that German spies never call themselves Siegfried. Relieved, Campbell taps him on the shoulder, explaining: "Just thought I'd mention it." Rivers thanks him: "Much appreciated."

Burns: failures of analysis

The life of a chrysalis

Sassoon's anger is nothing compared to the violence reigning in the ward, and Rivers' helplessness in the midst of it. Burns is creating havoc. He is constantly vomiting since he was thrown in the air by the explosion of a shell and landed head first on a German corpse, rupturing its gas-filled belly. The fact that was unable to heal him "drained [Rivers] of energy that rightly belonged to his patients."

In Chapter 4, Burns puts on his mackintosh and goes out. The nurses let him leave. He takes the bus, travels across Edinburgh and trudges through a muddy field fenced in with barbed wire. He is soaked, seeks shelter under some trees, sits down to rest, and sees animal corpses hanging from a tree: foxes, magpies, weasels, ferrets. He hears Rivers' voice telling him: "If you run now, you'll never stop." But he wants to be in this place where he feels he belongs. His body remembers the trenches. After untying all the "ghosts in the making" – referenced in the title of the third book – he lays the corpses on the ground in a circle around him. He takes off his clothes, folds his uniform and waits, naked, for the whistling of shells, surrounded by his companions.

The hospital staff is panicked when he does not return, fearing he might have committed suicide. When he comes back in the evening, he is scolded by a nurse, who warms him up, gets him food and calls Rivers. Burns will see what's what. Rivers sits at Burns' bedside while he sleeps and smiles at him when he opens his eyes. Observing him stealthily, Burns realises that he has come back "for Rivers" (R, pp. 38–40), for a witness to what he did. By enacting an experience impossible to convey in words, he transformed it into a ritual that Rivers, the anthropologist, is able to authenticate. But ten chapters later, the reader learns that Burns has relapsed to his initial state (R, p. 167).

He has returned to his family's seaside home. Rivers, exhausted, has taken a vacation, and visits him at his request. Burns is still unable to eat. Rivers is struck to see that "a prematurely aged man and a fossilized schoolboy seemed to exist [in him] side by side," giving him a "curiously ageless quality." And now Burns disappears once again, on a stormy night, after a distress rocket was sent up and sandbags were piled up to protect the house. This time he went to bury himself in the moat of a medieval castle, where violent deaths had occurred when the site was a battlefield in various wars – the perfect site for re-enacting the trenches in France. Rivers carries the emaciated body back to the house; in his arms, the body loses its stiffness and becomes a rag doll. Rivers puts him to bed and then prepares him breakfast, thinking that "nothing justifies this." But this time, when Burns is himself again, he tells Rivers, for the first time, about the Battle of the Somme, a futile attack in a place that was not on the map, and his field promotion, when all he could hope for to avoid atrocious mutilation was a bullet in the heart.

For the first time, Rivers sees the possibility that he might be healed, for he is now able to put into perspective the decomposed body into which he fell, by remembering more bearable events. Rivers knows only too well how closely the first stages of improvement resemble deterioration. To describe this paradox, he uses an image that should be taught to every "embryo analyst," as Bion, who fought in the same battles, calls his young colleagues: when one cuts a chrysalis open, there is a rotting caterpillar inside. The chrysalis' transformation resembles decomposition. After this transforming episode, Burns thinks he can go back to his studies, now that he has been able to face, at last, his war experiences in France, where "he has missed his chance to be ordinary" (R, p. 184).

Anderson and Billy Prior: the analyst's dreams

Despite the idealised view others had of him, Rivers did not consider himself a saint. He could involve himself with experiences of this kind because they had something to do with him, as shown by his own dreams, elicited by patients. Gaetano Benedetti called them "therapeutic dreams," the birthplace of a "transitional subject."[13] Anderson's dream is particularly unexpected since he hates psychoanalysis. A surgeon in civilian life, he can no longer bear the sight of blood after he was unable to save a young Frenchman covered in mud, screaming in pain and bleeding to death. Anderson never tells Rivers his dreams, although on his floor everyone awakened by his screams knows about them, especially his room-mate, who is getting worse.

In his dream, Anderson is threatened by snakes, the ones on Rivers' caduceus; Rivers himself is dressed like a forensic pathologist. When his analyst asks the routine question: "Do you often dream of snakes?" Anderson goes into a harangue against "Freudian Johnnies" and their stupid interpretations. This dream haunts Rivers while he makes his rounds in the ward. He asks himself whether being attacked by the serpents on the rod of Asclepius, and therefore unable to work as a surgeon and support his family, might not, at the same time, announce Anderson's possible suicide, offering up his corpse to the doctor in medical examiner's garb.

Rivers' feeling of powerlessness is amplified the next day when he meets Prior, another new patient on the ward, who is just as recalcitrant. The 22-year-old Prior is a fictional character, invented by Pat Barker based on Rivers' clinical notes. He comes from a working-class family in the North of England, speaks with a local accent, and is tied to the historical context of the social movement in that region during the war – the theme of the next book. When Rivers asks him what happened, because his file has not yet arrived, he indicates that he cannot speak by writing in capital letters on a notepad: "I don't remember."

Rivers examines his throat and Prior writes the diagnosis himself: "There's nothing physically wrong." Rivers suggests: "[…] we're going to have to try to get a history together […]. And that's not going to be easy. – Why? – Because I need to know what's happened to you. – I don't remember. – No, not at the moment, perhaps, but the memory will start to come back. A long silence. At last Prior scribbled something, then turned […] to face the wall. Rivers leant across and picked the pad up. […] 'No more words'" (R, p. 43).

The next night, Rivers has a dream that says a lot about his involvement with his patients, for it is triggered by both these patients: the medical examiner in Anderson's dream and the lack of words on Prior's notepad.

Experiment with Head on nerve regeneration

Rivers' second dream, which he analyses in two stages, brings back the neurological experiments he conducted between 1903 and 1907, as an assistant to neurologist Henry Head, well known for his discoveries on sensory-motor nerves. The book's title, *Regeneration*, is an explicit reference to these experiments that Head carried out on himself, while Rivers tested the regeneration of a nerve that Head had cut in his own arm.

In the dream, Head has his eyes closed and his arm bared, showing the full length of a purple scar. Rivers' task is to map the area of sensitivity to pain by pricking the forearm with a needle in different places, and with different degrees of intensity. In the dream, as he is pricking his arm, Head cries out with pain. Rivers would like to stop, but he knows he must continue.

So far, the dream describes the real experiment that led to the discovery of two stages of pain. At the first stage, called "protopathic," pain is extreme regardless of the intensity or nearness of the needle prick. At the second stage, called "epicritic," differentiated thresholds appear, making it possible to identify areas and variations of sensibility. Then Rivers' dream takes a different turn. He has to mark in pen, on the neurologist's arm, the outline of the protopathic area. Head hands him a scalpel, saying: "Why don't *you* try it?" Before he can utter a word, Head makes an incision near his elbow, drawing blood. At that point, he wakes up (R, pp. 45–46).

Rivers analyses his dream. The overt content is striking in its precision. It was he who suggested that Head become the guinea pig in an experiment that would require rigorous observation. It had been conducted for five years, and was extremely painful, especially at the protopathic stage, when pain was extreme regardless of the circumstances, in an "all-or-nothing" manner. Although at the time they never considered interrupting the experiment, the desire to stop was intense in Rivers' dream.

The dream's latent content brings into question Freud's theory. Although on the surface it seems to validate his conception of dreams as wish fulfilment – Rivers wanted to return to Cambridge to pursue his research – this interpretation overlooks the fact that the dream expresses fear and horror. Did the dream express Rivers' desire to torture one of his best friends? No doubt, the staunchest of Freud's supporters would have accepted this hypothesis, but Rivers could not. Instead, he felt the dream reflected his own conflict between his duty and the fact that he was inflicting pain, between his support for the continuation of the war and the horror to which Burns, Anderson and Prior were subjected.

Lately, all his dreams were about the conflict each patient triggered in the course of a treatment, which was, after all, his experimentation with psychoanalysis. Confronted with the paralysis of their sensibility, was he not awakening the protopathic pain of an unspeakable memory for the sake of an experiment?

Through transference, Rivers applies the neurological metaphor to emotional amputation. Something has cut off the circulation of information to which memory has no access. Dissociated states are reintegrated when he makes his patients talk, but at the cost of bringing back an overwhelming terror that could drive them to suicide. In his dream, he is experimenting on himself, as Head forced him to do, with the terror he tells his patients is not shameful, any more than the tenderness so prevalent between men fighting together. But, at the same time, his duty, after the epicritic stage of transference, is to have them sent back to the front line in France (R, p. 48).

Prior's psychoanalysis

Class struggle in analysis

The effect of Rivers' dream on his work with patients is immediate. Prior recovers his voice by screaming during the night: "Suddenly I realized I could talk." But Rivers' troubles are not over, since now his patient constantly questions him about himself. When the analyst tries to bring Prior back to his war memories, his patient replies: "All the questions from *you*, all the answers from *me*. Why can't it be both ways?"

His refusal to cooperate takes different forms: contempt for the analytic approach, to which he prefers hypnosis; contempt for the officers in the army – considered "one big family" – for the "WC" (working classes) (R, p. 52); and contempt for his father, about whom Rivers said, after having met him: "I liked him." "Oh yes," Prior agrees: "Outside the house. [Inside] I've seen him use my mother as a football" (R, p. 61). Rivers tells Prior that he is grateful to his father for having informed him that he has had asthma since childhood. He then examines Prior's lungs and cannot understand why he had not been found unfit for service.

The next night, Sassoon is woken up by screaming. Soon afterwards, he hears Rivers' and Prior's voices. As he goes back to bed, Prior is analysing transference: "I supposed most of them turn you into daddy, don't they? Well, I'm a bit too old to be sitting on *daddy's* knee. – Kicking him on the shins every time you meet him isn't generally considered more mature. – I see. A negative transference. Is that what you think we've got?" Rivers asks him where he learned all that: "I can *read*." The book beside his bed is entitled *The Todas*; Rivers wrote it after his second expedition to southern India in 1901 and 1902, two years after he participated in an expedition to the Torres Strait Islands, north of Australia, which revealed his vocation as an anthropologist.

Their conversation soon takes a more aggressive tone, when Prior launches into a harangue on class discrimination. He is enraged by snobbery in the military. Rivers is unable to bring Prior back to the nightmare that propelled him out of bed, leaving him crouching on the floor, as if he was trying to get through the wall – like Rivers had found him (R, p. 67).

Prior's hostility increases. He asks if he can smoke, and when Rivers refers to his asthma, he replies in a mocking tone: "Do you know how long an average officer lasts in France? – Yes, three months. You're not in France." Rivers has now read Prior's file and continues to question him about the nine days he refuses to talk about: "Do you remember the attack?" To his surprise, Prior gives in: "All right." The debriefing begins, and stops at the question: "What did you *feel?* [...] you're describing this attack as if it were a – a slightly ridiculous event [...] but you'd have to be *inhuman* to be as detached as that." "All right," Prior said with a smile: "It felt ... *sexy*" (R, p. 79).

Rivers tells himself that if he were to undergo the same questioning, he would have a similar reaction. After this implicit recognition, the unspeakable is about to emerge, from the shell-hole where Prior lost consciousness. But he pulls back and tells Rivers: "You always want to win." Rivers protests: "I had been [...] assuming we were on the same side," but in vain (R, p. 80). The class struggle gets the upper hand:

> Officers' dreams tend to be more elaborate. The men's dreams are much more a matter of simple wish fulfilment. [...] I suppose officers [have] a more complex mental life. – You honestly believe that that *gaggle* of noodle-brained half-wits [...] has a complex mental life? Oh, *Rivers*! – What you tend to get in officers is stammering [...] not just muteness. – It's even more interesting that you stammer.

Rivers is taken aback, and ventures: "It may even be genetic." But Prior suggests: "You might sit down and work out what it is you've spent fifty years trying not to say" (R, p. 97).

Regeneration of otherness

Late that night, Prior knocks on his door to apologise, and asks Rivers to hypnotise him. Rivers agrees. Under hypnosis, Prior is in a dugout; he has first trench watch, at dawn, and goes past two buddies making tea and grilling bacon. Then he hears a shell, a cry, and comes running back to see a conical black hole and nothing else – no kettle, no frying pan, no sign of the two men. He and another man shovel into a bag the mud mixed with human remains. He vomits. When they have almost finished, he finds himself staring into an intensely blue eye that he is holding between his fingers. It's the eye of one of the two dead men. "What am I supposed to do with this?" he asks. The man who is shovelling with him takes hold of his wrist, making the eye fall into the bag. "After that, my face became numb and I couldn't speak" (R, p. 101).

When he comes out of the hypnosis, Prior continues to deny what he felt:
"It was *nothing*." Then he starts to cry and pummel Rivers on the chest
with his fists. The analyst takes this to be the closest Prior can come to
asking for physical contact. Prior's story continues with the "friendly fire"
in which more men are killed by the British in trenches, where compasses
don't work because of all the metal in the barbed wire.

The regeneration of otherness, after all others had disappeared, was not
achieved through conversation, but by fist blows, after which Prior
continues to check if the other is solid. He does not accept his own
breakdown: "Most people could break down," Rivers tells him, "if the
pressure were bad enough, I know I could. – Did the wallpaper speak?"
Prior asks him, adding, as he is leaving the room: "He has very blue eyes,
you know ... we used to call him the Hun." Once again, Rivers reflects that
his patients are not mentally ill; they constantly test their analysts with
"shrewd X-ray eyes," to see if they can trust them (R, p. 107).

Changing places: prerequisite to accessing trauma

Prior's analysis culminates in the second book, *The Eye in the Door*, when
he insists that his analyst analyse his own symptom. They are both in
London, where Rivers now works in a hospital of the Royal Flying Corps,
and Prior in the Intelligence Service of the Ministry of Munitions. Prior has
had "fugue states," seven to be precise; he knows exactly how long they
lasted, but not what he did during that time. The analyst is back to square
one, as always happens in such cases, when all the previous progress is
followed by backsliding to the zone of death, from which other elements
have to be brought back to be regenerated. For all its familiarity, this
impasse is hard to bear each time it happens. Prior speaks to Rivers "as if
he was talking to the village idiot," and Rivers tells himself that they have
gone back to the worst moments at Craiglockhart (E, p. 133).

Prior's antagonism is so great that Rivers strikes back: "I'm not here to be
liked. – For somebody who isn't here to be liked you have the most wonderful
manner," Prior replies. Rivers sweeps his hand across his eyes: "... most
therapists are interested in dissociated states and so they [...] encourage the
patient further down that path. And that's dangerous. – Is that why you do
this?" Prior asks, imitating his gesture. "... it's just a habit. – No [...]. You do it
when ... something touches a nerve. It is a way of hiding your feelings. You've
just said it yourself, the eyes are the one part you can't turn into wallpaper."

Disconcerted, Rivers thinks that the confrontation is unavoidable, and he
finally admits that he has no visual memory. As a result, he can focus more
easily on what a patient says. Prior dismisses this rationalisation and asks:
"Have you always been like this?" It is now Rivers' turn to decide: "All
right." He stands up and changes seats with Prior. Surprised by the actual
enactment of what, in fact, has been going on for some time, Prior asks:
"Isn't this against the rules? – I can't think of a single rule we're not already

breaking. [...] I'm going to show you how boring the job is," Rivers answers. "Go on," Prior prompts him in an empathetic tone, adopting the pose of his analyst, his hands crossed under his chin (E, p. 136). Rivers does not intend to reveal anything other than what he has already published. But Prior's quality of listening would abolish these limits. In the meantime, the history-taking begins.

"When I was five ..." Rivers describes their house in Brighton, and stops at the top floor, where, facing the stairs, he sees his father's priest's gown hanging. "... something happened to me [...] that was so terrible that I simply had to forget it." Having learned from the best, Prior proposes an interference with his own story: "You were raped. Or beaten." Rivers dismisses this interpretation, saying that things happen to children of that age which seem terrible to them, but would seem neither terrible nor important to adults. "And equally things happen to children which are genuinely terrible. And would be recognized as terrible by *anybody at any age*," Prior answers.

Transference has changed direction. Now it's Rivers' turn to ask: "How old were you? – Eleven." We naturally think of mutual analysis, tried by Ferenczi, who at the same period was serving as an army surgeon in a hospital in Hungary. In the exchange between Rivers and Prior, child sexual abuse is placed on the same plane as war trauma: "It was on the tip of Rivers' tongue to say that no doubt Prior had been 'raped' in a number of places."

For the first time, Prior talks about being raped by the parish parson, to whom his mother gave a shilling a week – which she couldn't afford – as tuition for his instruction. And he tries to joke: "He got paid in kind, that's all. [...] Don't look so shocked, Rivers. – I am shocked," Rivers answers. Prior cannot bear the condescension often hidden behind indignation, and reinstates equality between them by grasping Rivers' knee and asking:

> This terrible-in-big-black-inverted-commas thing that happened to you, what do *you* think it was? [...] How old were you when you started to stammer? – Fi-ive. – For god's *sake*. Whatever it was, you *blinded* yourself so you wouldn't have to go on seeing it. [...] And what do you feel? – Fear.

Prior applauded. Three loud claps.

After some hesitation, Rivers suggests the image of medieval maps in which unknown spaces are filled with monsters. A more astute analyst than Rivers in this instance, Prior asserts the existence of real monsters and of images that stand in their way – Aby Warburg's surviving images – like the dressing gown on the threshold of the unknown. And he concludes: "Do you know, Rivers, you're as neurotic as I am? And that's saying quite a lot" (E, p. 140).

The birth certificates of ghosts

Reflecting on this exhausting session, Rivers admits that Prior is a "formidable interrogator" who uncovered the doubtless traumatic origin of the loss of his visual memory. Prior made him face a deep division in himself that had oriented his research with Head (E, p. 142).

A nightmare confirms this interpretation: Head is performing an autopsy, but something is wrong. Rivers tries to say: "No, he is alive." Head doesn't hear him and continues. A hand grabs his wrist, and the cadaver stands up, displaying all his hideous nudity. So, Head, the kindest of men, who had a gift for involving his patients in the study of their own conditions, could also set his empathy aside and work in a completely dissociated state.

Prior has in fact told Rivers: "Your case interests me." He has read his analyst's writings, and makes use of his geographic metaphor of unmapped zones where the subject disappears in the presence of real monsters. He now acts as the principal investigator of their co-research, and makes use of Rivers' own method by asking what happened just before, and holding up the mirror of his own story when there are no more images.

The child Prior was comes to the aid of the child Rivers was. But unlike Rivers, who blocked out all visual images, as a child, Prior lost himself in the yellow glow of a barometer on the wall, when the atmosphere in his home was too frightening. This yellow light attracts him again as he drinks a glass of beer in a pub, after reading in *The Times* about the death of a friend on the front line. He would have liked, just then, for a tank to come through the door and crush all these "prosperous-looking men" with their contented smiles, as it crushed the wounded at the Front who could not get out of the way in time. Then he dissociates for three hours, absorbed in the yellow light: "He had about twenty minutes left, the rest was blank" (E, p. 122).

Prior arrives at his next session speaking of himself in the third person, and ends up announcing, in the first person: "I was born in the Flanders clay two years ago, in a shell-hole in France. I have no father." Then he describes, in the third person, a violent scene between his parents, in which he tried to intervene and was thrown against a wall. After that, he started staring at the barometer and blotting everything away: "He wasn't there." To prove it, he burns his hand with a cigar, remaining totally impassive. Rivers tells him: "And now you have taken your little blue-eyed boy back." Prior had a dazed, faraway look, like that of a drug addict. Abruptly, his features convulsed with pain. Rivers dresses his wound, gives him brandy as an anaesthetic, makes up a bed for him in the hospital, calls him Billy, and says, leaving the room: "... and don't get depressed. We've made a lot of progress" (E, p. 242).

Instead of observing the foreclosure of the name of the father, Rivers is for Prior, and Prior for him, a warrior double – the *Iliad*'s definition of the *therapon*: second in combat and ritual double, charged with funeral rites. For the first time, Prior dissociated in the session, bringing back the child lost in the yellow glow, to regenerate him, literally, by having him be born in the shell-hole, with his dead buddies, and with the analyst as a reliable witness.

Another dream Rivers has the following night gives shape to the transference. While turning restlessly in his bed, thinking that he is dreaming the dreams of his patients rather than his own, he sees himself in a dreadful place where nothing human could live, and he is completely alone. Then he sees the mud begin to move, to gather itself together: "It rises and stands before him in the shape of a man who turns and starts walking towards England." Rivers tries to call him, but "the mud takes the shape of a man again, and then of many more men, until the night is filled with creatures made of Flanders mud, moving their grotesque limbs in the direction of home" (E, p. 244).

Time is set in motion

Prior had been able to create a persistent psychic state free of fear and pain, inaccessible to normal consciousness. Still, he and Rivers brought back from the Flanders clay those who had disappeared there, and took them home. The next morning at breakfast, Rivers decides to have Prior revisit the landing at the top of the stairs in the house where the barometer had been.

> ... when you were quite small you discovered a way of dealing with a very unpleasant situation [...]. And then in France, under that *intolerable* pressure, you rediscovered it. All I'm suggesting is that you rediscovered a method of coping that served you well as a child. [...] I think there has to be a moment of ... recognition. Acceptance. There has to be a moment when you look in the mirror and say, yes, this too is myself.

Traumatic memory gives way to memory that forgets, and can therefore remember, as Wilfred Bion would say.[14] Childhood memories come flooding back to Prior, who feels "like a sort of lifelong hopeless neurotic," like he'll never be able to do anything. Instead of invoking the Oedipus complex of the little boy who defended his mother against the father, Rivers, who is in touch with the child's helplessness – now cut out – gives Prior hope: "I shouldn't worry about that. Half the world's work's done by hopeless neurotics." Without prolonging the anamnesis, he testifies to a similar experience, in his own life, and offers him an initial mirror for a situation when time stops. Prior starts to feel more consolidated and he offers to type Rivers' texts, telling him that he writes like he stammers (E, p. 256).

The only thing that actually matters to him now is "new loyalties," formed in the Picard clay, which swallows up the living but creates new ties to which civilians and their good conscience have no access. Prior agrees:

> none of them is the same person he was before the war, the person his family still remembers. If you asked those who fought in France if they were the same when they came back, *all of them* would say no.
>
> (E, p. 255)

Rivers has created a new loyalty to his patients and to their ghosts, who may come home now. Contrary to Lacan – not much younger than they were – who could not bear the fact that he hadn't recognised his father when he returned from the Front (twelve years later, Lacan turned to psychiatry, introducing a new diagnosis: "self-punishment paranoia"), and who stopped practising psychoanalysis during World War II – Rivers and other analysts of psychosis and trauma created new ties of loyalty with people who had abandoned all hope. One of these analysts was Françoise Dolto (1908–1988), who had been a child during World War I. Seven years younger than Lacan, she was 6 years old at the onset of the war and wrote letters to her beloved godfather who was on the front line. When he was killed in 1915, she declared she was a "widow," like the women around her, who were mad with grief after the loss of a son or of a husband. She became a child analyst, and during World War II worked with children such as Leon, a Jewish boy.[15] All day long he was attached to a chair, in his parents' clandestine tailor shop, so that they could go on working. He was unable to stand on his feet, until Dolto spoke to the chair, which had become part of his self. The family escaped deportation. Like Rivers, in desperate situations Dolto made use of the dissociation she experienced as a child during the previous war.

In the transference, what takes place is the encounter of two dissociations. At this unpredictable point of coincidence, the meeting of two disconnections, which Rivers calls "suppressions"[16] – distinct from "repression" – there is likely to be a connection in the arrested time where patients wait for us.

First electric shocks

The other method, very widespread today, consists of deepening dissociation by mechanical means, using electric shocks, administered under anaesthesia nowadays. In Rivers' era, this procedure was known as faradisation. Pat Barker illustrates its use at the end of *Regeneration*, through the portrayal of the famous psychiatrist Lewis Yealland, who claimed that shell-shocked men were degenerates (R, p. 115). Today, it is more polite to speak of "genetic defects."

Rivers accepts Yealland's invitation to visit him at the National Hospital in London, and makes the morning rounds with him and two young doctors. Their attitude is cheerful; they are not interested in the patients' psychological state and they ask no questions, since the only thing that matters is rapid suppression of the symptoms, which are supposed to disappear within a week. The learned party stops before a man who has become catatonic after a shell exploded next to him, burying him up to his neck. Since then, he has remained in the same position, unable to lie in his bed, his torso leaning forward, his head twisted to his side, seeing lights dance before his eyes, although he suffered no physical wounds. Yealland informs him, "in an almost god-like tone," that he will receive an electric treatment that afternoon, and warns: "The electricity may be strong, but it will be the means of restoring your lost powers. – Will it hurt?" asks the young man, seized with a fear Rivers remembers only too well. Yealland dismisses it with an impatient gesture: "I am sure you understand the principals of the treatment [...] questions, never" (R, p. 225).

The last bed is occupied by Callan. He has become mute, like Prior had been, and is "very negative," according to Yealland, who recites the names of the places where he was stationed: "Mons, the Marne, Aisne, Ypres [...] Neuve-Chapelle, Loos, Armantières, the Somme and Arras." He broke down while feeding the horses, remained unconscious for five hours, and came round shaking all over and unable to speak. Very strong electric current had been applied to his neck and throat, and lighted cigarettes to his tongue. "I'm sorry?" Rivers protested. "What was that?" Callan smiled. Yealland admonished him: "I understand your [indifference] and it makes no difference to me [...]. You must recover your speech at once." He asks Rivers if he has time to witness a treatment, on condition that he shows no reaction: "The last thing these patients need is a sympathetic audience" (R. p. 228).

The treatment room is in darkness, except for a small circle of light around the battery. Yealland locks the door and puts the key in his pocket: "you will not leave me until you are talking [...]. Remember you must behave as the hero I expect you to be." He straps him in the chair. After an hour of weak current, Callan managed to say: "Ah." Yealland encourages him: "Do you realize that there is already improvement?" The electrode is applied again, and Yealland asks Callan to repeat the sound of the letters of the alphabet after him. Callan is falling asleep after a half hour of only saying: "Ah." Yealland brings him out of the chair and forces him to walk up and down in the room, repeating the letters endlessly. Callan runs to the door. "You do not understand your condition as I do," says Yealland, whose desire to strike is obvious to Rivers, as is the patient's submission. He is strapped in again and told: "You must speak, but I shall not listen to anything you have to say."

Once he is back home, Rivers realises that he is sick. During the night, he has a nightmare in which a man is tortured by having a horse's bit forced into his mouth – like the slaves in the novel *Beloved*[17] – the horse might have been the one Callan was feeding when he collapsed. He screams. This dream is certainly not wish fulfilment of a sexual nature: it depicts oral rape. The next day, Rivers stutters when he sees Yealland again. Of course, he remembers that Prior's silence had exasperated him, but the pain he had inflicted was not in any way equivalent. That treatment aimed at controlling patients engaged in self-destructive behaviour. In fact, Callan later committed suicide. The first part of Rivers' nightmare reiterated Sassoon's Declaration (R, p. 258).

Sassoon's psychoanalysis continued

Visions

What would have happened if Sassoon had been given faradisation? In a meeting with another doctor who is sceptical about his method, Rivers declares: "I am not going to give him electric shocks, or subcutaneous injections either. I'm simply asking him to defend his position" (R, p. 175). Sassoon continues to write poetry. There is another poet at Craiglockhart, young Wilfred Owens, Dr Brock's patient. He also stutters when he asks his idol for an autograph for his mother. Sassoon alludes to his own mother, devastated by the death of his brother, killed at Gallipoli in 1915. We also learn that Siegfried's father died when the boy was 5, after having gone away two years earlier. Siegfried tells Owen that he owes his first name to his mother's love of Wagner, adding in jest that fortunately he was not a girl, for he might have been named Brünehilde.

Sassoon's conversations with Rivers go beyond the former's intentions, when he hears himself describing a strange impression: "Sometimes when you're alone, in the trenches, I mean, at night you get the sense of something ancient. As if the trenches had always been there." Outside of time, he perceives that the skulls around him are those of Marlborough's men:

> as if all other wars had somehow ... distilled themselves into this war. [...] It's like a very deep voice saying: "Run along, little man. Be thankful if you survive." [...] A hundred years from now, they'll still be ploughing up skulls. And I seemed to be in that time and looking back. I think I saw our ghosts.
>
> (R, p. 84)

Speak of a Memoir of the Future![18]

Pat Barker has read *Tristram Shandy*.[19] Her Captain Rivers resembles Captain Shandy, who served under General Marlborough. In her *Trilogy*, Rivers even repeats Toby Shandy's famous gesture of setting a fly free by letting it fly out a window, telling it: "Go poor devil, get thee gone, why should I hurt thee? – This world surely is wide enough to hold both thee and me." Toby Shandy was to be reincarnated in Captain Bion in *A Memoir of the Future*, written fifty years after he had fought in the same places[20] – like Françoise's grandfather, a stretcher-bearer – in the Vosges, at Verdun, in the Arras mud and on the Chemin des Dames ridge. He would whistle "The Sombre and Meuse Regiment," evoking the confluence of the rivers where Uncle Toby, in *Tristram Shandy*, "had the honour to receive his wound."

Sassoon sees in Owen a junior officer, like Bion and Wittgenstein had been, and like all the patients in Pat Barker's novel are. Sassoon asks the young poet what he is writing. Owen admits that he is not writing about the ugliness of war. Sassoon takes him to task, telling him that he has to face the facts, and offers to publish him in the hospital's literary magazine. "You've got to sweat your guts out. [...] You don't wait till you *feel* like doing it" (R, p. 125).

Not long before, Sassoon himself had had to face the death of a buddy: "Gordon's death had woken him up [...]. That moment when he'd [...] glanced at the casualty list and seen Gordon's name had been a turning point ..." The ghosts he glimpsed from the future are coming home. The scene takes place in Owen's room, where Sassoon is helping him rework one of his poems. The young poet has made progress sweating his guts out; he no longer stutters. The wind has risen. Sassoon looks up: "What's that noise?" Owen hasn't heard anything. "Must be imagining things," Sassoon says, adding at once: "They don't *wail*. They hiss. [...] I hear hissing" (R, p. 142).

The next night, he hears tapping: "On such a night it was impossible not to think of the battalion." Memories of his last weeks in France resurface in a flood: "He saw his platoon again, and ran through their names [...]. Many of them were almost incapable of lifting their equipment [...]." He sees himself "pushing two of them in front of him [...] [kneeling] to inspect their raw and blistered feet." Of this little band, how many were still alive? The windows rattle; he thinks he hears tapping. Rats? How is it that he can't sleep here, where he is safe, when in France he slept anywhere?

When he wakes, Orme is there, standing just inside the door, wearing his beige coat, not the colour of the British army uniform: "After a while he remembered that Orme was dead, which did not seem to trouble him as he stood quietly on the threshold." But it troubled Sassoon. After a moment, he turned towards the window, then looked back at the door. Orme was gone: "I need to talk to Rivers." The next morning, Rivers was not there. Sassoon looked in the mirror and saw the face of a small child, himself around 5 years old. A day of shouting and slammed doors. The day his father died? Or rather the day he left home: "Sassoon smiled, amused at the link he'd discovered [...]. Rivers had [...] come to take his father's place. [...] After all, if it came to substitute fathers, he might do a lot worse," he thought, beginning to shave (R, p. 144).

A story of spirits in Melanesia

Rivers had been to London, where Head had offered him a position in an Air Force hospital. When he returned to Craiglockhart, he met Sassoon, who downplayed his visions: "Oh, it was nothing. I just ... saw something I couldn't possibly have seen." Rivers can see that he is afraid of ridicule for being irrational, so he goes first: "I did once see ... well, not see ... hear something I couldn't explain." And he recounts an episode from his stay in the Solomon Islands (first in 1907–1908 and then in 1914). Somebody had died, and spirits came in canoes to carry away his soul. The whole village was gathered together, sitting in silence. Suddenly, the house was filled with whistling sounds, heard by everyone: "I could see all the faces. Nobody was making those sounds. [...] That doesn't mean that there *isn't* a rational explanation. Only I don't think [it] fits all the facts" (R, p. 188).

Now that his analyst had created this context, Sassoon was able to tell his story in detail: "What happened to me started with a noise," up to the moment when Orme appeared, then vanished: "Nice lad. Died six months ago." Rivers asks him to be specific: "The same man?" Sassoon ventures to go further:

> No. Various people. – What do you feel when you see them? – I don't feel anything – You're not frightened? – No. That's why I said they weren't nightmares. – Afterwards? – Guilt. – Do they look reproachful? – No. They just look puzzled. They can't understand why I'm here.

After a pause: "I wrote about this. I'm sorry. I know you hate this." Rivers takes the sheet of paper: "I don't hate it. I just feel inadequate." He reads the poem:

> When I'm asleep, dreaming and drowsed and warm,
> They come, the homeless ones, the noiseless dead.
> While the dim charging breakers of the storm
> Rumble and drone and bellow overhead,
> Out of the gloom they gather about my bed.
> They whisper to my heart; their thoughts are mine.
> "Why are you here with all your watches ended?"
> "From Ypres to Frise we sought you in the line."
> In bitter safety I awake, unfriended;
> And while the dawn begins with slashing rain
> I think of the Battalion in the mud.
> "When are you going back to them again?"
> "Are they not still your brothers through our blood?"

This last verse echoes Sterne's question when he took a stand against slavery, while Voltaire was investing in the slave trade: "Am I not a brother and a man?" The phrase was adopted by the abolitionists at the end of the eighteenth century, etched on Wedgwood medallions, and distributed widely.[21]

"Don't feel you have to say something." Sassoon's courtesy turns out to be superfluous. Rivers is not capable of saying a word, since he is choked up with tears. The poet doesn't know what to do. "Does the question have an answer?" his analyst finally asks, wiping his eyes. "Oh, yes. I'm going back."

They would resume their meetings in the next book, after Sassoon is repatriated to London, with a head injury. Prior returns to the Front as well. Yet neither he nor Sassoon like war, any more than Rivers does. But there is something stronger than pacifism. What is it? To help the reader understand it, Pat Barker describes the political and social context in

England, at a time when what dominates the news is the prosecution of conscientious objectors and homosexuals.

Social movements

In *The Eye in the Door,* the second book of the *Trilogy,* Billy Prior makes use of his official status at the Munitions Ministry to return home, near Manchester, and visit a woman in prison. She was falsely accused of having intended to poison Lloyd George. He knows her well – this generous neighbour who owned a grocery store and took care of him while his father brutalised his mother and cheated on her, buying his son's silence with sweets, which he regularly threw up. Prior wants her to speak to him, so that he can obtain a retrial for her. She intends to say that she had bought curare to paralyse dogs and free conscientious objectors, including her son, Prior's childhood friend, held in another unheated cell, naked, with his uniform lying beside him.

"The eye in the door," which looks through the peephole of the cell, is the eye Prior wants to pierce with his "I." The drama is Cornelian. Rivers understands that Prior's fugue states are more frequent now, taking him down another road than that of political and psychoanalytic clichés. Another "I" emerges in this situation: that of a plural body of survival, in an exchange of mutual care, both physical and psychological, including an intimate relation between the living and the dead, like the buddy whose eye he picked up in the trenches (E, Chapter 3).

By this yardstick, Freud's interpretation of repressed homosexuality in the army seems secondary, as does the prison cell holding Prior's childhood friend, a cell Prior describes to his mother, to her great shock, as being more comfortable than the mud, the cold and the smell of bodies in the trenches. While strikes were multiplying in the munitions factories in the North of England, Prior was witness, on the battlefield, to bullets rendered useless and cannons destroyed by their own shells. Both Prior and Sassoon, who is strongly supported by pacifists, find their words hollow in respect to the men left behind on the front line.

In the meantime, Rivers goes up in a plane with Dundas, a pilot who takes him on board to show him his symptoms. Rivers sits in the observer's seat and observes his own fear. Pilots are said to be less susceptible to war neurosis because they are kept active. This does not apply to the observer. Dundas strokes the plane's fuselage, smiling. Rivers tells himself that he is part of the experiment, and that a researcher's hypothesis is rarely confirmed by his gut. On this occasion, his gut does its best to confirm his hypothesis. When Dundas loses his sense of the horizontal, Rivers understands what is meant by gravity squashing your head into your body. Still, when the plane drops and the pilot seems to have trouble focusing on the instruments, he feels very calm, telling himself there are worse ways to die, yet shouts: "DOWN!" The landing is chaotic, but not worse than others he has known. On the tarmac, his legs are shaking. He is annoyed to be in such a state, minimises his fright; in short, does everything he tells his patients not to do (E, p. 65).

Another trial is making headlines in London: that of Noel Pemberton Billing, who is accusing homosexuals and Jews of demoralising the nation. He is acquitted. It is soon learned that a paranoid forger, Captain Harold Sherwood Spencer, had been circulating a Black Book with the names of 47,000 British citizens supposedly collaborating with German propaganda (E, p. 24). At the same time, a million young men had died in France. A justice system that acquits scoundrels destroys the link between the living and the dead.

Billy Prior picks up Charles Manning in Hyde Park, apparently in a quasi-fugue state, since he doesn't recognise him, although they work in the same Ministry. Prior plays the working-class bloke to seduce him, and after their sexual encounter he asks him where his leg wound comes from. The name "Passchendaele" jogs his memory. They were both treated by Rivers at Craiglockhart and are pursuing their therapy with him in London. Together, they attend a banned performance of *Salome*, which according to rumour is supposed to be shocking, but they remain unmoved, wondering if Oscar Wilde could have imagined that for some spectators, severed heads were not made of papier-mâché (E, p. 78).

Manning's psychoanalysis

A shell-hole speaks

Manning is hospitalised due to panic attacks triggered by the war, about which he refuses to speak, and by the fear of being denounced, because he is married. Seeing an opportunity to bring together his two fears, Rivers asks him if he is familiar with Freud's text on homosexual and sadistic drives, released during battle. "I am not a repressed homosexual," his patient objects. Rivers' objective is not to confront Manning with his sexuality, but to reveal suppression, precisely because it is not repression. He gives him the example of Sassoon, whom Manning knows well, who "contrives to be two totally different people at the Front: [...] a tremendously successful and *bloodthirsty* platoon commander, and yet [a poet who afterwards writes] another anti-war poem."

Rivers offers him the company of the poet, which he accepts; he then speaks in the first person plural:

> We *all* hate [the war]. [...] It's just a bloody awful job, and we get on and do it. I mean, you split enormous parts of yourself off, anyway. – Is that what you did? [...] You know we are going to have to talk about the war.

The occasion presents itself the next night. London is being bombarded. The target is Vauxhall Bridge. "Though we don't need to worry when they hit it. Only when they miss," Manning comments laconically, when he runs into Rivers during his night rounds. The nurse asked the doctor to tell Manning not to smoke on the ward where there are men who have been gassed. "Yes, of course," says Manning.

Through the window, they hear the soft murmur of a song soldiers sing in the trenches. It triggers the bit-by-bit recall of a terrible scene, finally addressed to another, a scene where a shell will speak. Manning is standing before the shell-hole like in a waking dream: "It's nothing very much actually [...]. Just a line of men marching along duckboards wearing gas masks and capes. Everything's sort of greenish-yellow [...]. The usual ... porridge. If a man slips off [...] he just sinks." Rivers gets right to the point: "If you had to pick out the worst thing, what would it be? – There's a hand coming out of the mud. It's holding the duckboard and ... nothing else. Everything else is underneath." A short silence. "Oh, and there's a voice. [...] – What does it say? – Where's Scudder? It's a nasty, *knowing* little voice: Where's Scudder? Where's Scudder? – Do you answer? – No point. It knows the answer."

Silence. Gunfire is heard in the distance. Rivers suggests that they go to his room so Manning can smoke. "There," he says, putting an ashtray at Manning's elbow: "One of the reasons I don't talk about it, apart from cowardice, is that it seems so futile. – Because it's impossible to make people understand? – When you go into the Salient, you really do say goodbye to everything" – the title of Robert Graves' future book: *Goodbye to All That*. Rivers goes on relentlessly: "You were going to tell me about Scudder. – Was I? Their eyes met. [...] – He was a man in my company. [...] He was hopeless. He knew he was. [...] he'd been treated for shell-shock the previous year. With electric shocks. I didn't know they did that. – Oh, yes, Rivers said. They do. [...] – The night after he had the treatment he didn't dream about mines. He dreamt he was back in the trenches having electric shock treatment."

Manning goes on:

> He couldn't switch off ... function like an automaton. He couldn't ... turn off the part of himself that minded. [...] I can see the same sort of thing happening to me. [...] Anyway, we moved forward. It was raining. And we were told to report to the *graveyard*. [...] there were corpses everywhere. The whole business of collecting and burying the dead had broken down. Scudder was fascinated by these people [who] were *really* dead, and the corpses by the road weren't. Any more than we were really alive.

The lady of thoughts

The narration goes on for a long while, until the day Scudder disappears. The men look for him everywhere, and finally find him. Then there's an attack. They advance between crater holes. And again: "Where's Scudder?" Has he deserted? This time, he is in a shell-hole, mired to his waist, then to his chest. The men form a chain, but they slide as well and are unable to pull him out:

> I have never seen anything like his face. And it went *on* and *on*. He was slipping away all the time, but *slowly, pleading* with us to do something. I knew what I had to do. I got the men lined up and told him we were going to try again, and while he was looking at the others I [...] fired. [...] I missed. And that was terrible, because then he knew what was happening. I fired again, and this time I didn't miss. We spent the rest of the night there, in that hole. It was very odd. You know, I don't think any of the men would have said: "You did the wrong thing. You should have let him die slowly." And yet nobody wanted to talk to me. They kept their distance.

"A long silence. 'His mother wrote to me [...]. To thank me. Apparently Scudder had written to her and told her I'd been kind to him.' Rivers said firmly, 'you were',"" validating his action, like an inscription on the muddy soil. And then there was Hines: "We staggered down the road giggling like a pair of schoolboys [...] when the shell got us. [...] I crawled across to him. And he look straight at me and said, 'I'm all right, mum.' And died."

One of my grandfathers, who had been gassed during the war, had seen, as he sat astride his horse, soldiers mowed down in a wheat field, calling out "mummy" with their last breath. One of Rivers' patients perceives him, in his transference with them, as a masculine mother. This feminine agency, found in the pockets of soldiers on the battlefield in the letters addressed to their mothers, their wives, their sweethearts, their wartime pen pals, plays more than a maternal role. Don Quixote called her Dulcinea, the "Lady of his thoughts," the only reference that remains and allows one to think when the law of the fathers has collapsed. She was given this name in the time of the troubadours, by warrior poets. She is the earth that protects you and buries you, writes Erich Maria Remarque, a German veteran of World War I, in *All Quiet on the Western Front*.[22]

Sassoon's psychoanalysis continued in London

A head injury

The Eye in the Door also lets in through the door the gaze of the gods whose disappearance Plutarch deplored when a cry was heard on the Aegean Sea: "The great god Pan is dead!" amidst weeping and lamentations from every corner.[23] Rabelais evokes the scene in *The Fourth Book*,[24] and José-Maria de Heredia in a verse of his *Trophées,* speaking of "the purple shroud where dead gods sleep,"[25] a scene of mourning that would be taken up again by Ernest Renan at the end of his *Prayer on the Acropolis*.[26] Lacan also observes that what we have put in the place of "the sphere of the gods we Christians have erased is what is at stake here, in the light of psychoanalysis."[27] But Rivers does not put anything in the place of the gods. He makes them act directly in the transference with his patients. Rivers had mentioned the gods in his last session with Sassoon at Craiglockhart, when Sassoon had spoken of his visions and of his desire to return to France, and he himself had mentioned his experience with spirits in Melanesia. Now, when he sees him in London, hospitalised with a head injury, the gods are still there.

Sitting by his bed, Rivers waits for Sassoon to wake up. When he does, he touches Rivers' sleeve. "He's making sure I'm real," Rivers thinks. Sassoon starts to talk at once. He is different, his speech is rapid, his eyes riveted on Rivers. He complains about all the pacifists that have visited him, filling the room with treats that he would like to send to his men: "I don't belong here. [...] the Germans on the Marne, five thousand prisoners taken and all you read in the papers is who's going to bed with whom [...]. thirty yards of sandbags, that's the war." Now he can see all of it – as Don Quixote saw from the top of a hill, through a herd of sheep:[28] "vast armies [...] *millions* of people, *millions, millions*." A circling movement of his arms: "And it's marvellous in a way, but it's terrible too. [...] you'd have to be Tolstoy."

"How's the head?" Rivers asks, wanting to hear what happened. "It's a scratch. [...] the timing was perfect. Did you see my poem in the *Nation*? 'I stood with the dead'. BANG! Oops! Sorry. Missed. – I'm glad it did. – I'm not." Rivers wonders if it was a suicidal gesture. He has seen Sassoon's file. He does not understand how it could have happened and asks him where he was hit on the head. Sassoon attempts to explain: "I was in No Man's Land. – No, I mean *under the helmet*. – I'd taken it off." An awkward pause. "We'd [...] re-established dominance. [...] I was so *happy*. [...] Oh, god, Rivers, you wouldn't *believe* how happy. And I stood up and took the helmet off, and I turned to look at the German lines." Rivers was furious: "... you wanted to get killed. – I've told you, I was happy." Rivers took a deep breath, "schooling himself to a display of professional gentleness." Sassoon tries to joke: "I must say, I thought the standard of British sniping was higher than this. – *British* sniping? – Yes, didn't they tell you? My own NCO. Mistook me for the German army." He thinks about the raid his men are going on today: "They're not your men now, Siegfried. [...] You've got to let go. – I can't."

When he comes back the same evening, after having dined with Head, Rivers finds Sassoon sweating profusely in his bed, and talking without stopping. The partition between the separate parts of himself is gone: the commander who loves his men but doesn't hesitate to send them to their deaths, and the anti-war poet whom the latter supplies with material. Sassoon is aware of all this:

You know, Rivers, it's no good encouraging people to know themselves and ... face up their emotions, because out there they're better off not having any. [...] [People] need to be trained *not to care* because if you don't [...]. It's too cruel.

Rivers doesn't argue, and thinks only of calming him. After three hours, when Sassoon has fallen into a deep sleep, Rivers starts to think about what he said. His dissociation can't be called pathological, since his experience as an officer confers moral authority to his Declaration.

Rivers falls asleep on the unoccupied bed in Sassoon's room; he dreams he is in Melanesia, on a crowded ship. He wakes up feeling nostalgic, and realises that he too is split between his Melanesian self and his frustration, when he was back in Cambridge, at being unable to integrate that part of himself in his scientific work. Sleeping in a room with another person re-establishes the contact with his Melanesian self. He is lulled to sleep by the rhythm of Sassoon's breathing. When he wakes up, he finds Sassoon kneeling by his bed, completely calm: "I seem to have talked an awful lot of rubbish last night." He touches Rivers' sleeve: "I don't know what I'd do without you."

Rivers' Melanesian "I"

And what would Rivers have done without the headhunters? His two expeditions took place in 1907–1908 and 1914, after the experiment conducted with Head. He came back from Melanesia transformed. Around the same time, art historian Aby Warburg had a similar experience. He travelled to the territory of Hopi and Pueblo Indians, to explore the "living archaeology" of the rites of Antiquity that surfaced again in Renaissance paintings. And later, during a period of psychic upheaval connected to the Great War, he used his research to cure his own madness. In Binswanger's clinic where he was a patient, he gave a one-hour lecture on Serpent Ritual among the Hopis, using this lecture for his own therapy.[29] He was helped in this by his disciple Fritz Saxl, who had just come back from combat. Rivers proceeds in the same way.

In the last chapter of *Regeneration*, a story he tells Head and his wife Ruth illustrates how he participates subjectively in the construction of kinship:

I don't know whether you've ever had the experience of having your life changed by a quite trivial incident. [...] It happened to me on that trip [in the Solomon Islands]. I was on the *Southern Cross* – That's the mission boat and there was a group of islanders there – recent converts. [...] and I thought I'd go through my usual routine, so I started asking questions. The first question was, what would you do with it if you earned or found a guinea? Would you share it, and if so who would you share it *with*? [...] to them it's a lot of money, and you can uncover all kinds of things about kinship structure and economic arrangements, and so on. Anyway at the end of this – we were all sitting cross-legged on the deck, miles from anywhere – they decided they'd turn the tables on me, and ask me the same questions: What would I do with a guinea?

(R, p. 241)

This question: "And you?" is regularly asked in the transference with madness and trauma. Prior asks it at Craiglockhart and Rivers does not dismiss it:

> I explained I was unmarried and that I wouldn't necessarily feel obliged to share it with anybody. They were *incredulous.* How could anybody live *like that?* And it was one of those situations [...] where one person starts laughing and everybody joins in and in the end the laughter just feeds off itself. [...] And suddenly I realized that *anything* I told them would have got the same response. I could've talked about sex, repression, guilt, fear – the whole sorry caboodle – and it would've got exactly the same response. They wouldn't have felt a twinge of disgust or disapproval [...] because it would all have been *too bizarre.* And I suddenly saw that their reactions to my society were neither more nor less valid than mine to theirs.

At that point, it's true, Rivers was in the same situation as these people, carried off their island by the British and drifting towards an unknown destination.

As it happens in this kind of critical session, the outcome is amazing for the analyst as well. Rivers bears witness to his own transformation:

> And do you know that was a moment of the most *amazing* freedom. [...] It was ... the *Great White God* de-throned, I suppose. Because we [...] quite unselfconsciously *assumed* we were the measure of all things. [...] And suddenly I saw not only that we weren't the measure of all things, but that *there was no measure.*

But nothing changed when he returned to England, where "*you* know you're walking around with a mask on, and you desperately want to take it off and you can't because everybody else thinks it's your face." He would recover this freedom in his interactions with his patients: "[They] have done for me what I couldn't do for myself." He smiles: "You see healing *does* go on, even if not in the expected direction" (R, p. 242).

World War I was the crucible of the psychodynamic psychoanalysis of madness and trauma; William Rivers was one of its pioneers, along with others who were "trained" by the war, such as Sándor Ferenczi, Thomas

Salmon, Harry Stack Sullivan, Frieda Fromm-Reichmann, Françoise Dolto and Wilfred Bion.

Katherine Rivers, "Alice in Hysterialand"

Prior's question: "What about you?" led Rivers to the unexpected exploration of his lack of visual images. His thinking differs from Freud's interpretation, presented in his analysis of Hoffman's tale "The Sandman," who tears out children's eyes: "This infantile fear is a frequent substitute for the fear of castration."[30] It may also reveal the analyst's blindness when he refuses to see the traumas affecting his lineage. In September 1897, when Freud abandoned his "Neurotica," his psychoanalysis of trauma, "so as not to incriminate the fathers, including his own," he blinded himself to a fact he had confessed to Fliess the previous February: the sexual abuse inflicted by their father on his younger brothers and sisters.[31]

The Ghost Road leads us down a path where children betrayed by their relatives are likened to young veterans betrayed by their command and by civilians when they come home. Betrayal by one's own people is Jonathan Shay's definition of trauma,[32] which holds the analyst accountable for his blind spots, transmitted along his lineage. This word, "lineage," usually designating peoples we no longer call primitive or savage, has been banished since the disastrous attempt of last century's totalitarian regimes to purify the line of descent and create a "new man." Nevertheless, Rivers contends that ancient peoples like headhunters have preserved funeral rites that were lacking for millions of the dead in civilised countries in World War I, and again in the next war.

He decides to visit his younger sisters Katherine and Ethel, who live in Ramsgate. The three of them, and their brother Charles, are the children of Reverend Henry Rivers, a minister specialised in the treatment of stuttering, a practice passed down to him by his father-in-law Thomas Hunt and his brother-in-law James Hunt. The latter had also founded the Anthropological Society of London, where his racist theories were well known. One of Reverend Rivers' famous patients was Charles Dogdson, better known as Lewis Carroll, who often stayed at their home. In *The Ghost Road*, Rivers' childhood memories and his expeditions to Melanesia are intertwined with the treatment of patients like Moffett, whose legs remain paralysed without any organic reason, and Wansbeck, whose olfactory hallucinations resist all treatment. In that context, he is ready to examine his own family history more closely.

His sister Katherine had been exceptionally beautiful; she "combined a childlike innocence with a child's sharpness of perception" and was a model for *Alice in Wonderland*.[33] Indeed, Charles Dogdson almost never stammered when he was talking with the girls or reading them his stories. Rivers wonders: "Was it because these were his words and he was determined to get them out?" One day, the writer confessed to their mother that he loved girls and hated boys. His phrase "boys are a mistake" haunted Rivers for a long time.

When he was over 50, a thought occurred to him: suppose that an "innocent young boy becomes aware that he is the object of an adult's abnormal affection. Put bluntly, the Rev. Charles [...] Dogdson can't keep his hands off him, but – thanks to that gentleman's formidable conscience nothing untoward occurs" (G, p. 90). Rivers pursues his train of thought:

> The years pass, puberty arrives [...]. In the adult life of that child no abnormality appears, except perhaps for a certain difficulty in integrating the sexual drive with the rest of the personality. – What do you mean "perhaps"? he asked himself.
>
> (G, p. 25)

Indeed, although "sometimes he understood Katherine's childhood better than his own," he began to find an answer to the questions the islanders had asked about him on the boat, while roaring with laughter. He thought especially about their loneliness: both his and Katherine's.

"Poor Kath, she's had little enough to smile about" since the time they called her the Cheshire Cat because of her wide grin as she "sat enthroned in Dogdson's lap," on so many occasions. Her vital essence drained by the writer's love, her life had been constricted into a smaller and smaller space, until she was confined to her bedroom, and then to her bed. In the meantime, her brother had gone around the world as a ship's doctor: Australia, India, the Solomon Islands, the New Hebrides. He had also lived in Germany. "Yet she was no more neurasthenic than he was himself. But he had found his nourishment out in the world, while she had fed on herself" (G, p. 91).

Moffett: a failed magic treatment

Rivers' patient Ian Moffett can't leave his bed any more either, since he suffers from "hysterical" paralysis for which there is no organic cause. He had collapsed at the first sound of a cannon. Could he have applied for dispensation? In his family, that was inconceivable. Rivers can't help thinking of his sister, "Alice in Hysterialand." After having tried everything with Moffett, except electric shock and injections, he suggests a therapy inspired by Njiru, his informer, witch doctor friend on the Solomon Islands: after a massage, he performed the concrete extraction of the illness, "literally drawn out of the body" (G, p. 49).

Rivers enacts a similar scenario by sketching on Moffett's legs the tops of stockings, which he rolls down each day by a few fingers, drawing the ink circle lower and lower, removing with it the veil of paralysis. His patient asks him ironically if he knows what century they are in. Although he himself is not convinced, Rivers uses the power of suggestion, and says with authority that the area freed from the stocking would recover normal sensation the next day. Moffett does not believe it, but it works.

At the same time, Major Telford, another patient who plays a role in the story, complains, after a riding accident, that his penis is missing. Nurses have amputated it and put it in a jar, like a pickle in brine. After a futile discussion, Rivers finally asks what part of his anatomy he urinates with: "M'cock, you stupid bugger, what do you pee out of?" Before slamming the door as he leaves, he asks Rivers to call him "Major," saying that of the two of them, he is the better doctor – which soon proves to be true (G, p. 55).

Now Moffett can walk again, and takes a few steps. Later that afternoon, the Major informs Rivers in a conspiratorial tone that someone has been locked in the bathroom for hours and keeps groaning. Rivers kicks in the door and finds his patient in the bathtub, his wrists slashed, a bottle of whisky by his side. "Dead, is he? The major asked cheerfully? – Dead drunk. I think he'll be all right." Indeed, Moffett recovers, but the mechanical suppression of his delusion has resulted in pushing him to suicide. The death of his legs protected him from actual death. At the same time, Rivers hears a metallic jangle that reminds him of the offerings of seashells in the skull cave where Njiru had taken him. Rivers realises that when he used Njiru's magic recipe, he left out the witch doctor's skills with ghosts, who would soon confront him as well.

Rivers' psychoanalysis

They manifest themselves the next weekend, when he is visiting his sisters in Ramsgate. The town had been bombarded heavily; many civilians, men, women and children, had been killed. Katherine's health had dramatically deteriorated. Ethel leaves William alone with Katherine, going off to have a few days' rest. The brother and sister remember each other's childhood. William recalls that once, on the river, Dogdson had tried to pin up Kath's skirts so she could paddle. But that time she had pushed him away: "Some intensity in his gaze? Some quality in his touch? Their mother had spoken sharply to her, but Dogdson had said, 'No, leave her alone'." Katherine regrets the loss of Dogdson's letters and drawings. That is when she mentions the painting of Uncle Will, at the top of the stairs.

Although he is ten years older than his sister, he doesn't remember the painting: "What was it of?" The painting marks the place where his visual memory stops. Proud to have a better memory than her older brother, Katherine describes the picture to him. It depicts the amputation of Uncle William's leg, while somebody waits nearby with a cauldron full of hot tar to cauterise the stump. Rivers can hardly believe his ears: "Are you sure?" Katherine assures him that he hated the painting (G, p. 92).

Memories came flooding back. As the eldest child, he had served as a guinea pig for their father's treatment of stammering, which in the young boy's case remained unsuccessful. Rivers has a vague sensation of being carried by his father to look at something. How strange that he finds it impossible to remember this painting, although he knows its subject very well. Their ancestor, named William Rivers like him, was the midshipman who shot the man who shot Lord Nelson on the *Victory*, at the Battle of Trafalgar, on October 21, 1805. According to family legend, the admiral's words had been: "Look after young Will Rivers for me." When he had been wounded himself, he had to have his leg amputated with no anaesthetic other than rum. Another family legend said that he had not once said a word or cried out.

Now Rivers remembered. His father had carried him to the top of the stairs to see this painting. It was the day when the boy had had his hair cut for the first time. At the barbershop, he had cried loudly, embarrassing his father, who finally slapped him on the leg, and later took him up the stairs to show him the painting. "He didn't cry," his father had said [...]. "He didn't make a sound." That is when his stammer began. Although the Napoleonic Wars meant nothing to a 5-year-old, he had perhaps concluded that this was what happened to you if your name was William Rivers. Indeed, as he had said to Prior, "children can be terrified by things which do not seem important to adults" (G, p. 95).

Trafalgar, mournful sea![34] which swallowed up all visual images. Yet his father was not at all a sadist. What had terrified the boy was not the blood, the knife or the hot tar, but that resolutely clenched mouth. Now, every day of his working life he told his clench-mouthed patients:

> Go on [...] cry. It's alright to grieve. Breakdown's nothing to be ashamed of [...]. But he also said: "... stop crying. Get up on your feet. Walk." He both distrusted that silence and endorsed it [...] being his father's son.
>
> (G. p. 96)

Here, discourses on castration lose their meaning. In the Battle of Trafalgar, in London and in Ramsgate, dispersed body fragments were not fantasies. The silence the child was being taught brings to mind the French poet Alfred de Vigny, author of *Military Servitude and Grandeur*, who ends his poem "The Death of the Wolf" by verses we used to learn by heart when we were children:

> To, groan, to cry, to seek for aid
> Is cowardice. With energy and strength
> Perform thy long and often heavy task.
> And walk [...] along
> The way where fate has placed thee [...].
> Then, after that [...], without complaint
> Suffer and die [...].[35]

All my relatives

The recollection of this episode in his life – a decisive flaw – makes Rivers aware of his patients' stoicism. Despite their symptoms, they keep their mouths clenched, not on repressed fantasies, but on real events glued to their retina, and thus rendered invisible. Rivers recovers such an event in his own life, after validating his sister's impression of something strange in Lewis Carrol's attitude towards her, which their mother had denied. In their happy family, a child's life was sacrificed to the work of the great man, as were the lives of the men lying on the battlefield, whose deaths Prior informs Rivers about in the letters he sends him from the Front.

The absence of cathartic rites, to purify the stain of deaths and abuses, awakens, for Rivers, the teaching he received from Njiru, his crippled informer, the son of a chief and, like himself, unmarried: "His abilities [as a healer] would have made him remarkable in any society." Njiru told Rivers about his suppositions and doubts when their ritual ways of dealing with death were labelled cruel by the civilised world, and he allowed him to attend their funeral rites (G, Chapter 10).

The body of a chief was propped up in a sitting position on the beach, in an enclosure of stones. Njiru has destroyed all his possessions except his axe. Now he prays: "Be not angry with us, be not resentful, do not punish us. Let them drink and eat [...]. Let the children eat, let the women eat, let the men eat." Then Njiru takes Rivers into a cave full of bats, where the new ghost will be brought, to be greeted by old ghosts. In the village, they would wait about eighteen days for the body to decay, in the midst of stench and flies, until the sound of a conch announced the return of the headhunters with a captive to be sacrificed. This time it was a child from a neighbouring island. This is when Rivers had heard the whistling sounds he told Sassoon about. After this, the skull of the dead man is brought to the skull house where Njiru takes Rivers. The anthropologist is relieved to see that the captive child is there alive, with the mortuary priest. After a prayer of purification, there is an abrupt transition to everyday life, although not quite like before, when the victim was sacrificed.

The destruction of the islanders' rites by civilising humanism has resulted in lethargy, loss of meaning, forgetting of lineages and, above all, a dramatic increase of infertility, as if they were dying of no longer waging the ritual war of headhunting. In their culture, knowledge is linked with power, measured by the number of spirits who are your allies. This was also what we heard medicine man Joe Eagle Elk say on the Rosebud Indian Reservation in South Dakota, where his tribe of Lakota warriors, the famous Sioux Indians, are confined. "All my relatives" was the ritual formula used during ceremonies; it linked the participants to the living, to spirits in nature and to the souls of the dead, including soldiers fallen in recent wars.[36] Rivers revives his Melanesian teachings to reconnect with "all his relatives" and appease the ghost that haunts Wansbeck.

Psychoanalysis of Wansbeck and Harrington

The stench Wansbeck has been hallucinating since killing a German prisoner with a bayonet is gone, only to be replaced by an apparition standing by his bed every night. Rivers asks him if he believes in life after death: "Not since I saw the unburied corpses swarming with flies on No Man's Land, the smell ..." Rivers remembers the ritual words spoken by Njiru, as well as the flies and the smell. He asks Wansbeck what he thinks is happening to him. Wansbeck rationalises, saying: "A projection of my own mind. – Of your guilt? – No, guilt's what I feel [...]. Guilt as objective fact" (G, p. 226).

Like in ceremonial theatre all over the world, in Antiquity during the Middle Ages, or in Noh theatre today, the embodiment of psychic agencies by concrete characters makes it possible to address them, to feel and put into words that which cannot be said. Why couldn't the unspeakable forces that haunt us have the right to concrete existence as beings endowed with language?

Njiru would have agreed completely with this description of the spirit of Guilt. Rivers applies this animistic logic, asking Wansbeck:

> What language does it speak? [...] – English. Has to be. – So why don't you speak to it? – It's only there for a second. – You said it was end-less. – All right, it is an endless second. – You should be able to say a lot, then. – Tell it my life story? – It knows your life story. – All right, it's bloody mad, but I'll have a go.
>
> (G, p. 226)

In the "vision quest" among the Lakota people, the one who is searching for a vision is taken to the top of a hill and left there alone, naked under a star blanket. One of them told us: "When you see or hear something, you better not remain spellbound, but speak to it."

When Wansbeck leaves, Rivers remembers the severed heads, torsos and limbs that assailed Harrington at Craiglockhart. The face of a buddy blown up next to him, without lips, without a nose or eyelids, would lean over him and make him vomit and soil his bed. The interesting thing had not been the analysis of the nightmares themselves, but the fleshing out, night after night, of his buddy's face, while Harrington spoke to him of his life at the hospital and of his psychiatrist. After several weeks, he woke up with the memory of the hour after the explosion. He had crawled through artillery fire to pick up fragments of the body, and he had sent his buddy's mother the pieces of his gear that he had found. The fact that Rivers pointed out his loyalty to the friend killed in the explosion produced a great improvement, and culminated in him waking up one morning in tears, "crying not only for his own loss but also for his friend's, for the unlived years" (G, p. 229).

Matthew Hallet's death

By relaying the messages of his patients' ghosts, Rivers considers himself "a conduit," a pipe, at the risk of combining their stories into a single story, and blending their voices into a single cry of pain. A whispered cry came from young Hallet. In Prior's diary entry dated October 5, 1918, he recounts how he followed a gurgling sound that led him to Hallet in a shell-hole, with half his face blown away: "He's going to die anyway. I think I thought about killing him [...]. Bastards, bastards, bastards [...]. Die, can't you? For God's sake, man, just die. But he didn't" (G, p. 197). They had sailed to France together; it was Hallet's first time. And Prior had had a premonition: "Ghosts everywhere. Even the living were only ghosts in the making. [...] in trench time [...] a generation lasted six months, less than that on the Somme [...]. He was this boy's great-grandfather" (G, p. 46).

Hallet is taken to a hospital in London, where Rivers goes to see him, and speaks to his family, gathered around his bed and waiting: "Keep talking to him. He *does* recognize your voices and he can understand" (G, p. 265). They hear a heart-wrenching whisper: "Shotvarfet." Bending over his gargoyle face, Rivers thinks: "Why are you alive?" Njiru would have seen him as being dead already. His father asks: "Not long now, eh? – No, not long." On the night before he left Melanesia, Njiru had said: "And [...] now you will put it in your book." But the war had broken out, and he hadn't had time. Instead, he had put it all in his patients' therapy.

Hallet starts to cry louder and louder. His family tries to soothe him. Behind the screens shielding his bed, they hear chanting murmured by the patients in the common room, "each man lending the little strength he had to support Hallet in his struggle." And on the same November day in 1918, Prior and Owen die defending a bridge during a useless offensive. Rivers was finally able to make out Hallet's mumbling: "Sotwafet: It's not worth it," which he kept repeating. And then suddenly it was over. Rivers raised the sheet, arranged his arm by his sides and withdrew silently. On the edge of the canal, Owen and Prior's regiment, the Manchesters, lie, "eyes still open, limbs not yet decently arranged, for the stretcher-bearers have departed with the last of the wounded, and the dead are left alone" (G, p. 275).

At dawn, when he leaves the hospital exhausted, Rivers sees Njiru, who is dead, not as a ghost, but as he was in life, coming towards him to sing the words that tell ghosts to depart:

> There is an end of men, an end of chiefs, an end of chieftain's wives, an end of chief's children – then go down and depart. Do not yearn for us, the fingerless, the crippled, the broken. Go down and depart, oh, oh, oh.

Bent over Rivers, he stares into his face with his piercing eyes, then fades into the light of day (G, p. 276).

Man is a ceremonial animal

The end of the last book of the *Trilogy* is an ascending movement towards death, like Bach's *St John Passion*: "*Ruht Whol*, Rest in peace," endlessly repeated. Hallet's cry was taken up by the other soldiers, whose rhythmic chant supported him in his final struggle. Gregory Nagy tells us that in Homer's epic the *Iliad*, the name Achilleos is composed of *Achos*, meaning pain, and *Laos*, meaning the people armed for war. Nagy's book gave us the word *therapon*, taken from the *Iliad*, meaning the second in combat and the ritual double charged with funeral duties. Rivers personifies both these functions, and relays the murmur of his peers, *philoi*, singing an Elegy, which in ancient Greek means "Alas! Alas!" endlessly repeated.[37]

A place was created apart, where Oedipus wants to die, at Colonus: a sacred place, *chôro sieros*, holy ground removed from daily life where the collective and the singular are entwined. Oedipus enters this sphere and says that this is where he will stay.[38] This retreat is also sought by patients who must accomplish a nomination ritual, the "ceremony of the name," as Laurence Sterne calls it, not because they fear other people, but in order to be in a protected place. This enclosure, clearly demarcated in tragedy, delimits the nucleus of the political. When the social fabric starts to come apart, a place must be found for a second, symbolic death, where the social link can be recreated.

At the psychiatric hospital, we meet people who have been looking for this place for generations. When they encounter someone like Rivers, who has been taught the need for such a place by the headhunters, they know that they do not have to kill themselves to accomplish the sacrifice required on the brink of a new nomination. All that is needed is that their analyst sacrifices a part of his neutrality. Here, Freud tells us in *Moses and Monotheism* that the unconscious is neither that of repression nor a collective unconscious. Its dynamic is aimed at producing the subject of historical truth, where everything has been erased, like Pharaoh Akhenaton's civilisation.[39] This subject is not collective, but the subject of a plural body of survival, which is vital in catastrophic times and cannot be fitted into the opposition between normal and pathological.

Socrates, a veteran of the Peloponnesian War, tells us in *Phaedrus*:

> The greatest blessings come by way of madness, *dia manias*, that is heaven sent. [...] these trials, the most rigorous of all, carrying old resentments, *menis*, bred in certain lineages, *genos*, will lead the one with right delusions, *orthôs menenti*, to perform purification rites which deliver him of present ills.

To illustrate, American Indian rites called "potlatch" on the West Coast of the United States and "giveaway" ceremonies among American Indians of the plains are not quid pro quo arrangements. In catastrophic situations, we do not bargain with the gods, but carry out ceremonies addressed to them. Cathartic rites are meant to wash away stains; as for ceremonies, *telestai*, their name comes from *telos*, the goal, the accomplishment, not an obsessive routine: *telomai* means "I set myself in motion."[40]

Once the limits of this space have been set, the therapeutic and political stakes can be expressed, as Wansbeck says when he invokes the Guilt of England instead of dragging the smell of putrefaction everywhere. Harrington can tell Rivers about the gesture of piety he accomplished after his buddy was blown up, as a funeral rite. Psychoanalysis allowed these young men who had gone through the looking glass to perform a *Nekuia*, a visit to the dead such as that made by Ulysses to the Elysian Fields, where Achilles' shadow tells him: "Say not a word in death's favour; I would rather be a paid servant in a poor man's house and be above ground than king of kings among the dead."[41]

By listening to his patients, Rivers felt he had become a pipe through which "the hard-earned experience of a man for his self healing was made available to another."

This space produces time originating from the temporality of *aion*, the eternity of arrested time, provided that the analyst, like Rivers, testifies to experiences he has had himself. This artfulness – *ararisko*, the etymology of "art" – points to and articulates clearly what is not acceptable in the social link, or in classical science. When Erwin Schrödinger wrote the equations of the new paradigm for quantum mechanics in Arosa, Switzerland, he felt great joy, as if he were receiving "a gift from a fairy."[42] Rivers experiences extraordinary freedom when he leaves behind the dogmas of anthropology and mainstream psychoanalysis.

Ground zero of objectivity

This is my tribute to all the soldiers who might be forgotten. Not out of an obligation to remember, now that remembrance has become a slogan, but because of a particular transference with those who are called mad, with whom I speak about the *Trilogy*, celebrating its author, Pat Barker, who introduced me to Rivers. The transferences he describes, which Bion will call "psychotic transferences," come from confrontation with trauma, in the most brutal sense of "inexplicable blows."

When one recovers one's wits, it is clear that they have been scattered, and that gathering them together is not so easy. I will summarise that task in two stages.

The first stage of analysis consists of resisting negative forces by connecting the dispersed elements in a fictional narrative, which keeps trauma at bay for some time, in an attempt to conjure malediction. At the second stage, the analyst steps into the area of death. Rivers becomes aware that he has been changed by his field of enquiry, in anthropology and in therapy. Affected, as a first witness, by what he is shown, through resonance, he discovers that trauma speaks to trauma, and only to trauma, in an artistic adjustment, where things get stuck and crackle, as the poet Sassoon shows him when he fills his anti-war poems with his combat experience. This second stage generally unfolds in one or two critical sessions, for one does not linger in the sphere of the sacred. When the birds have made their omens in the celestial space drawn by the augur's wand, they can go on to peck in neighbouring fields.

In conclusion, I shall quote Wittgenstein, who was drafted into the Austrian army in the same war, and came back in a state similar to that of Rivers' patients. Indeed, although Lacan went so far as to call him psychotic,[43] in *Remarks on Frazer's Golden Bough* Wittgenstein provides a special perspective on Rivers' contribution to this seminar. His aphorism "One could almost say that man is a ceremonial animal" is based on his experience with ghosts: those of his three older brothers who committed suicide, and that of his English friend Pinsent, a pilot who crashed during the war. As Rivers knows, Wittgenstein states that "there is something in us which speaks in favour of those savages," and he goes on, contradicting Frazer's "objective approach": "Nothing shows our kinship with those savages better than the fact that Frazer has at hand a word as familiar to us as 'ghost' or 'shade' in order to describe the views of those people." The aim is "to make death die," and to do so: "Personification will, of course play a large role, for, as everyone knows, men (hence spirits) can become dangerous to mankind." As a result: "One could very easily invent primitive practices oneself, and it would be pure luck if [...] we did not happen to encounter [them] somewhere in the real world."[44] This is just what Rivers brought about.

William Rivers died in 1922, the year when Aby Warburg was shouting, in Binswanger's Bellevue clinic overlooking Lake Constance, that all the Jews would be assassinated. The "Long Week-End" between the two world wars had begun. But the madness would go on, with Hannah Arendt as a witness, as we will see in the next seminar.

Notes

1 Barker, P., *The Regeneration Trilogy*, Hamish Hamilton, 2014.
2 The three separate books of the *Trilogy* will be referred to as "R" for *Regeneration*, "E" for *The Eye in the Door* and "G" for *The Ghost Road*.
3 Tison, S. and Guillemain, H., *Du front à l'asile, 1914–1918*, Alma, 2013.
4 Faulkner, W., *Absalom, Absalom!* Random House, 1966.
5 Duroselle, J. B., *La grande guerre des francais, 1914–1918*, Perrin, 1994.
6 Audoin-Rouzeau, S. A, *Quelle histoire*, Gallimard, 2013.
7 Graves, R., *Good-Bye to All That*, Vintage, 1958.

8 Heller, J., *Catch-22*, Simon & Schuster, 1994.
9 Sassoon, S., *The War Poems*, Rupert Hart-Davis, 1983.
10 Biagini, A. and Motta, G. (Eds.), *The First World War: Analysis and Interpretation*, Vol. 2, Cambridge Scholars Publishing, 2015, p. 203.
11 Sheppard, B., *A War of Nerves: Soldiers and Psychiatrists in the Twentieth Century*, Cambridge University Press, 2001.
12 Sullivan, H. S, *Schizophrenia as a Human Process*, W. W. Norton & Company, 1962.
13 Benedetti, G., *Psychotherapy of Schizophrenia*, Jason Aronson, 1977.
14 See *infra*, Seminar 8 on Wilfred Bion.
15 Dolto, F., *L'Image inconsciente du corps*, Seuil, 1984, pp. 288–299.
16 Rivers, W. H., "The Repression of War Experience," *Lancet*, 2 (1918): 531–533.
17 See *infra*, Seminar 4 on Toni Morrison and Frieda Fromm-Reichmann.
18 Bion, W., *A Memoir of the Future*, Routledge, 1991.
19 Sterne, L., *The Life and Opinions of Tristram Shandy, Gentleman*, Alma Classics, 2017.
20 Bion, W., *A Memoir of the Future*, op. cit.
21 Ross, I. C., *Laurence Sterne: A Life*, Oxford University Press, 2001.
22 Remarque, E. M., *All Quiet on the Western Front*, Ballantine Books, 1987.
23 Plutarch, "On the Obsolescence of Oracles," in *Moralia*, Loeb Classical Library, 1936.
24 See *infra*, Seminar 12 on François Rabelais and Yvette Guilbert.
25 De Heredia, J.-M., *Sonnets from The Trophies*, HardPress Publishing, 2013.
26 Renan, E., *Prayer on the Acropolis*, Culture Edition, 1963.
27 Lacan, J., *The Seminars of Jacques Lacan: The Ethics of Psychoanalysis*, W. W. Norton & Company, 1997.
28 De Cervantes, M., *Don Quixote*, Canterbury Classics/Baker & Taylor, 2013.
29 Warburg, A., "A Lecture on Serpent Ritual," *Journal of the Warburg Institute*, 2 (1938–1939): 277–292.
30 Freud, S., *The Uncanny*, S.E. 17, Hogarth Press, pp. 217–252.
31 Masson, J. M., (Ed.), *The Complete Letters of Sigmund Freud to Wilhelm Fliess, 1887–1904*, Harvard University Press, 1985.
32 Shay, J., *Achilles in Vietnam*, Touchstone Books, 1995.
33 Carroll, L., *Alice in Wonderland*, Firefly Books, 2006.
34 Hugo, V., *Selected Poems of Victor Hugo: A Bilingual Edition*, University of Chicago Press, 2001; Blackmore, E. H. and A. M. (Trans.). "Waterloo," which starts: "Waterloo! Waterloo! Waterloo! Mournful Plain ..."
35 De Vigny, A., *Military Servitude and Grandeur*, University of California Libraries, 1919; "The Death of the Wolf," in *A Sheaf Gleaned in French Fields*, Dutt, T. (Ed.), C. Kegan Paul, 1880.
36 Mohatt, G. and Eagle Elk, J., *The Price of a Gift: A Lakota Healer's Story*, Nebraska University Press, 2000.
37 Nagy, G., *The Best of the Achaens*, Johns Hopkins University Press, 1979.
38 Sophocles, *Oedipus at Colonus*, Dover Publications, 1999.
39 Freud, S., *Moses and Monotheism*, Jones, K. (Trans.), Vintage Books, 1996.
40 Plato, *Phaedrus*, Focus Publishing/R. Pullins Co., 2003.
41 Homer, *The Odyssey*, Book XI, Classic Books Library, 2007.
42 Moome, W., *Schrödinger: Life and Thought*, Cambridge University Press, 1989.
43 Lacan, J., *Seminar of Jacques Lacan. Book XVII: The Other Side of Psychoanalysis*, W. W. Norton & Company, 2007.
44 Wittgenstein, L., "Remarks on Frazer's Golden Bough," in *Wittgenstein: Sources and Perspectives*, Luckhardt, C. G. (Ed.), Cornell University Press, 1978.

7 Seminar 7: 1999–2000
Hannah Arendt (1906–1975)

Reading madness with Hannah Arendt: the production of freedom

The subject of this seminar is not Hannah Arendt. I do not read Hannah Arendt through the prism of madness, but rather explore madness through the prism of Hannah Arendt's thought. *The Origins of Totalitarianism*[1] was conceived with Heinrich Blücher in New York during the war, published in 1948, and only twenty years later in France, as if, to quote Claude Lefort's title *Complications*,[2] translating her analysis would have been too complicated. Whereas, in fact, reading her work allowed me to come to the simple conclusion that madness *is* a resistance to totalitarianism on whatever scale.

Hannah Arendt and her second husband Heinrich Blücher, a former communist militant, experienced both forms of totalitarianism. In 1933, she went into exile in France with her first husband Gunther Anders, whom she later divorced. In 1940, she was sent to the Gurs internment camp with many German Jews, and escaped *in extremis* during the summer, before deportations began. In May 1941, she immigrated with Blücher to the United States, where she wrote *The Origins of Totalitarianism*, in American English with German syntax, since she continued to think in her mother tongue.

The connection between the psychoanalysis of madness and Arendt's analysis of totalitarianism

One point of entry into this discussion is our 1993–1994 seminar "Madness: A Social Pre-Science,"[3] which discussed Charlotte Beradt's book *The Third Reich of Dreams*,[4] published in the United States, and later in Munich, in German. In 1932, one year before Hitler came to power, this journalist undertook to keep a record of the dreams of those around her, harbingers of the terrible things to come.

The intensity of these dreams with their clear-cut contours, like traumatic dreams, testified to the fact proclaimed by Robert Ley, head of the German Labour Front and organiser of the Nazi Party: "The only person in Germany who still leads a private life is the person who sleeps." These dreams revealed a freedom prohibited by propaganda and by the police, among dreamers of various social origins. They show that which cannot be said and cannot be repressed but is recorded in a cut-out unconscious, after the destruction of all otherness – except a ruthless other for whom there is no other.

Despite the danger posed by the regime, Charlotte Beradt collected dreams secretly, calling Hitler "Uncle Henry" and the Nazi Party "the family." She hid 300 dreams in the books in her library, which she sent to the United States in 1938, before going into exile herself. In New York, she befriended Hannah Arendt and joined the small group of German immigrants who came together every week to talk, among other things, about the creation of the State of Israel.

Hannah Arendt encouraged Charlotte Beradt to publish her book in 1966, while she herself was in a difficult situation after the publication of *Eichmann in Jerusalem* in 1963. Her use of the expression "banality of evil" and the mention of the role played by Jewish Councils, *Judenrat*, in the deportations created a scandal. The controversy that followed led her to write a postscript to the 1964 edition, in which she defends her right to judge:

> The argument that we cannot judge if we were not present and involved ourselves seems to convince everyone everywhere, although it seems obvious that if it were true, neither the administration of justice nor the writing of history would ever be possible. In contrast to these confusions, the reproach of self-righteousness raised against those who do judge is age-old; but that does not make it any the more valid.[5]

In the same way, during an analysis of madness or trauma, the analyst must exercise judgement in the face of abuses most often trivialised, including his own at critical moments, instead of hiding behind "benevolent neutrality."

Our second meeting with Hannah Arendt's work takes place on the battlefield of wartime psychoanalysis. Hannah Arendt did not like psychoanalysis. But in this seminar, I will contend that her thinking was close to the psychoanalytic approach of Frieda Fromm-Reichmann (1889–1957).[6] Exiled like Arendt in the United States, she became an analyst of psychosis at Chestnut Lodge, after her experience with treating soldiers with head injuries during World War I in the military hospital of her hometown, Königsberg.

War traumas, as well as the abuse of women and children, raise the question of the collapse of the symbolic order, and make it necessary for psychoanalysis to change its paradigm. We discovered this new approach in 1980, at the clinic of the Austen Riggs Center, where we met analysts treating psychosis, such as Otto Will and Martin Cooperman, who had been veterans of Guadalcanal during World War II, and introduced us to Harry Stack Sullivan and Frieda Fromm-Reichmann.

In fact, this new paradigm was discovered during the previous war.[7] Still, we need Hannah Arendt's analysis to apply this approach to our work with patients who bring us situations marked by lies, secrets, betrayals and the crumbling of the given word. We are confronted with the impossible to say, to imagine and to inscribe, situations that Arendt does not cease to challenge by writing relentlessly. This paradigm, as old as war, is illustrated by the following two stories.

In Chapter 55 of Rabelais' Fourth Book,[8] published in the middle of the sixteenth century, telling the story of Pantagruel's voyage to the Oracle of the Holy Bottle to learn whether Panurge would be made a cuckold if he married, Pantagruel hears voices. The pilot informs them that a "great and bloody battle" took place on that site on the frozen sea the previous winter, during which the clamour of the war was frozen as well. Indeed, frozen, silenced words fall on the deck like sweets of various colours, which thaw when Pantagruel catches "them in his hands: the red ones crying out from sliced throats," and others coming from women, children, horses, even the sound of cannons. Henceforth, they all find an inscription in Rabelais' tale.

The need for an inscription of surviving images, voices and visions is also the theme of Masaki Kobayashi's film *Kwaidan*,[9] which takes place on the other side of the globe, on the site of the Battle of Dan-no-ura in the twelfth century, during which the Minamoto clan was defeated by its rival clan, the Taira. Here, frozen words are warmed in the mouth of a blind monk who plays the biwa in a convent nearby. One night, a ghostly samurai hijacks him to sing before the phantom court that had sunk into the sea in front of the convent. Haunted by these ghosts, he languishes during the day, until the abbot makes him confess what has been happening, and covers his body with inscriptions, forgetting his ears. This renders the rest of him invisible, but the next night the sight of his ears infuriates the samurai, who tears them off. Now blind and deaf, he continues to sing his epic poem, enhancing the fame of the convent. Like in an analysis of trauma, terrible words from a timeless time are called upon to make themselves heard and be inscribed in memory. Such words can only be transmitted using special instruments in a specific transference.

Hannah Arendt's writing unfreezes the "ice-cold reasoning" of ideologies and the terror felt by men "squeezed together violently," when the social link is completely destroyed. With great foresight, at the end of *Totalitarianism*, she speaks of "an ever-present danger." I suggest that we call totalitarian "the death zones" – an expression coined by Benedetti[10] – explored in transference by our patients' folly.

Madness explores totalitarian zones trivialised by psychoanalysis

Of course, as Hannah Arendt stresses, totalitarian regimes are an invention of the twentieth century, while madness has existed since the beginning of time, long before Nazi and Stalinist regimes assassinated the mad, "in a temporary alliance between the elite and the mob." But she adds that "in this present calamity, the seeds of freedom" continue to exist in madness since one must be mad not to follow the movement, especially when it pro-claims its good intentions.

Arendt speaks of the seeds of freedom, not of "the limits of freedom," to which Lacan referred at the Bonneval conference, on September 28, 1946, published under the title "Comments on Psychic Causality" in *Écrits*:[11] "Not only can man's being not be understood without madness, but it would not be man's being if it did not bear madness within itself as the limit of his freedom." At this conference, organised by psychiatrist Henri Ey to condemn the organicist approach to psychosis, Lacan named as an advocate of brain supremacy neurologist Kurt Goldstein who, on the con-trary, had been greatly influenced by psychoanalysis, and had also been Frieda Fromm-Reichmann's teacher. He remained a model for her psycho-dynamic psychoanalysis of psychoses at Chestnut Lodge.[12]

Lacan's doctoral thesis, "Paranoid Psychosis and Its Relation to the Per-sonality," praised by Joë Bousquet, Léon-Paul Fargue and "dear" René Crevel, gives the impression that he was unaware of the psychoanalytic approaches to trauma and psychosis practised since the previous war, not only by Fromm-Reichmann, but also by Harry Stack Sullivan and Thomas Salmon in the United States, Sándor Ferenczi in Hungary and William Rivers in England, to name just a few. The war, during which Lacan stopped practising psychoanalysis, seems to offer him an excuse:

> For several years I have kept [...] from expressing myself. The humiliation of our time under the subjugation of the enemies of human kind dissuaded me from speaking up, and following Fontenelle, I abandoned myself to the fantasy of having my hand full of truths so as to better close it on them. I confess that it is a ridiculous fantasy, marking, as it does, the limitations of a being who is on the verge of bearing witness.[13]

After this brief allusion, the war is never mentioned again in his presenta-tion. Still, "the enemies of humankind" and "the limitations of their beings" did not dissuaded the analysts I mentioned – including Wilfred Bion, whom Lacan would visit after the war[14] – from opening their hands and warming up their patients' frozen words, bringing to bear their clinical practice in wartime. Eight years later, in his "Response to Jean Hyppolite's comments on Freud's text *Negation*," Lacan speaks of *Verwerfung*, the future "foreclosure," *retranchement* in French[15] – meaning "cutting out." In *Écrits*, the phrase "What does not come to light in the symbolic appears in the real"[16] applies to the case of the Wolf Man, whose analysis was inter-rupted on the day of the Sarajevo assassination in 1914.[17] When the young Russian patient came to see Freud again in 1919 to talk about his financial ruin during the 1917 revolution, his analyst sent him to some colleagues. Then the famous patient started to have delusions, raising the question of transference in psychosis, considered impossible until then.

But Freud did not keep his hand closed on that question. Twenty years later, he wrote *Moses and Monotheism*,[18] after his books were burned on May 10, 1933 in an auto-da-fé on the Opera Platz in Berlin, in front of the university, organised by Goebbels and the totalitarian regime that was to kill four of Freud's sisters in 1942. At the end of the book, he wrote: "We have long since understood that in every delusion there is a kernel of forgotten truth [...]. We have to admit such a context of 'historical truths'." This is the challenge he set for psychoanalysis before his death in 1939. Yet in 1954, in his "Response to Jean Hyppolite," Lacan still persisted in believing that "what is foreclosed to the subject, appears in the real erratically in relations of resistance without transference, or as a punctuation without text." For their part, Hannah Arendt had analysed the deliberate foreclosure of true speech by totalitarian agencies, and Frieda Fromm-Reichmann had stated long since, from her experience of totalitarianism, that "where there is no transference, everything is transference."[19]

The foreclosure of the name of the father, which Lacan pointed out during the case presentations we attended at Sainte-Anne Hospital, stands in sharp contrast with the analysis of the transference of "surviving images," ousted from the symbolic chain, and submitted to the analyst's "seismograph of the soul," as historian of Renaissance art Aby Warburg called it.

Aby Warburg went mad at the start of World War I; confined in Binswanger's clinic, he shouted that all the Jews would be assassinated. His prescience was rooted in knowledge stored in traumatic impressions recorded by the seismograph of his soul when, in the aftermath of the Franco-Prussian War of 1870, he had witnessed, as a child, the rise of "mass anti-Semitism" – which Hannah Arendt dates to that period – a threat to his family of Jewish bankers in Hamburg. During the war, his mother and himself had almost died of typhus; after France lost the war, the overflow of gold coming from French reparations had destabilised German banks and Jewish bankers were held responsible. The first Antisemitic League was created in Hamburg by the anarchist Victor Marr, when Aby was 13 years old. This is also when he made a pact with his younger brothers to relinquish the directorship of the bank against their promise to buy him all the books he wanted, for the rest of his life. Hence the famous library built by his brothers in Hamburg, according to his plans. The library became the Warburg Institute in London when the books were smuggled there in 1933, after his death. His delusional cries in the early 1920s were expressing the historical truth, which no one wanted to see.[20]

In *Moses and Monotheism*, Freud also refers to "surviving images," a phrase coined by Warburg: "The strongest obsessive influences derive from those [early] experiences, while the child's psychic apparatus is incompletely fitted for accepting them." Freud compares them to photographic negatives, which "can be developed after a short or long interval." In Aby Warburg's case, this interval lasted as long as the period between two wars, 1870 and 1914. Speaking of this phenomenon, Freud quoted E. T. A. Hoffmann, who "explained the wealth of imaginative figures in his stories by citing the quickly changing pictures and impressions he had received during a several weeks' journey in a coach, while he was still a babe at his mother's breast."

This pre-Oedipal analysis was familiar to the writers Freud advises us to read at the beginning of his *Gradiva*, since they "are valuable allies, *Bundes genossen.*"[21] Laurence Sterne in *Tristram Shandy*,[22] Bion in *A Memoire of the Future*[23] and Carlos Fuentes in *Christopher Unborn*[24] have all created prenatal characters – speaking gametes that Sterne calls "*Homunculus,*" and Bion "*Somites.*" Not only do they keep the score of intergenerational traumas, but they may bring about new beginnings. Hannah Arendt calls them by the Greek term *oi neoi*, "the new ones."

Christopher Unborn (*Cristobal Nonato*)

The model for Carlos Fuentes' book is clearly *Tristram Shandy*, which begins with the hero's first cry as an embryo: "I wish." He wishes that his parents "had minded what they were about when they begot me." Like Sterne, Fuentes starts off with this incredible "I," spoken by a character barely out of his father's testicles and his mother's egg. From this place, he raises the question of the radical novelty of a newborn, a central theme for Hannah Arendt, who had no children.

Conceived on a beach in Acapulco by his father Angel and his mother Angeles, Cristobal, – whose birth is planned to coincide with the anniversary of Christopher Columbus' arrival in the New World – would cling desperately to his mother's oviduct, during nine months of solitude, like the embryo of the future Tristram, terrified by the "long, long months" he would spend without holding, "in his way alone" – as Winnicott was to remember – an unaccompanied "little gentleman."

Following, like Sterne, in the footsteps of Cervantes in the author's preface to the second *Don Quixote*, and of Wittgenstein in the preface to his *Philosophical Investigations*, Carlos Fuentes speaks directly to the reader – *lector* in Spanish, whom he calls *elector*:

> It's time I reveal myself before you, Reader, and tell you I have already returned by way of *my genes*, which know all, remember all, and if, a bit later, I, like you, forget everything when I'm born and have to learn it all over again before I die, who would deny that in this instant of my gestation I know everything because I am here inside and you, Reader, are you out there?

> (p. 64)

The fertilised ovule asks his father: "But my grandparents, Dad, tell me about my grandparents" (p. 54). Angel is the son of the Mexican equivalent of Pierre and Marie Curie, "The Curies of Tlalpan." "They believed in science with all the love of novelty and all the fury of liberal, emancipated

Mexicans and rejected both inquisitorial shadows and the sanctimonious-ness of the past." Moved by the scientific and humanitarian desire to put an end to hunger in Mexico, they invented the Inconsumable Taco, made of a tortilla that could not be eaten by rodents. The two scientists fell victim to this invention, which ended up choking them, but in the meantime they had invented a mousetrap for the poor that needed no cheese. Instead, their idea was to slide a photograph of a piece of Roquefort in the mousetrap, which they placed in the basement. The next day they hurried downstairs to see what happened. The trap had worked: the photograph had disappeared, but in its place they found the photo of a mouse.

A make-believe universe

Cristobal's grandparents never intended to foster their procedure on the whole society by creating what Hannah Arendt calls a *fictitious* universe, founded on absolute faith in science – whether embodied by racial laws or by historical determinism. She insists on the absurdity of such beliefs held to varying degrees: from the "abnormal credulity" of companions who maintain "contact with the normal world in an atmosphere of honesty," to the cynicism of the party elite, constituting a "hierarchy of scorn" for the useful idiots.[25]

In the third part of *The Origins of Totalitarianism*, entitled "Totalitarian-ism," Hannah Arendt borrows many terms from the sphere of madness: concentration camps are "an experimental madness" she describes as "insane." For her, the word "madness" is not a metaphor, since metaphors do not function when the symbolic chain is broken. The camps are not "like" an experimental madness; life without freedom is not "like" life in a concentration camp. The expression "It's like" does not apply here. No other meaning is hidden behind the actual word.

Magritte pointed out that in his painting of a man wearing a bowler hat seen from behind, one must not try to imagine what the face is seeing. Behind the head, there is the canvas; thank goodness, since there might not have been anything. Beyond the illusions maintained by the hidden face of "secret societies established in broad daylight for the conquest of the world or for world revolution," Arendt says, "there is the void."

On the other hand, the analyst of madness and trauma provides a canvas on which images without reflection may begin to leave an imprint on the background of the analyst's story. Hannah Arendt's relentless writing, which springs from her own story, constitutes this backdrop on which she catches the productions of totalitarianism ruled by the principle of "everything is possible," which she differentiates from "everything is permitted" in imperi-alism, where a law exists and is broken. When everything is possible, "the delusion of omnipotence" gives "the most aberrant procedure a chance to succeed," and provides the certainty that "power of organization can des-troy power of substance."

Totalitarianism where everything is possible encounters the obstacle of madness as a technique and art of survival. For instance, it allows the prisoner incarcerated by the Argentinian junta to hallucinate in his cell that his friends are there to visit him, so that solitude does not drive him mad.[26] Regimes of terror know this well and kill the mad at once, whether their madness is real or feigned. Any unpredictability threatens their system.

Indeed, Folly is unpredictable with unforeseeable manic and depressive phases, or traumatic revivals that attempt to show what cannot be said. When the only answer is electric shock and medication, after some respite the result is a feeling of annihilation, of belonging to a subhuman species. According to Hannah Arendt, the destruction of symbolic bearings by totalitarian systems renders human beings "superfluous," mere material for the production of the new man. Individuals are reduced to a collection of compressed identities, $1 + 1 + 1 + 1$. Percentages and statistics prevail, without ancestors and with a falsified language, analysed by Victor Klemperer in his book *LTI: Lingua Tertii Imperii*, (*The Language of the Third Reich*).[27] Explanations for the world's unhappiness, bearing no relation to reality, uphold an atemporal system, limitless and without borders, like "communism in a single country" or *Lebensraum* on a planetary scale.

In such systems, psychoanalysis has no right to exist. Arendt shows the systematic "attacks on linking," as Bion calls them, carried out against the given word, and sworn faith in totalitarian systems that spread forgeries. When madness is reduced to genetic, statistical or structural categories that dismiss transference, how can a therapist reach the other side of an Iron Curtain where everything seems unreal, Arendt asks, but where folly waits for a second in combat with whom to fight perversion?

The analyst's commitment

When encountering madness, we conduct research in a sphere we describe as totalitarian, in search of another, a witness to an unimaginable world. Hannah Arendt is this witness. To explore this field of research, she cannot adopt objective detachment. When she conceives her book in 1943 with Blücher in New York, where they arrived stateless in 1941,[28] the Nazi and Stalinist camps are operating at full capacity. She is not content to give descriptions, but speaks as a subject, using the words of the philosophical and literary tradition, maintaining a tension between her analyses and the therapeutic process they prompt.

In the chapter on propaganda,[29] she describes a "psychological war" waged by means of subliminal images: "people are threatened by Stalinist propaganda with missing the train of history, with remaining hopelessly behind their time [...] just as they were threatened by the Nazis with living against the eternal laws of nature and life" (p. 349). The laws of historical determinism or racial purity spare no one: "Stalin prepared the physical liquidation of deviationists, representatives of 'dying classes'" (p. 73). Hitler exterminated Jews, Gypsies, homosexuals, the mad and the incurably ill (p. 74). A rhetoric of scientific prophecy "shapes the life of their people according to the verdicts of genetics," or economic forces that have the power of a verdict of history, promoting "gigantic lies and monstrous falsehoods as unquestioned facts" (p. 333).

Words are tantamount to actions. Aryan children are produced in the *Lebensborn* or kidnapped in great numbers among Polish blonde, blue-eyed tots (p. 68). The expression "the living dead" is the demented reality of "the mass production of corpses" in Nazi and Soviet concentration camps (p. 441). The term "experimental madness," which Arendt employs often, describes real experiments conducted by perverse imaginations, which defy all "common sense, whether of a psychological or sociological nature" (p. 441).

In these conditions, her therapeutic process is inspired by Karen Blixen's phrase: "All sorrows can be borne if you put them into a story or tell a story about them." Mary McCarthy said of her friend Hannah that she had the magnetism of an actress, but had learned to control her stage fright by placing herself in the service of History and of the stories she told. Arendt held storytellers in high regard and admired the formal perfection of their art.[30] She found this admirable talent in Danish author Karen Blixen, who used the pen name Isak Dinesen. Arendt met her in New York a short time before Blixen's death in 1963:

> She was very old, terribly fragile, magnificently dressed. She narrated, without any notes, passages from her book *Out of Africa*,[31] almost word for word. She seemed to be an apparition from some unknown time and place.

It was this grand Lady who provided Arendt with the phrase, quoted above, at the start of Chapter 5 of *The Human Condition*.[32]

When it is impossible to speak and to imagine, stories allow impossible things to enter the body of the storyteller sideways, through the action of storytelling. Creating fiction is radically opposed to falsification, on condition that one trusts one's own impressions.

The fearful imagination

> Only the fearful imagination of those who have been aroused by such reports but have not actually been smitten in their own flesh, of those who are consequently free from the bestial, desperate terror which, when confronted by real, present horror, inexorably paralyzes everything that is not mere reaction, can afford to keep thinking about horrors.
>
> (p. 441)

Hannah Arendt asserts this impression without letting it paralyse her judgement. She states: "The fearful imagination has the great advantage to dissolve the sophistic–dialectical interpretations of politics which are all based on the superstition that something good might result from evil."

Arendt is clear in her radical condemnation of any attempt to erase traces, a question that concerns the psychoanalysis of madness and trauma most particularly:

> Such dialectical acrobatics had at least a semblance of justification as long as the worst that man could inflict upon man was murder. But, as we know today, murder is only a limited evil. The murderer who kills a man leaves a corpse behind and does not pretend that his victim has never existed; if he wipes out any traces, they are those of his own identity, and not the memory and grief of the persons who loved his victim; he destroys a life, but he does not destroy the fact of existence itself.
>
> (p. 442)

The deliberate disappearance of the dead goes hand in hand with that of the living:

> The real horror of Nazi and Soviet concentration and extermination camps lies in the fact that the inmates, even if they happen to keep alive, are more effectively cut off from the world of the living than if they had died, because terror enforces oblivion. [...] David Rousset called his report on the period he spent in a German concentration camp *Les Jours de notre mort*, The Days of our Death.[33] [...] nobody is supposed to know if they are alive or dead.
>
> (p. 443)

Descartes' evil spirit is embodied in reality:

> The human masses sealed off in [the camps] are treated as if they no longer existed, as if what happened to them were no longer of any interest to anybody, as if they were already dead and some evil spirit gone mad were amusing himself by stopping them for a while between life and death [...]. It is the skilfully manufactured unreality of those whom it fences in, that makes extermination look like a perfectly normal measure.
>
> (p. 445)

The emergence of totalitarian systems in the twentieth century is "an unprecedented phenomenon" which she distinguishes from the tyrannies and imperialism that had existed previously:

There are no parallels to the life in the concentration camps. Its horror can never be fully embraced by the imagination for the very reason that it stands outside of life and death. It can never be fully reported for the very reason that the survivor returns to the world of the living, which makes it impossible for him to believe fully in his own past experiences. It is as though he had a story to tell of another planet.

(p. 444)

Except if the survivor encountered a witness to these "events without a witness," whom Dori Laub – co-founder with Steven Spielberg of the Fortunoff Video Archive for Holocaust Testimonies – calls a "passionate witness," who shakes off the fascination with horror and can hear, against all odds, stories that had remained impossible to tell until then.

The therapeutic art

The only text possible – from *textum* in Latin, from the verb *texere*, to weave – when there are no more words or images is to interweave a new weft in the warp of a text in the making. To create otherness where there is no inscription is the true objective of *The Origins of Totalitarianism*.

Part 1, "Antisemitism as an Outrage to Common Sense," opens Arendt's discussion on the "dubious honour" conferred upon the Jewish problem "of setting the whole infernal machine in motion." Given the actual events:

> all explanations of antisemitism [be it the scapegoat theory or the revival of Dark Ages superstitions], look as if they had been hastily and hazardously contrived, to cover up an issue which so gravely threatens our sense of proportion and our hope for sanity.[34]

Part 2, "Imperialism," prepares the reader for the emergence of the Totalitarian System, which she considers an enactment of Jonathan Swift's *Modest Proposal*, quoted at the end of Part 3, "Totalitarianism." Swift suggested solving the problem of famine in Ireland by raising children in view of eating them:

> The Nazis and the Bolsheviks can be sure that their factories of annihilation demonstrate the swiftest solution to the problem of overpopulation, of economically superfluous and socially rootless human masses. [...] Wherever it rose to power, [totalitarianism] destroyed all social, legal and political traditions of the country, and established a foreign policy openly directed toward world domination.[35]

The beginning, *archè*, through which each new birth reinvents the world, is replaced by the elimination of individuals, for the sake of creating "One Man of gigantic dimensions" as the ultimate product of the regime (p. 466).

How can one report on that which defies imagination? The fearful imagination is what drives Hannah Arendt to think and write constantly. In his article "Art and Trauma," Dori Laub differentiates "a depository art," which traumatises the reader or spectator, from "therapeutic art," whose goal is psychic survival.[36] On this point, Arendt's writing coincides with the analytic scene, which is also the tragic scene of ceremonial theatre. According to Aristotle, the fearful imagination, together with pity, was a therapeutic incentive of the tragedies that Greek citizens were required to attend. Many of these tragedies depicted the madness of war, *experienced by their authors*. Aeschylus had fought in the Battles of Marathon and Salamin; Sophocles acted as *"strategos"* on two occasions; and Socrates, his contemporary, fought bravely as a hoplite in the Peloponnesian War, as Alcibiades praises him for doing at the end of *The Symposium*.

The madness of Ajax, in Sophocles' tragedy, is that of someone traumatised by war, since he rightly asks for the arms of Achilles, which have been given to Ulysses. To take revenge on the commanders of the Greek army for their betrayal, Ajax kills their cattle and sheep – vital food supplies – while hallucinating that he is slaying Agamemnon's companions. When he recovers from his delusion, Ajax kills himself.[37] Likewise, Euripides' Heracles also carries out a massacre. When he goes off to capture Cerberus in Hades, he leaves his wife and his children with their putative father Amphitryon. In his absence, his enemies are plotting to kill his heirs in order to seize power, but Hera has sent Lyssa, the goddess of rage, to drive him mad, so that he kills his wife and children while he is hallucinating. When, emerging from his delusion, he wants to end his life, his friend Theseus stops him.[38]

In Ancient Greece, authors of epic tales and tragic theatre have the gods intervene in the excess, *ubris*, of the heroes, and they do not reduce madness to the brain.[39] Gregory Nagy,[40] quoted by Jonathan Shay in *Achilles in Viet Nam*, describes Achilles' wrath, at the beginning of the *Iliad*, as a response to the betrayal of Themis, Fairness, by his commander Agamemnon when he claims the captive Briseis, who should have been rightfully his. Homer's epics were recited every four years during the Athens Festival, *Panathénaia*, by a bard who was identified to Homer while he sang. The rhythm and the tales were a therapy of war traumas for citizens who had been in battle. According to Gregory Nagy, expert on the Hellenistic period teaching at Harvard, epics are war stories told by veterans to their grandchildren, in the present tense of trauma, over the heads of their immediate descendants, who are fed up of hearing such stories over and over.

Hannah Arendt strives to transmit what cannot be transmitted, in the face of an ever-present threat. Her purpose is not to inform people by the documents she gathers, but to create, for herself and for her readers, an otherness to which one can speak. Although she did not like psychoanalysis, she gives us tools not only to analyse the "iron logic" that transforms humans into things, but also to resist it (p. 120). Systematic destruction of man's civic and moral identity produces "the submission of populations rendered apathetic and compliant" (p. 291). The historian and the analyst do not escape this fate. How can we resist apathy and not be compliant with rationalisations that make us lose our bearings? How can we reach our patients in their abysmal solitude?

From loneliness to the creation of otherness

David Rousset wrote: "Here, hundreds of thousands of us know that we are living in absolute solitude" (p. 191). In the last chapter of *Totalitarianism*, "Ideology and Terror," Hannah Arendt discusses the difference between solitude and loneliness: "What makes the loneliness so unbearable is the loss of one's own self," whereas in solitude "identity is confirmed by the trusting and trustworthy company of my equals." In loneliness, "man loses trust in himself as the partner of his thoughts. Self and the world, capacity for thought and experience are lost at the same time" (p. 477).

Our task, says Dori Laub, is to "re-establish the lost internal *Thou* – as Martin Buber, in *I and Thou* (1923), calls this "you" which allows one to speak to oneself[41] – when loneliness is incommunicable, when total absence of empathy has destroyed alterity.[42] "Real loneliness," which cannot be conceptualised, is often experienced through cut-out feelings that another may feel in your place.

"On Loneliness" is the title of Frieda Fromm-Reichmann's last article. The manuscript was found on her desk in her cottage at Chestnut Lodge after her death in 1957.[43] In this article, she speaks of her patients' isolation at a period when she herself is afflicted with deafness, as were both her parents. Before immigrating to the United States in 1935, she had worked as a neurologist at the Königsberg hospital where Hannah Arendt's father, suffering from syphilis, was a patient between 1911 and his death in 1913. His condition had deteriorated to the point where he no longer recognised his daughter, who was 6 years old. The child's fright at the sight of him was trivialised by her mother, as the latter admitted later. The words she often uses – "insanity, lunacy, abnormal and senseless" – testify to her early loneliness upon witnessing her father's madness.[44]

Frieda Fromm-Reichmann's father committed suicide by throwing himself down an elevator shaft after losing his job due to his deafness. How can a child understand a parent's suicide, remarks Jane Tillman,[45] without being drawn into the zone of death that entraps her in the incomprehensible "mysterious object"?

Arendt rejects the attraction of endless speculation in the face of absurd political terror, which triggers an endless search for causes and swallows up life. According to her, the most effective weapon of totalitarianism is logical seduction, which traps the masses in the "ice-cold reasoning [of] the mighty tentacle of dialectics." Both appear falsely as the last support in a world where no one can be trusted and nothing is reliable:

What prepares men for totalitarian domination in the non-totalitarian world is the fact that loneliness, once a borderline experience usually suffered in certain marginal social conditions like old age, has become an everyday experience of the evergrowing masses of our century.

In everyday life, perversion takes people in distress as its target of choice.

The three words Hannah Arendt uses to describe this psychical experience – "solitude, isolation, loneliness" – and their opposite – "consolation" – do not have a common etymology. "Isolated" comes from *insula*, island; "solitude" comes from *solus*, alone; and "console" comes from *solari*, to soothe. Loneliness is the exclusion of all others, in which abused children and victims of trauma take refuge, when they no longer expect anything of anyone. Out of despair, they may then become attracted to the infernal machine of totalitarian discourses, which "use reason to destroy reason by teaching and glorifying the logical reasoning whose content is nothing more than a refusal of contradictions."

She describes a situation resembling a psychotic experience, in which time stops after the suppression of ancestors and private life:

> Isolation and loneliness are not the same. I can be isolated – that is in a situation in which I cannot act, because there is nobody who will act with me – without being lonely; and I can be lonely – that is in a situation in which I as a person feel myself deserted by all human companionship – without being isolated.
>
> (p. 474)

The dying classes, races and individuals, unfit to live, no longer have a past and their future is programmed elimination.

Space is both destroyed and limitless:

> By pressing men against each other, total terror destroys the space between them. The ability to think is abolished by a logic without a subject, which eliminates the limits of the self. Isolation is different from loneliness, which preserves the limits of the self; isolation creates confusion.

Psychosis-like states are induced, and the self deserts the individual.

In order to differentiate these states from the philosopher's solitude, Hannah Arendt cites the anecdote about Hegel on his deathbed, saying: "Nobody has understood me except one; and he also misunderstood" (p. 477). But under totalitarian conditions, the only way to avoid madness is to yield to organised dementia by surrendering one's singularity to terror, which annihilates "even the productive potentialities of isolation" and eliminates the chance that loneliness may become solitude, by "eradicating the love of freedom from the hearts of men" (p. 466).

For Hannah Arendt, love of freedom is the way out of the hopeless double bind that blocks the future through a fascination with the end of the world. In the last page of *Totalitarianism*, she says: "… such considerations as predictions are of little avail and less consolation." Following advice from Kafka,[46] who tells us that to write is to "leap out of the ranks of assassins," she leaps out of the "iron band" of totalitarian assassins, to call for "a new beginning" (p. 478). Without quoting him, she also follows in the footsteps of La Boétie, who beseeches us not to fall into voluntary servitude: "Ô foolish people! … What evil change has so denatured man that he, the only creature really born to be free, lacks the memory of his original condition and the desire to return to it?"[47]

The production of freedom

Folly aims for freedom, in a battle against ruthless agencies that treat human beings like things. Hannah Arendt points out that common sense remains powerless against crimes of unprecedented magnitude, as powerless as the human sciences, including mainstream psychoanalysis, whose "stock phrases" and failures with extreme trauma she criticises. Still, she received the Sigmund Freud Prize, awarded to German-language writers. And this recognition was well-deserved, since her writing supports the psychoanalysis of madness and trauma, which has elicited severe criticism from colleagues shocked by this involvement in "psychotic transference," as Bion calls it.

In her postscript to *Eichmann in Jerusalem*, which she added in response to the controversy triggered by the book, she rejects the maxim still in vogue today: "One should not judge." Defying her own critics, she defends tooth and nail her *thou*: "That which you say to yourself to exercise your judgement," whose loss, Dori Laub confirms, characterises a totalitarian world. "If you invoke," she writes, "the argument that we cannot judge if we were not present," or worse, "in his place, I would perhaps have done the same," you are lost (p. 137). The production of freedom which acknowledges soul murder, honours the dead without a grave and detects lies enshrouded in silence involves risks she is willing to take. In the span of time between her two books (1948–1963), her tone has changed. She is now attacked for her arrogance and her persiflage.

Eichmann in Jerusalem is the result of Arendt's self-analysis, which she calls *cura posterior* in a letter to Mary McCarthy. Her initial reaction at the trial was a state of shock at discovering how normal the accused looked in his glass booth. She had expected to see, for the first time, a flesh-and-blood Nazi responsible for the deaths of millions of Jews transported to extermination camps thanks to his zealous organisation. Stunned, she has to admit that Eichmann is incapable of self-analysis, although he consented "enthusiastically" to being interviewed by an Israeli officer. The tale of his life is a series of exculpatory stereotypes, downplaying his role in the Nazi Party; he refuses responsibility for the crimes of which he is accused by arguing that he never killed a Jew with his own hands, and that he even had a certain admiration for them. Arendt concludes her portrait with La Rochefoucauld's maxim: "It is very difficult to live with a criminal, especially when he is you."

The controversy surrounding her book concerns her criticism of the legal characterisation of facts in Eichmann's prosecution. Although the charge "crimes against humanity" had been created in 1945 for the Nuremberg trials, the Israeli court did not make use of it. Arendt is accused of putting herself in the place of the judges when she writes in the epilogue what the court should have told the accused:

> And just as you supported and carried out a policy of not wanting to share the earth with the Jewish people and the people of a number of other nations – as though you and your superiors had any right to determine who should and who should not inhabit the world – we find that no one, that is, no member of the human race, can be expected to want to share the earth with you. This is the reason, and the only reason, you must hang.
>
> (p. 139)

The psychiatric evaluation was inconclusive. One of the psychiatrists even went so far as to state: "He is more normal than I am, at any rate, after having examined him." This does not surprise Hannah Arendt, since to be normal in this system means to be a criminal prompted into action by the commandment: "Thou shalt kill." The trial confirmed her analysis in *Totalitarianism*. She admitted this to Mary McCarthy, writing to her, while assailed by critics: "You were the only reader to understand [...] that I wrote this book in a state of euphoria."

Her confidence in her own analyses allowed her not only to weather the storm, but to reaffirm, in the postscript, her criticism of human sciences and psychoanalysis: "True, we have become very much accustomed by modern psychology and sociology, not to speak of modern bureaucracy, to explaining away the responsibility of the doer for his deed in terms of this or that kind of determinism" (p. 139), such as the unfairness of the Treaty of Versailles, an unhappy childhood, or obeying orders. After listing other excuses, she adds:

> Another such escape from the area of ascertainable facts and personal responsibility are the countless theories, based on non-specific, abstract, hypothetical assumptions – from *Zeitgeist* down to the Oedipus complex – which are so general that they explain and justify every event and every deed.
>
> (p. 140)

Hannah Arendt insists on the need for a new paradigm when dealing with "an unprecedented crime" that requires testing the limits of legal discourse, and concepts such as the "subjective factor" taking into account "intent to do wrong. Where this intent is absent, when the ability to distinguish between right and wrong is impaired, we feel no crime has been committed" (p. 110). But when the abolition of this distinction is raised to the status of an absolute principle by a system that annihilates millions of people, holes in memory are created to swallow up murders without a trace.

The analyst must testify to events fallen into the trash bin of History, not from a position of neutrality, but out of analogous zones in his own story. Then a subject may emerge, able to judge and take responsibility. This transformation is performed in the third part of Aeschylus' *Oresteia*, "The Eumenides,"[48] when, during the trial of Orestes, Athena votes to exonerate Orestes from matricide, taking him from a guilt transmitted through generations, to his responsibility as a subject, according to Solon's laws (636–558 BC) on individual responsibility. Then the Erinyes, goddesses of revenge, become the Eumenides, goddesses of benevolence.

Hannah Arendt ridicules the contemporary obsession with finding excuses for criminals, "as if our humanity resided in this sceptical attitude."

"Consent lights up the face. Refusal gives it its beauty."

This phrase, written by René Char in "Leaves of Hypnos" during World War II,[49] shows the kinship between psychotic transference and Hannah Arendt's work. They have in common the "consent" to truths that have been cut out and the refusal to eradicate traces.

René Char was writing while he fought in the French Resistance, and his words echo those of Hannah Arendt, written at the same period:

> This war will stretch beyond platonic armistices. The implanting of political concepts will proceed with the convulsive stealth of an hypocrisy certain of its rights. Don't smile. Thrust aside both scepticism and resignation and prepare your mortal soul to face an intramural confrontation with demons as cold-blooded as microbes.

Five years earlier, going beyond the ready-made phrases to which psychoanalysis had been reduced, Freud expressed his loneliness, in the prefatory note of the *Moses* dated "before March 1938" and written in Vienna:

> All that [...] would probably lead to our being forbidden to work in Psycho-analysis. [...] I know that this external danger will deter me from publishing the last part of my treatise on Moses. [...] So I shall not publish this essay. But that need not hinder me from writing it. [...] Thus it may lie hid until the time comes when it may safely venture into the light of day, or until someone else who reaches the same opinions and conclusions can be told: "In darker days there lived a man who thought as you did."[50]

Hannah Arendt echoes the same loneliness in Chapter 7, "Truth and Politics," of her book *Between Past and Future*[51], in which she identifies three
types of truths: "rational truths," which are mathematical and moral; "opin-
ion truths," which politics endeavour to change; and "factual truths," which
Lenin called stubborn, since that which existed cannot be erased. And yet,
she says, this is exactly what happened in Russia and in Germany, as well as
in France, where "the majority of the population denied facts when they
contradicted ideology." No one cares about a factual truth that is crushed
by the steamroller of pseudoscience. Everyone ceases to see people cut out
from the photographs, as well as pages torn out of schoolbooks, so that history can be rewritten.

One could easily think that the destruction of all truth – so that nothing
is guaranteed by anything any longer, "nothing is any truer than any other
thing," no one can count on anyone, and peoples are manipulated by
propaganda – is a hopeless phenomenon. Yet Arendt maintains, in conclusion: "Truth, though powerless and always defeated possesses a power of its
own: the voice of the truth teller," of the herald who has found refuge in
the solitude of research, or among famous storytellers like Isak Dinesen,
who bring us joy (p. 259). One of the places for truth-telling, we might add,
is the psychoanalysis of madness and trauma.

Hannah Arendt's first husband, Gunther Anders, whom she met while
attending Heidegger's lectures, wrote two open letters to Eichmann's sons,
under the title *We, Sons of Eichmann.*[52] The first letter was addressed to the
17-year-old adolescent, and the second to the man he had become twenty-
five years later. Gunther Anders, whose actual family name was Stern, came
from a family of child psychologists with ties to Piaget, and he was Walter
Benjamin's cousin. The intention of his letters, signed by "the Jew Anders,"
the personified Other, is to bring the son of a monster back into the realm
of truth thanks to the pronoun "we." In his second letter, he writes: "We
know not what we do; we could be the sons of Eichmann, and participate
in horrors without being able to imagine it." In the background, Anders'
vision of the world is apocalyptic: "We are threatened by a universe of
machines, and the bombs dropped on Hiroshima and Nagasaki are only the
beginning."

But Hannah Arendt never agrees with doomsday prophecies. In her postscript to the second edition of *Eichmann in Jerusalem*, she expresses her
opposition to those "who will not rest until they have discovered an 'Eichmann in every one of us'" (p. 458). In her view, there is no excuse for ignor-
ance: "We must be conscious of what we do." So, she asks herself what she
is doing when she uses the German language.

The gift of language

In the United States, she continues to write and to think in German. After
having almost completed (except for the last two chapters) the manuscript

of her thesis on *Rahel Varnhagen: The Life of a Jewess*,[53] she left Germany for Paris in 1933 and reflected on the fact that, as a Jew, like Rahel, she could not do without the German language, although it carried the orders of the Führer's killing machine. "Language has not gone mad, all the same," she says, but some work is needed to deal with the stigmata left by what it was forced to do. *The Life of the Mind*[54] discusses these questions.

Reflecting about thought, she uses the Greek expression *logon didonai*, to give *logos*, which she translates as: "to give account is to justify in words" (p. 102). Before the mind can travel through the words, *poreuesthai dia logon*, as Plato says: "The sheer naming of things is the human way of appropriating and, as it were, disalienating the world into which, after all, each of us is born as a newcomer and a stranger" (p. 99). In order to appropriate the world, the subject needs "plurality." There can be no subject without otherness, including that of other peoples and civilisations: "The crime of totalitarianism consisted in the total suppression of an element of this plurality, the Jewish people, condemned to disappear from the surface of the earth."

It is essential to give the other his place, even in catastrophic times. "*Wo es war, sol Ich warden*," Freud writes:[55] "Where id was" – the obscure and impenetrable part of our psyche – "there ego must be." *Sollen* is an ethical imperative. According to Arendt, "thoughts do not have to be communicated in order to occur, but they cannot occur without being spoken – silently or sounded out in dialogue." She knows that speech comes from the place of the Other: "To reason silently with oneself is to come to terms with whatever may be given to our senses in everyday appearances; the need of reason is to give account, *logon didonai*, as the Greeks called it with great precision" (p. 101). Even in the face of a totalitarian movement that does its best to destroy the *logos* and the gift of it, we feel that language is there, even if it is contaminated, even if it can only enumerate "elements without reason, *stoicheia aloga*," as Socrates states in the *Theaetetus*.[56] It strives with wild freedom – like children do when they learn to speak – to interweave these elements with those coming from a potential other, in order to create *logos*.

The one who has been ousted from *logos* strives at once to rejoin the order of language. This task is carried out, everywhere in the world, through cathartic ceremonies that perform the destruction of the thing, *das Ding*, in order to allow its name to exist "without a bearer," as Wittgenstein says.[57] The word "dog" does not bite, the word "mouse" eats no cheese, the word "grinder" doesn't grind anything." Arendt writes: "no language has a ready-made vocabulary for the needs of mental activity. [...] Language is 'vitally metaphorical', as Shelley says" (p. 102). "The life of the mind" manifests itself through "the carrying over – *metapherein* – of an intuitive perception of similarity in dissimilarities." For instance, "Kant gives an example of a despotic state as a 'mere machine', like a hand mill, since it is 'governed by an individual absolute will'" (p. 103).

But in the language of the Third Reich, this metaphor is impossible, because words are taken literally and the concentration camp machine actually crushes living corpses without a tomb. Cristobal Nonato's mice had grasped this strategy when they were given photographs of cheese to eat, and they sent back photographs of mice caught in the trap. Totalitarian torturers would not have appreciated the joke, since they lack all sense of humour, and when they give people lies to eat, they have already transformed them into lifeless *Figuren*.

To define this unprecedented regime of terror, Hannah Arendt refers back to the principles of action attributed by Montesquieu to different regimes: honour for the aristocracy, virtue for democracy and fear for tyranny. According to her, the action principle of totalitarianism is logic: an ice-cold logic for Hitler, a metallic logic for Lenin, about whom Stalin said that he was not a great speaker, but fascinated the crowds with his iron logic. In either case, this kind of logic allowed Eichmann and other "apparatchiks" to justify their actions by claiming to be mere cogs in the wheel of the system.

Subverting the principle of neutrality and objectivity

The second chapter of *Beyond Past and Future* is entitled "The Concept of History." Hannah Arendt examines her experience as a subject of history, in the face of totalitarianism. The name *Istôr* appears in Song 18 of the *Iliad*, in the description of the shield of Achilles, made for him by Hephaestus. It is one of the Wonders of the World and depicts Greek society. *Istôr* appears in a scene where two judges compete, so that the best judge can be chosen. He is the judge of judges, the one who confers the prize and testifies to the judgement.

In the fifth century BC, Herodotus, a contemporary of Socrates and Pericles, wrote the story of the Greco-Persian Wars, calling his work *Istoria*, meaning "Enquiries." Hannah Arendt's enquiry is that of a witness horrified by the monstrous deeds of man. *Deinos anthopos*, sings the choir in *Antigone*: "Of all terrifying things, nothing is more terrifying than man." Arendt translated the Greek adjective *deinos* correctly: "terrifying." She observes that for the Ancient Greeks, history:

> is not seen as parts of either an encompassing whole or a process; on the contrary, the stress is always on single instances and single gestures [...] which interrupt the circular movement of daily life. The subject matter of history is these interruptions – the extraordinary, in other words.[58]

Mnemosyne, the muse of history, mother of all the muses, allows facts and feelings condemned to non-existence to come to light, in order to be inscribed in the past and the future, particularly facts and feelings eradicated by totalitarian logic, according to which: "What was originally nothing but a hypothesis to be proved or disproved by actual facts, will in the course of consistent actions always turn into a fact, never to be disproved."[59] But coherence is no guarantee of truth. We have only to consider the overused Oedipus complex that may serve to ignore the factual truth of traumatic events, of which Oedipus has had his fair share. The analyst cannot simply remain silent behind the patient on the couch, saying: "I am listening to you," but has to enter the cut-out scene and say: "I," even if his colleagues don't like it.

To shed light on this point, Hannah Arendt refers to the Feast of the Phaeacians in *The Odyssey*.[60] After the shipwrecked Ulysses, who has lost his identity, has been led by Nausicaa to her father's palace, he is invited to the king's table, where he listens to the blind bard Demodocus, who sings the epic of the Trojan War. Hearing his own name mentioned when he enters the conquered city, he begins to weep. Homeric tradition comments that the tears running down his face are those of Andromache seeing the death of Hector, knowing she will be sent into slavery. The voice of the bard, at the scene of his present trauma, allows him to recover his senses. Arendt notes: "The scene where Ulysses listens to the story of his own life is paradigmatic for both history and poetry."

This scene was invoked again by Gregory Nagy, when he spoke in our seminar, at Nicole Loraux's invitation. He connected it with a similar situation in the first chant of the *Aeneid*, which contains the famous verses: "*Sunt lacrimae rerum, et mentem mortalia tangent*" – "There are tears of things, and mortal things touch the mind."[61] Gregory Nagy analysed this verse, describing Aeneas' psychical state when, after leaving behind the destruction of Troy, and after the loss of his companions at sea, he landed in Carthage. While waiting for Dido, he contemplates the temple built by the queen. When he sees himself on the bas-relief recounting the Trojan War, he begins to weep as well. As was the case for Ulysses, another has entered the scene of his present traumas. This other is Dido, about whom we will learn that she has also escaped massacres in her native Phoenicia. In both cases, a witness was needed, allowing the heroes to become the subjects of their stories, after crying tears impossible to shed.

Tears remain in things, when mortal things lose access to the mind, after the falsifications of history. The analyst, called upon – like *Istôr* – to testify to these cut-out things, may be affected by the tears of the things. He has to give them back – *sollen* – to the one who is then able to come out of traumatic numbness and become the subject of his story. This solution, which Hannah Arendt considers "paradigmatic for history and poetry," concurs, she says, with that offered by quantum physics – developed between the two world wars, as were her own ideas and those of Schrödinger, who disagrees with the principle of objectification and includes the observer in the field of observation. Arendt refers to this explicitly, pointing out that "there could be no answers independent of a question-asking being. The old quarrel, therefore, between the 'subjectivity' of historiography and the 'objectivity' of physics has lost much of its relevance."[62]

Her criticism of social sciences and psychoanalysis, "when they treat human relations more carelessly than natural sciences do," agrees with Wittgenstein's assessment at the end of his *Philosophical Investigations*: "The physicist sees, hears and informs us about these phenomena, while the psychologist merely observes external reactions" (section 571). That is why Schrödinger, in his *Tarner Lectures* at Cambridge in 1956, launched an appeal to analysts to relinquish the illusion of neutrality.[63]

Hannah Arendt concludes her chapter on "the concept of history" by condemning the confusion between the social and the political, which reached its paroxysm with "the experimentation of a classless society organised among human beings when they maintain relations with each other but have lost the world of common experience they once shared." This confusion is also maintained by psychoanalysts who rely only on the social treatment of madness, refusing any involvement in the political challenge their patients bring them, such as the erasure of traces.

By dismissing transference in psychosis, as Lacan did at the end of his "On a Question Preliminary to Any Possible Treatment of Psychosis,"[64] analysts ignore History and their own history, "as if the best thing to do with history," in Arendt's words, "is to forget this sad affair for the sole purpose of eliminating oneself." Still, if we do not have access to history, we can turn to mythology.

The madness of the daughter of Minos and Pasiphae

In a lecture entitled "History, Turbulence and Temporality," I spoke of *Hippolytus*, Euripides' play.[65] In this tragedy, the characters are sick, *nosoi*; their illness, which affects their *phrèn* – the diaphragm, solar plexus – is closely tied to the existence of gods. Phaedra has gone mad, and when her Nurse hears her delusions she cannot believe that "the daughter of Minos and Pasiphae" could be in love with her stepson. When the Nurse informs the young man, he hurls insults at his stepmother. Phaedra hangs herself, after accusing Hippolytus of raping her. Having returned from the underworld just in time, Theseus curses his son and banishes him, while Poseidon sends a sea monster to devour the boy. When Artemis tells Theseus the truth, the father forgives his dying son and promises to avenge him.

There are certain words that "speak to" this seminar. Standing in front of his wife's corpse, Theseus cries and analyses madness, invoking fate: "*O Tucha!* Fortune! [...] How heavy this Fate has fallen upon my house! Upon my head! Some unspeakable stain, *aphrastos*" (verses 818–820). There are no words. Theseus cannot say what struck him, literally, something coming from a place that doesn't forget, *ex tinos alastorôn* – the privative prefix "a" precedes the past participle of *lanthanô*, to forget. The Erinyes, with their serpent-entwined hair, are the goddesses of a memory that doesn't forget.

Theseus' life has become "unlivable, *abiotos biou*," through a tragic fault, *amartia*, coming from the dawn of time. *"Aïai! Aïai! Melea, meleapathè!"* Theseus cries out in agony: "How can I bear the horror of this Fate? This is the doing of some ancestor! The evil deeds of long ago brought back by a demonic fate, *tuchan daimonôn*" (verses 831–832). Traumatic memory has broken through actions without words, and returned in the form of a monster sent by Poseidon. Phaedra's lineage is not devoid of monsters either. Her mother Pasiphae slept with the white bull of Crete, and gave birth to her sister Ariadne as well as to the Minotaur.

The gods inhabit a sphere without words and without forgetting where there is betrayal. Minos, Phaedra's father, betrayed his brother Rhadamanthus. Likewise, Hitler and Stalin created regimes where brother kills brother and children betray their parents, but these tyrants are not gods. Indeed, Zeus, who guarantees the Oath, *orchos*, sleeps with whoever pleases him, but he is a god, and in the sphere of the law his function is not threatened by his whims. The word "oath" involves a commitment, just as the word "link" involves the given word, *logon didonai*, and refers to alliances. The term "social bond" involves a bond tied by the given word. The word "oath" is linked to the guarantee provided by the god. Without it, the whole symbolic chain is broken, and nothing more can be said.

The French word for oath, *serment*, comes from *sacramentum*, a deposit given in the form of money or livestock by a plaintiff at a trial, which will be offered to the god if the plaintiff loses his case – hence the need to tell the truth. Totalitarian systems function inversely. Hannah Arendt speaks of "complete retextualisation of the order of discourse" by propaganda that eliminates not only factual truth, but even the possibility of lying, since generalised lying has become the norm. Words such as lineage, *genos*, kinship and contract become meaningless.

The breakdown of the symbolic order is also that of morality. Today, this word has been replaced by the more elegant term "ethics," which means the same thing in Greek – the Latin *mos, morisis* being the equivalent of the Greek *ethos*. But no matter: when morality is replaced by criminality, there will always be Don Quixotes to rise up, driven by the political necessity to defend the honour of women and defiled young girls, of abused men and children, and of the dead without a grave.

Madness attempts to weave the social link when the words connecting people through interest – *interesse*, that which is in between – and with their ancestors have been devalued. As Erasmus says in his *In Praise of Folly*, Folly knows what she is doing when she drives the analyst to occupy the places where true speech can start again.

Archè: the commandment of a commencement

In "Moral Considerations," Hannah Arendt insists on the double meaning of the word *archè*: to command and to begin. In totalitarian systems, belief in the causality of natural or historical determinism is a way of denying any new beginning. Hannah Arendt concludes the third volume of *The Origins of Totalitarianism* with these words: "This beginning is guaranteed by each new birth; it is, indeed, every man" (p. 222). She bases this statement on a quote by Luther: "Man, before whom there was nothing, was created so that there may be a beginning."

There are solitary children having to begin again a lineage destroyed by murder and betrayal, so that arrested time can be set in motion: "The time is out of joint: O cursed spite that ever I was born to set it right."[66] Hamlet plays the fool to this aim. Arendt refers to children as "the new ones," *oi neoi* in Greek, who reset the limits needed for the law. *Orchos*, "the oath," also means "enclosure." Similarly, work with madness consists of setting limits when faced with the unleashing of hate, which in totalitarian systems creates constant instability through "attacks on linking" – Bion's expression – which these children try to weave again.

Chapter 5 of *Between Past and Future*, entitled "The Crisis in Education," takes a critical look at the disappearance of parents' authority when they delegate responsibility to their children:

> as though parents daily said: "In this world, even we are not very securely at home [...]. You must try to make out as best you can; in any case you are not entitled to call us to account. We are innocent, we wash our hands of you."
>
> (p. 245)

Arendt's tone is very sharp; she uses the words "betrayal" and "abandonment" when speaking of parents who treat children like adults, and act like their children's buddies or rivals, to give themselves an illusion of youthfulness. Under the pretext of making their children independent, they do not preserve the home as a secure place. The public sphere invades the private space, whereas "the child requires special protection and care so that nothing destructive may happen to him from the world" (p. 241).

Her conclusion is an apparent paradox:

> Exactly for the sake of what is new and revolutionary in every child, education must be conservative. [...] And education, too, is where we decide whether we love our children enough not to expel them from our world and leave them to their own devices, nor to strike from their hands their chance of understanding something new, something unforeseen by us, but to prepare them in advance for the task of renewing a common world.

She objects to the manipulation of children when they are used to serve the causes of adults, seeing this as a confusion between the sphere of the social and the political.

This is the paradox of the production of freedom discussed in the previous chapter, "What Is Freedom?" It is the ability to seize the unexpected and break the unalterable chain of causality, like in an analysis of madness where the analyst breaks the chain of genetic and structural causes, in order to grasp interferences that often emerge by chance. Hannah Arendt recommends the creative use of "coincidences stranger than fiction," which accomplish miracles by subverting automatic reliance on historical and biological determinism. This is what initiates a new beginning.

Thus, freedom is not simply free will, but the freedom "to act," a verb to which she confers a double etymology: Greek and Latin. In Latin, *agere*, "to set in motion," and *gerere*, which links the actions to those of ancestors, *res gestae*, without any determinism. And in Greek, *prattein*, meaning to complete what was started. In both languages, freedom is associated with authority, implied by the Greek verb *archein*, "to command" and "to start," and by the Latin word *auctoritas* – the origin of the word "author" – coming from the verb *augeo*, "to increase." In Arendt's words:

> [Education] must preserve what is new in every child and introduce it as a new thing into an old world, which, however revolutionary its actions may be, is always from the standpoint of the next generation, superannuated and close to destruction.

On this condition, a new political self may emerge.

A political self[67]

One of the first to create confusion between the social and the political sphere was Seneca when he translated Aristotle's phrase "*Anthôpos phusei politikon zoon*" – "Man is by nature a political animal," by "*Homo est naturaliter politicus, id est socialis*" – "Man is by nature a political animal, that is, social." The loss of this distinction – which Arendt strives to restore – has serious consequences for the treatment of madness.

Indeed, this distinction has existed since the Middle Ages. Of the many discourses on madness produced in that era, be they theological, legal, medical or literary, as they are presented by historian Jean-Marie Fritz in a fascinating book,[68] we will examine two more closely: the one he calls "literary discourse: madness in the space of the marvel," and "the discourse of medicine, an infinite discourse." The first is political, since it concerns breaks in the social link; its dwelling place is literature, where the madman becomes "the Savage Man" on the outskirts of the civilised world. There, he fights monsters and meets fairies who reveal unheard-of truths, abolished by denial, in a space where time stands still. When he returns, he is literally as out of date as the Knight of the Sad Countenance.

Medical discourse has never stopped making use of humoral theory, still manifest today in mood stabilisers and in an organicist approach that looks for the cause of madness inside the skull or in the genes. Now, as then, the treatments are more or less the same, medication and shock, in an attempt to reintegrate madness socially into the collective, though with a difference. Equal access to care distributes the same old shocks, but under anaesthesia and reimbursed by insurance companies or by social security, in a confusion between the social and the political, if I am to believe Folly as presented by Erasmus, whom I take as an authority on the subject. At the end of his *Praise*,[69] she claims: "But I forget myself and run beyond my bounds [...]. If I shall seem to have spoken anything more boldly or impertinently than I ought, be pleased to consider that not only Folly but a woman said it."

Aristotle did describe man as: "*Zôon politikon*," but he added "*logon echôn*," endowed with speech. In Latin, a second misinterpretation was introduced when the second part of the phrase was translated as *animal rationale*: "man is a political and rational animal." Still, when Aristotle wrote that "man is endowed with speech" – that is, able to relate to his fellow men, *omoioi* – he excluded women and slaves, who are part of the household, *oikos*. Citizens must be free of domestic cares, so they may go to the agora where they speak.

So, when Erasmus' Folly speaks "as a woman," she oversteps the bounds of her social role, refuses to become a statistic, and begins by stripping her analyst of all his social attributes, in order to reveal in his place the totalitarian agency she is fighting. Then a political subject can emerge at this critical moment, provided the analyst is able to acknowledge his failing and pass judgement on this agency overtly. This is how a new freedom and a new otherness emerge. In Hannah Arendt's words:

> totalitarian government does not just curtail liberties or abolish essential freedoms; nor does it, at least to our limited knowledge, succeed in eradicating the love for freedom from the hearts of man [...]. But it cannot deny the fact that each man *is* a new beginning, begins, in a sense, the world anew.

The political theatre of Fools in the Middle Ages, called *sotties* in French, was led by Mother Folly,[70] who calls her children – the *Sot* and the *Sottes* – "jesters" in English. They come bumbling onto the stage to show the abuses of the times through their brilliant delirious words and gestures, and to judge political crimes. At some point, they drag on the stage some worthy personage whose fancy clothes they tear off to reveal the fool's costume hidden under the double-talk. This theatre illustrates the paradigm of the psychoanalysis of madness as a fight against perversion.

For Hannah Arendt, the stakes are the same. Her book *Rahel Varnhagen: The Life of a Jewess*[71] reveals the existence of a reality hidden under the ideals of equality promoted by the Enlightenment.

Hannah Arendt, psychoanalyst

Although she did not like psychoanalysis, her biography of Rahel (1771–1833), which she started to write in 1932 and published in New York in 1958, resembles an analysis taking place between Hannah and Rahel, her "closest friend though she has been dead for some hundred years." Arendt read Rahel's diary and her correspondence published in *Ein Buch des Andenkens für ihre Freunde* (*A Souvenir Book for Friends*), after ending her liaison with Heidegger, during the year she attended his courses in Marburg in 1924, when she was 18, seventeen years younger than him.

Through her transference to Rahel, she discovered – as did Frieda Fromm-Reichman, (also 17 years her senior), in Hannah Arendt's home town of Königsberg – a new paradigm for psychoanalysis, focusing not on the repressed unconscious, but on injury to otherness. Rahel, a German Jewess like her, a writer like her, infuriates the young Hannah Arendt, who hurls passionate invectives at her, mocking her stupidity and naivety, born, like in her own case, of an obsessive desire for assimilation. The chapter "Day and Night" is dedicated to the analysis of Rahel's recurrent dreams, like visions persisting into wakefulness. They open a space where Jewishness manifests itself, cut out from her ancestry during the day.

Who dreamed these dreams? The transitional subject of this analysis is also Hannah Arendt, for whom these dreams are a way to express melancholia and nocturnal terrors after her separation from Heidegger. She experiences the absolute loneliness described by Frieda Fromm-Reichmann in her last article, which finds an address thanks to Rahel's dreams that explore a catastrophic area cut out by denial. We come to know these dreams, with their prophetic dimension, through the friendship, *philia*, Hannah Arendt felt for Rahel, who had been, like her, the target of anti-Semitism – overtly professed by Heidegger's wife Elfriede, who was a member of the National Socialist Party.

Arendt starts Rahel's analysis in a chapter entitled "Jewess and Schlemihl," which reveals at the outset the cutting out of age-old history through assimilation:

> It had taken her sixty-three years to come to terms with a problem which had its beginnings seventeen hundred years before her birth, which underwent a crucial upheaval during her life, and which one hundred years after her death – she died on March 7, 1833 – was slated to come to an end.
>
> (p. 19)

Described as a Schlemihl, the beggar by the roadside, Rahel deliberately chose to live a lie: "Lying is lovely when you choose it" (p. 49). At the end of her life, she had fallen prey to "loneliness that drives you mad" because she had shielded herself against the course of events, and "retreated from the society that had made her an outcast." But despite herself, she recorded in her diary and in her letters the impact of facts not subjectively integrated. Her torment comes from having "deprived the other of any possibility of responding to her, in order to preclude rejection" (p. 41).

Arendt restores Rahel's authority as an author, and becomes "the other" for her across the distance of a century, especially by analysing her dreams, in the chapter "Day and Night" (p. 161). These are traumatic dreams that Freud would agree do not follow his theory of dreams as wish fulfilment. In 1920, he writes in *Beyond the Pleasure Principle*:

> If, in spite of the quality of dreams or traumatic neuroses, we want to maintain the conception of dreams as wish fulfilment, we have to acknowledge that in such states, the function of the dream has been greatly disturbed, that it has been diverted from its aim.

The new aim of the dream had been discovered by analysts like Frieda Fromm-Reichmann, William Rivers and Sandor Ferenczi during World War I in military hospitals, and by Thomas Salmon who worked with immigrants at Ellis Island. Unknowingly, Arendt's approach follows his principles of proximity, immediacy, expectancy and simplicity, in the psychotherapy of traumatised soldiers.

The subject of Rahel's first dream is closeness, *proximity*, with an undefined animal that "loved me tremendously," and stayed with her when she found herself cut off from the company of others. This animal is a white sheep – *tragos* in Greek, the root of the word tragedy. She alone knows that it can speak, in a society that not only ignores her soul and the history of her ancestors, but would later cooperate in the plan to murder them all. Arendt is reading Rahel's testimony while Hitler is writing *Mein Kampf* in jail. At the end of her dream, Rahel finds the animal dead at the foot of a tree, reduced to nothing but black fur (p. 170).

The second dream is a scene announcing an imminent ordeal, *immediacy*, in which she is hurled like a scapegoat from the last rampart of a fortress in an ancient city (p. 174). The earth is parched, a "waste land" where nothing grows, and the "too bright shafts of the sun [...] pierce their way through no bracing air." This dazzling light, compared by Arendt to the ideology of the Enlightenment, which, in order to preserve its purity, sacrifices singularity through assimilation, gives Rahel the impression that the story in the dream is true. Her march towards the abyss, dragged by the mob, is made possible by the complicity of her Spanish lover Urquijo, whom she keeps asking: "You won't say yes, will you?" In the face of his hesitation, which foreshadows other deadly indecisions, Rahel "fell from stone to stone," murdered by "the collusion, between the elite and the mob," Arendt would later write in *Totalitarianism*.

In another "dream of the same sort," Rahel kills her lover and thinks of killing herself: "What use was the day [...] when the 'other land' of night, forever presented opaque riddles and again and again conjured up delusory visions of 'freedom, truth, unity, native soil'?" (p. 176).

The fourth dream is cathartic; it renews hope, *expectancy*. Rahel is no longer alone: "I lay on a wide bed [...] on the edge of the world." Another woman is there with her. They are sharing their thoughts:

"Do you know mortification?" and we asked each other if we had ever felt this particular form of suffering in our lives. We said: "Yes, that I know" [...] and the particular form of suffering we were speaking of was rent from the heart [...] we were rid of it forever and felt wholly sound and light.

(p. 177)

Hannah Arendt has taken that place beside Rahel, on the edge of the world.

These dreams were repeated, with great clarity, for ten years. Like the ones collected by Charlotte Beradt, they testified to Rahel's history – a history of shame about her origins – intertwined with History. Contrary to Heraclitus' *Fragments*, where the world shared with others in the daytime, *koinos*, is contrasted with retiring, at night, into a singular world, *idios*, Hannah Arendt points out that Rahel's dreams are not only connected to the world at large, but reveal elements of it that are suppressed during the day. Rahel "could no longer trust her opinions because she had become lost to herself." Still, "Unhappiness, banished from the day, flees into the night, [where it] contracts into a tightly sealed container of despair" (p. 168). Thus, the repetition of dreams, where "phantoms and shadows" that pursue her during the day have taken refuge, is a dynamic, starting with the loss of her soul, reduced to an empty skin, towards regeneration started by her writing, all the way to the emergence of the subject of cut-out history, in the hope – as Freud says in his *Moses* – "that some day, somebody will say 'in dark times there was a [woman] who thought like you.'"

Beyond the "stock phrases" of mainstream psychoanalysis, and the abstractions inherited from the philosophy of the Enlightenment, which Arendt strongly opposes, she analyses her special transference to Rahel and interprets her dreams as a means of searching for the historical truth. This analysis no doubt provided the fundamental elements of *The Origins of Totalitarianism*, just as his war experience provided Bion with the elements of his psychoanalysis of madness and trauma. When she pursues her search for historical truth, Arendt is agreeing with Freud who, at the end of his life, persecuted by the Nazi regime, like she was, designated this truth as the goal of psychoanalysis, in *Moses and Monotheism*. At the end of *Rahel Varnhagen*, Arendt too emphasises that dreams are fearless: "... night turns into a specific night, when dreams insist [...] upon certain contents, darkening the day with excessively distinct shadow-images, again and again reverting to things past ..."

Notes

1 Arendt, H., "III: Totalitarianism," in *The Origins of Totalitarianism*, World Publishing Company, 1962.
2 Lefort, C., *Complications: Communism and the Dilemma of Democracy*, Columbia University Press, 2007.
3 Unpublished.
4 Beradt, C., *The Third Reich of Dreams*, Quadrangle Books, 1968.
5 Arendt, H., "Postscript," in *Eichmann in Jerusalem*, Viking Press, 1964, pp. 280–298.
6 See *infra*, Seminar 4 on Toni Morison.
7 Rivers, W., "The Repression of War Experiences," *The Lancet*, February 1918; see *infra*, Seminar 6 on Pat Barker.
8 See *infra*, Seminar 12 on François Rabelais and Yvette Guilbert.
9 Kobayashi, M. (Dir.), *Kwaidan*, 1964. Based on Hearn, L., *Stories and Studies of Strange Things*, Rutland Publishing, 2005.
10 See *infra*, Seminar 2 on Gaetano Benedetti.
11 Lacan, J., *Écrits*, Fink, B. (Trans.), W. W. Norton & Company, 1966, p. 144.
12 Hornstein, G. A., *To Redeem One Person Is to Redeem the World: The Life of Frieda Fromm-Reichmann*, The Free Press, 2000.
13 Ibid., p. 660.
14 Lacan, J., "La psychiatrie anglaise et la guerre," in *Autres écrits*, Seuil, 2001.
15 Lacan, J. *Écrits*, op. cit., p. 386.
16 Ibid., p. 324.
17 Freud, S., *Five Lectures on Psycho-Analysis*, S.E. 11, Hogarth Press, 1910.
18 Freud, S., *Moses and Monotheism*, S.E. 23, Hogarth Press, 1939.
19 See *infra*, Seminar 4 on Toni Morrison.
20 Chernow, R., *The Warburgs*, Vintage Books, 1993. See *infra*, Seminar 11 on Robert Musil.
21 I thank Jeanne Wolff Bernstein for the German literal meaning: "enjoyment companions."
22 Sterne, L., *The Life and Opinions of Tristram Shandy, Gentleman*, W. W. Norton & Company, 1980.
23 Bion, W., *A Memoir of the Future*, Karnac Books, 1991.
24 Fuentes, C., *Christopher Unborn*, Farrar, Straus & Giroux, 1989.
25 Arendt, H., *The Origins of Totalitarianism*, op. cit.
26 Vinar, M. and Vinar, M., *Exil et torture*, Denoël, 1989.
27 Klemperer, V., *The Language of the Third Reich*, Bloomsbury Academic, 2006.
28 Young-Bruehl, E., *Hannah Arendt: For Love of the World*, Yale University Press, 1982, p. 183.
29 Arendt, H., "III: Totalitarianism," in *The Origins of Totalitarianism*, op. cit. p. 342.
30 Joung-Bruehl, E., *Hannah Arendt: For Love of the World*, op. cit.
31 Dinesen, I., *Out of Africa*, Modern Library, 1992.
32 Arendt, H., *The Human Condition*, University of Chicago Press, 1998.
33 Rousset, D., *Les jours de notre mort*, Pluriel, 2005.
34 Arendt, H., *The Origins of Totalitarianism*, op. cit., p. 3.
35 Swift, J., *A Modest Proposal for Preventing the Children of Poor People from Being a Burden to Their Parents, or the Country, and for Making Them Beneficial to the Public*, Nonesuch Press, 1968, p. 460.

36 Laub, D., "Art et Trauma," *Le Coq-Héron*, 221 (2015): 35.
37 Sophocles, *Ajax*, Cambridge University Press, 2001.
38 Heraclitus, *Fragments*, Viking Press, 2001.
39 Shay, J., *Achilles in Vietnam*, Scribner, 1995.
40 Nagy, G., *The Best of the Achaeans*, Johns Hopkins University Press, 1998.
41 Laub, D. "Reestablishing the internal 'Thou' in testimony of trauma," lecture, Portland, May 9, 2013.
42 Felman, S. and Laub, D., *Testimony: Crises of Witnessing in Literature, Psychoanalysis and History*, Routledge, 1992.
43 Fromm-Reichmann, F., *Psychoanalysis and Psychotherapy*, University of Chicago Press, 1959. See *infra*, Seminar 4 on Toni Morrison and Frieda Fromm-Reichmann.
44 Young-Bruehl, E., *Hannah Arendt: For Love of the World*, op. cit., p. 18.
45 Tillman, J., "The Intergenerational Transmission of Suicide: Moral Injury and the Mysterious Object in the Work of Walker Percy," *Journal of the American Psychoanalytic Association* 64/3 (2015).
46 Kafka, F., *The Diaries of Franz Kafka, 1910–1923*, Schocken Books, 1988.
47 La Boétie, É., *Discourse on Voluntary Servitude*, Kurtz. H. (Trans.), Columbia University Press, 1942, p. 187.
48 Aeschyles, *The Oresteia*, University of California Press, 2014.
49 Char, R., "Leaves of Hypnos," in *Furor and Mystery and Other Writing*, Commonwealth Books, Black Widow, 2011, p. 133.
50 Freud, S., *Moses and Monotheism*, op. cit.
51 Arendt, H., *Between Past and Future*, Penguin Books, 1977.
52 Anders, G., *Nous, fils d'Eichmann*, Payot & Rivages, 1999.
53 Arendt, H., *Rahel Varnhagen: The Life of a Jewess*, Johns Hopkins University Press, 1997.
54 Arendt, H., *The Life of the Mind*, Harcourt Brace, 1978.
55 Freud, S., *New Introductory Lectures on Psycho-Analysis*, S.E. 22, Hogarth Press, 1933.
56 Plato, *Theaetetus*, Liberal Arts Press, 1955, 202 b.
57 Wittgenstein, L., *Philosophical Investigations*, Oxford University Press, 1983, section 43.
58 Baehr, P. (Ed.), *The Portable Hannah Arendt*, Penguin Books, 2000, p. 279.
59 Arendt, H., *Between Past and Future*, op. cit., p. 88.
60 Homer, *The Odyssey*, Penguin Classics, 1999, Song VIII, verses 62–64.
61 Virgil, *The Aeneid*, Penguin Classics, 2003, Song I, verse 442.
62 Arendt, H. *Between Past and Future*, op. cit., p. 284.
63 Schrödinger, E., "The Principle of Objectivation," in *What Is Life? with Mind and Matter*, Cambridge University Press, 1967.
64 Lacan, J., *Écrits: A Selection*, Sheridan, A. (Trans.), Tavistock/Routledge, 1977.
65 Euripides, *Hippolytus*, Focus, 2001.
66 Shakespeare, W., *Hamlet*, Simon & Schuster, 1992, Act II, Scene 5, verses 189–190.
67 Tweedy, R., *A Political Self*, Karnac Books, 2017.
68 Fritz, J.-M., *Le Discours du fou au Moyen Âge*, Presses universitaires de France, 1992.
69 Erasmus, D., *The Praise of Folly*, Aeterna Publishing, 2010.
70 Davoine, F., *Mother Folly: A Tale*, Stanford University Press, 2014.
71 Arendt H., *Rahel Varnhagen: The Life of a Jewess*, op. cit.

Conclusion

Madness and the Social Link

The birth of a political subject able to inscribe historical truths erased by the "banality of evil" – a term coined by Hannah Arendt – is what opens the future in a psychoanalysis of madness and trauma, at critical moments when the analyst is pushed out of his entrenchment behind mainstream discourse. The authors with whom we conversed in this book showed us the way to a process of "psychotic transference" – Wilfred Bion's expression" – consisting in joint research into the unsymbolised matters that are at stake, for the patient and the analyst, in the dynamic process of madness and trauma. Jean-Max Gaudillière used to say that on these occasions, "trauma speaks to trauma," allowing events that made a powerful impression, recorded in a flash but cut out of speech, to be validated. An underground "intelligence" finds its expression through the discovery of otherness, and resonates with the art of the storytellers who accompanied us throughout the seminars.

These authors, in their various ways, all portray the emergence of a political subject who comes back from exile, as we shall see in the next volume, *The Birth of a Political Self.*

Index

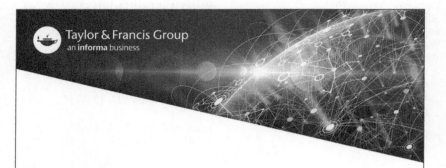